Advance Praise for *Dottoressa*

"While sharing the many difficulties she's faced as an outsider to the Italian healthcare system—with its piles of paperwork, unwritten rules, and old boy networks—Levenstein also writes a love letter to Italy . . . The first chapters recount, with a combination of exasperation and humor, the years-long obstacle course she encountered in her quest to practice medicine in the country. She proceeds to talk about everything from what a well-dressed Italian physician should wear, to, in a particularly wise and witty chapter, love and sex from both an Italian and an American perspective. A timely epilogue discusses the Affordable Care Act from her unique position as an American expat and an Italian physician, with Levenstein reflecting on how Italians, despite widespread dissatisfaction with their own health system, manage to live more healthily than Americans."

 —*Publishers Weekly*

"Dr. Levenstein's gripping account of her experience as an American doctor in Rome is more than a memoir, it is a portrait of a changing country and the evolution of healthcare as seen from behind her stethoscope. It is as funny as it is poignant. A must read for anyone who thinks they understand medicine, Italy, or humanity."

 —**Barbie Latza Nadeau, Italy bureau chief of**
 The Daily Beast **and author of** *Roadmap to Hell: Sex, Drugs and Guns on the Mafia Coast*

"Susan Levenstein's *Dottoressa* is a smart, funny, charming, highly readable memoir of practicing medicine in Italy and is full of astute insights into the way Italy works. Approaching Italy from the vantage point of the medical profession and its health system is actually a great way to understand important aspects of Italian society. There is corruption and cronyism, the dysfunctional university system that produces a massive oversupply of doctors (many of whom remain unemployed), but at the same time an often quite efficient national health system that treats everyone and often with better results than the more expensive American system."

—Alexander Stille, author of *Benevolence and Betrayal*, *Excellent Cadavers*, and *The Force of Things*

"We waited for a writer who never arrived. We expected—in vain—a sociologist who would study and explain us. We hoped for a historian to deconstruct and re-construct the euphoric and problematic 'life in Italy.' Then along came Dr. Levenstein, apparently confined to a world of physicians and patients. Luckily she kept notes, and has written a book that must be read. It proves that a stethoscope can be a good instrument to explore not just a person, but a society."

—Furio Colombo, formerly of NYU, Columbia University, and editor of *The New York Review of Books* in Italy, author of *Immigrants: The Hunt Is On* and *Trump Power*

"Susan Levenstein gives us a fascinating account of her life as an American doctor in the Eternal City, including an analysis of Italian healthcare that is both informed and terrifying. A must read for anyone who contemplates relocating to Rome—if they want to live long enough to enjoy their Italian dream."

—Matthew Kneale, author of *English Passengers* and *Rome: A History in Seven Sackings*

"Susan Levenstein is arguably the wittiest internist on earth, whose droll, mordant voice comes through even in papers she writes for technical medical journals. In *Dottoressa*, Levenstein offers a memoir of her years as a decidedly unconventional doctor in a decidedly unconventional setting. She is a born raconteur, and has the observational skills of a sardonic cultural anthropologist. This is a wonderfully fun read."

—**Dr. Robert Sapolsky, Stanford University,**
**author of *Why Zebras Don't Get Ulcers* and *Behave:*
*The Biology of Humans at Our Best and Worst***

"One woman's story of her medical journey from Harvard to Rome and her experiences, in medicine and life, as she practiced her profession in Italy. Her intelligent, candid, and witty observations, with some moving and courageous insights, lead her and the reader to ask what medicine is and could be."

—**Wallis Wilde-Menozzi, author of *The Other Side of
the Tiber, Reflections on Time in Italy***

"So far as medicine is concerned, Italy really is a foreign country, where definitions of what ails you, expectations of the physician, and standards of medical practice may come as a surprise. This sharp-eyed, deeply thoughtful, often exhilarating book will enlighten you not only about what it's like to be an American doctor in Italy but about the whole dolce vita way of life."

—**Frederika Randall, journalist, translator, critic,
and long-time denizen of Rome**

Dottoressa

An American Doctor in Rome

SUSAN LEVENSTEIN, MD

pb

PAUL DRY BOOKS
Philadelphia 2019

First Paul Dry Books Edition, 2019

Paul Dry Books, Inc.
Philadelphia, Pennsylvania
www.pauldrybooks.com

Library of Congress Control Number: 2019935866

ISBN 978-1-58988-139-6

to my patients

CONTENTS

PROLOGUE

I first crossed the Italian border in January 1970, at the wheel of a Volkswagen Beetle, heading for Milan to hear my friend Ursula Oppens perform at the Piccola Scala. When I cheered at the end of the concert people turned around to stare. Only years later did I understand why: I had yelled "Bravo!" instead of "Brava!" making it seem I hadn't noticed the pianist was a woman.

My first fully functional word of Italian came from the roadside. Gas stations open for business all had signs with an easy word, *APERTO*, while shuttered ones said, unpronounceably, *CHIUSO*. When I hit Milan at lunchtime needing to change money, I found a building auspiciously labeled *BANCA* but locked up tight. I stopped a passerby and hazarded, "A-pert-oh?" He shook his head and pointed to half past two on his watch. Bingo, I was charmed already. Next challenge was the street signs. Since half the streets in the city had an arrow pointing to the *SENSO UNICO*, I figured that must be a very important United Nations agency. This was one translation error that could been deadly: what it really meant was *ONE WAY*.

I was wandering through Europe on a mission that year, weighing medical school yes, medical school no. I'd tell people I met, "I'm going to be a doctor," and stand back to see how they reacted. Germans were skeptical, English polite, French indifferent.

Italians were gratifyingly enthusiastic. For me, they ran the best country in Europe. They dazzled you with style, overdosed you with pasta, and applauded your Joan Baez imitations. It was a haven where the great King Judgment had been dethroned, "A" was always awarded for effort, everybody appreciated my first ten stumbling words in their lingo instead of watching hawkeyed for me to slip up. All of which did wonders for my mental health and self-image.

I had been raised on the New York edge of America by psychotherapist, more or less Jewish, nitpicking, *different* parents whose idea of a fun family outing was going to Manhattan on Saturday afternoon to chant "Ban the bomb." In 1965 I bussed down to the March on Washington and in 1967 lay down in front of Secretary of Defense McNamara's car at Harvard. That is to say, I was half a stranger in my own land and, at twenty-two, primed to embrace Italy *in toto*. I imitated the locals shamelessly by donning a wide-brimmed hat at a rakish angle, knocking back espressos on the fly, talking endless politics, and bringing empty bottles into the alcohol-seeped air of wine shops to be loaded up with pale red swill.

More inebriating than that low-octane wine was the ubiquitous beauty: from Michelangelo to Giotto, Saint Mark's to the Trevi Fountain, backstreets like movie sets, women with perfect earrings, men with their shirts half unbuttoned, pop songs that married the operatic with the topical. I loved how their beaches had coral sand under see-through water, how they called fruit cups Macedonias because like that country the dessert was a hodgepodge, how you could eat spaghetti every night and never get tired of it, how workmen burst into song, how children ran around in restaurants, and especially how all of a sudden, abracadabra, it was April in Rome, with a non-stop soundtrack of screaming swallows, and there had been no winter. I remember feeling my first mouthful of pesto bless my body like a naked sunbath on warm fresh-cut grass. I was so bowled over by Italy I even briefly considered going to medical school in Sardinia, a fate professionally worse than death that I escaped chiefly by being too disorganized to arrange it.

Once home from Europe it took a year of premed science courses in Berkeley, filling out my credits with the oddest subjects I could find in the catalogue, such as Northern Indian Classical Music, before I could enroll in the Mount Sinai School of Medicine in Manhattan, intending to become a psychiatrist until I decided regular medicine was more interesting. After three more years, at Montefiore Hospital's Residency Program in Social Medicine in the Bronx, I was a committed primary care internist, ready to cure the world.

All through my medical training I would turn my memories of Italy over and over like a rabbit's foot to keep my sanity during nights on call. So in September 1978, when I found myself Board Certified in internal medicine and married to a Roman engineer, it was logical to dust off the old dream, drag Andrea back to his home town, and give Italian life a try.

November 1978, eleven at night, just inside Tanzania. The two soldiers who stopped our truck were so drunk they barely managed to keep their bayonets pointing in our direction. Andrea and I, about to close a six-week African parenthesis before settling in Rome, obediently clambered out to be escorted at riflepoint to the tent of an equally sloshed camp commander, who dressed us down and ordered the protesting truck driver to haul us back to Kenya.

Our dreams of watching lions stalk wildebeest at Ngorongoro Crater and smelling the cloves in Zanzibar had been dashed by an abrupt closing of the Tanzanian border, due to fighting near Uganda. Public buses between the two countries had been halted, railway lines had never existed, Andrea's awkward stab at bribing a ship's captain had fizzled, and this, our final attempt to cross the border, by hitchhiking, had now met the same fate. The trucker fumed all the way back across ten miles of no-man's-land and dumped us at the Kenyan border station.

There were two benches outside, narrow, wooden, and painful, where we got snatches of sleep until a workingman's bus stopped at dawn, en route to Mombasa, and picked us up. In my dreams that night I said farewell to my American life. That dusty nowhere in Africa seemed to straddle not just the edge between two countries, but a watershed between my old world and my new one. Perhaps it was facing those bayonets as a couple that hammered it home: I really had thrown in my lot with my Italian husband, and with the unknown. When our plane took off from Nairobi a week later, I was ready to leave all certainties behind and begin a joyful adventure in chaos.

preludio

1

Eternal City, Eternal Wait

When I migrated from the banks of the East River to the Tiber shores the path was strewn with bureaucratic boulders, landmines, and pitfalls. I offer the tale of my odyssey as an object lesson to would-be fellow cosmopolites in that art of abandoning all hope the Italians like to call *pazienza*.

The idea was to try working in Rome for a year and see how it went. This sensible American plan collapsed under the weight of Italian bureaucracy.

Luckily I didn't investigate every angle before starting off; if I had known the true lay of the land I might not have kept going after that Italian medical license like a donkey after his carrot. I'd have taken a job in some clinic in the Bronx, where I'd be seeing four patients an hour to this day. Instead, I made those steps you can't retrace: gave up my three-bedroom apartment on the Upper West Side with views of the Empire State Building and the Triborough Bridge, and sold my Dodge Challenger convertible to a pinky-ringed Turkish importer-exporter who planned to strip it down to the skeleton of an Oriental low-rider.

Months beforehand I started focusing my Manhattanite efficiency on getting registered in Italy, Andrea leading me by the hand through the wilderness of Old World red tape. The first step was "getting my documents together," an Italian ritual repeated before every encounter with officialdom. Sticking to a list kindly provided by the Italian Consulate, I collected my birth certificate, passport, high school diploma, college diploma, college transcript, medical school diploma, medical school transcript, certificates of internship and residency, National Board Examination certificates, American Board of Internal Medicine test results, and specialization diploma. Then I got them transfigured into Italian by the one person in New York authorized by the Italian Consulate to crown his translation with an imprimatur. We judiciously gave him a set of our own translations as crib notes, tailored by my husband to match the Rome medical school curriculum.

I wrote a cover letter from Andrea's dictation. It had to be in my own hand, on a folded sheet of double-sized pale yellow ruled Italian paper embossed with a State seal, and had to be addressed "To the Magnificent Rector of the University of Rome." You have to live in Italy a while to appreciate the theatrical elegance of making every fiddler a *Maestro* and every teacher a *Professoressa*; even the most corrupt member of the Italian parliament is by definition Honorable, and every client of a parking lot is by default, for lack of any higher title, a Doctor ("Back up, *Dotto'*, turn the wheel hard to the left, *Dotto'*").

There came the proud day in June when I got to deposit the stack of documents in front of a smiling consular official in red nail polish and Armani. After expressing puzzlement that an American doctor would want to move to her country ("You medical people have it so good here"), she Xeroxed my certificates, transcripts, and diplomas, made squiggles on the back to certify the Xeroxes were "authentic copies," gave me back the originals, and assured me that she'd get things processed zip zip in Italy so that by the time I left for Rome three months later I'd have my Italian license and be ready to get a job. Don't call me, I'll call you.

When we were about to fly in September and I still hadn't heard from her, I went to check. Found the Xeroxes piled up on Signora X's desk right where I'd left them, and the Signora gone for a month's vacation. Slightly put out, I snatched up the stack to hand-carry over (re-inventing a common expatriate method for avoiding challenges to the efficiency of the Italian mails), prepared to do battle with the system on its own territory.

Glossary: *pazienza*

Patience squared. An essential Italian virtue, often invoked as a gentle reprimand for a foreigner's loss of cool. When the grocery is out of milk, or an unannounced bus strike cancels your next patient's appointment, the word to say (with palms upturned) is *pazienza*. It extends beyond the prosaic "keep waiting" to the philosophical: you have just experienced yet another reminder that the universe is fickle and, if not haphazard, certainly not designed with your benefit in mind.

In Rome, the person in charge of *equipollenza*, or training equivalency, was located at the Foreign Ministry. I got into that mass of marble by depositing my passport at the front desk, and was escorted through dimly-lit halls wearing a temporary ID badge on my lapel and clutching my little pile of documents. The diminutive official took a glance at my grimy Xeroxes and harrumphed a little laugh through his moustache. The colleague at the New York Consulate had unfortunately gotten several things wrong, he said.

First a procedural error: the "authenticating" squiggles on the back of the copies were meaningless. They didn't even vouch for the accuracy of the photocopying, much less prove the validity of the originals. All the documents would have to be sent back and scattered around the USA for proper authentication, by local Italian consulates. For example, the Italian Consul in Boston had to testify that Harvard was a degree-granting university.

Second, the Consular list had omitted a crucial document, the Certificate of Existence in Life. No, the mere observation of me stamping my foot and tearing my hair was not, for the Italian government, sufficient proof that I existed. Yes, a nonexistent person was unlikely to be asking for an Italian medical license, but rules were rules. The Consulate's final error was a bit of misinformation, bred, perhaps, of tenderheartedness. All these documents couldn't possibly get me an Italian license. They would merely get me a toehold in the University where they might, at best, be alchemized into an Italian medical degree, but an actual license would be another and rather more difficult question.

This was my first lesson in Italian bureaucracy. The Consular official in New York clearly hadn't had the faintest idea what she was doing and no intention of trying to find out, but she had found me too simpatica to disappoint—a sentiment not strong enough to keep her from abandoning my application to gather dust.

By this time various shady sources such as Italian medical professors and representatives of international foundations had suggested an alternative to my quest for the holy grail of doctorly legitimacy: just hang out a shingle and to hell with the license. Unfortunately, I'm such a coward that climbing on a bus without a ticket gives me palpitations, so practicing without a license would be a degree of "transgression" (as the Italians call it) far beyond my talents.

While my American documents winged their way across the Atlantic to their various destinations, got stamped, authenticated, and embossed, and made it back to Italy, I had my existence in life certified. Then I signed up as a medical student and waited for the Faculty Council to decide how many of my credentials to accept. Until then, the only thing I could do besides tour the Forum was take my official Italian language examination at the University. On appointment, I walked into a room where a man looked up from his desk and asked in Italian, "Are you really a physician?" and I said, "Sì." He asked, "What's an American doctor doing moving to this second-rate country?" I said, "Non so, I don't know." He waved me out the door. I had passed.

That language exam was probably as valid as any, and quicker. But I did begin wondering. In the years I'd kept their company, Italians had always seemed quite pleased with their own ways of doing things. What made maligning their own country become a national habit when faced by a would-be emigrant American physician?

It was five months before the Faculty Council held the meeting to review my papers, in line with the year and a half it took me to get a telephone. You have to accept the deliberate unspeed of Italian timetables if you want the right to be liberated by their correspondingly laid-back lifestyle. The Council ruled to accept virtually all my coursework, but at two points my husband's translations hadn't been clever enough: I had to take examinations in Public Health and in Forensic Medicine. The dinkiest subjects in the curriculum, but they cost me another three months. I didn't mind studying, anything to reconnect with medicine.

But I was afraid I might flunk. Oral examinations before an audience were the norm in Italy, whether you were trying to pass high school geometry or get a job as a street cleaner. A friend gave me a piece of advice: introduce yourself and your unusual situation to each professor beforehand, in your highest professional style and your best suit. This suggestion turned out to be right on target. Physicians in Italy may steal each other's patients and stab each other in the back for a job, but they will courteously address each other with an intimate collegial "tu," and when facing non-initiates they will band together. Once introduced to me as a Colleague, a professor could be counted on to refrain from treating me with the sarcasm or arbitrary Fs he might award to a mere medical student. (As the Red Queen said, "It isn't etiquette to cut any one you've been introduced to.")

All I remember from Public Health is how they make ultrapasteurized milk. Forensic Medicine gave me the temporary illusion I'd be able to tell whether a body had been dead or alive when it was thrown in the lake, and treated me to a lecture from my examiner, right up there on the little stage in front of thirty other students awaiting interrogation, on the virtues of the Italian legal approach to medical misdeeds. "All you Americans can do is sue for malpractice," he said. "An Italian surgeon who leaves a sponge in the belly can be charged with assault and battery, and a physician who prescribes a drug that causes his patient's death can be brought up for manslaughter." He chose not to mention that as of the day of our conversation this exemplary law had never been applied.

Safely past the examinations, I learned to my horror that I had to produce a doctoral thesis. My panic didn't last long, because I was assured that for medical students the thesis requirement is pretty perfunctory. I found a professor with a soft spot for New

Yorkers, radiologist Plinio Rossi, who was happy to provide not only his sponsorship but a pre-digested piece of research ready to be put into final form.

The thesis took six weeks to type up and print and get bound into the obligatory hard-cover book. Following a "thesis defense" that lasted about the time it took for handshakes all around, in August 1979 I officially became a Double *Dottoressa*, with a *Laurea* next to my MD. As proof of my new status I was given a transcript including only the two examinations I'd taken in Italy, dot-matrix printed in blue ink. And the diploma, to match the ones I had seen hanging on the walls of colleagues' offices, lettered in gold leaf and scarlet? Check back in a couple of years, *Dottoressa*.

My mother-in-law stopped by periodically at the medical school to wait along with other *mamme* on the line to the Diplomas window, but she eventually gave up. At a party in 1991 I was introduced to a woman who worked in the university administration, and I took the opportunity to ask whether they were likely to have kept my diploma after all these years or whether they'd have thrown it out. "What year did you get your *Laurea?*" she asked. "1979." "Oh, it'll be ready in just a couple more years."

It actually took until 1997. Seems every one of the thousands of diplomas conferred each year by the University of Rome has to be produced by a single authorized calligrapher, who churns them out according to the less-than-rigorous work schedule of the Italian civil service. A procedure like so many others in Italy, exasperating in its time scale, but producing exquisite hand-crafted results.

At this point, just one major barrier separated me from my medical license: the *Esame di Stato*, or State Examination, which my Guardian Angel at the medical school had assured me I could take in December. When I went to find out how to actually register for the examination, the GA said, "Of course, to sit the *Esame di Stato* you will have to present proof of having done six months of *tirocinio* (internship), two in internal medicine, two in surgery, and two in obstetrics."

My heart fell—this was a new one. "But I've already done not only an internship but a complete specialization, three years full-time in the hospital."

"Ah, but Dottoressa, you did only internal medicine. We Italians require a hospital internship that covers the other specialties as well."

"But in medical school I had three months each of surgery and obstetrics!"

He sighed. "Dottoressa, your transcript says those were *frequentazioni* (clerkships), not *tirocini*." Foiled by my own translation.

I felt despair: the *Esame di Stato* was given only twice a year. I was going to lose another ten months. "But you've promised me all along I could take the *Esame di Stato* in December!"

He raised his dusty head, and spoke slowly as though to a child: "*Dottoressa*, have patience, I know perfectly well there are only four months left. Note carefully what I said: you have to PRESENT PROOF of having done a *tirocinio*."

A light bulb went on in my thick American skull. I thanked him sincerely and went off to hunt up a *primario*, a Chief Of Service, who'd be willing to sign a false certificate covering the past two months. A surgeon friend of Andrea's family obliged without a moment's hesitation.

As for the other two undergraduate *tirocini*, I decided it would be fun to do them, and more relevant to my career than tossing coins in the Trevi Fountain. On the first day of September I showed up at the obstetrics division—a false start; the nurse turned me away for lack of a white coat. Some rules, at least, are writ in stone. The next day I made it past the bouncer and hunted from floor to floor until I found a doctor. I shook his hand, introduced myself, told him my story, told him how glad I was to have the opportunity to learn obstetrics, told him how the OB service at my own medical school was mostly private so I had only gotten to catch four babies with my own hands . . . I may have gushed a little. He gave me an ironic look, and said, "Colleague, go home. This is no place for you. I'm in my fourth year of specialization in obstetrics and I haven't touched a baby yet." So much for obstetrics. Another false certificate. And another lesson in Italian education: the purpose of formal training is to inculcate theory, all practical instruction being left for on-the-job.

Tirocinio number three, internal medicine. I passed under an ochre-colored arch into the grounds of the San Camillo Hospital and wandered down paths between crumbling buildings, rubbing shoulders with pyjama-clad patients, before finding the right squat plaster pavilion. In the six-bedded rooms a cloud of white-coated figures trailed in mute reverence behind their *primario* as he paused at each bed: "This gentleman was admitted a week ago for diabetes and heart failure and has not been improving . . ." "Notice the sunken look of this man's face, he's in end-stage renal failure . . ." The purpose of hospitalization seemed to be to observe the natural evolution of disease, not to treat it.

At the third or fourth bedside the *primario* mentioned a treatment that had been long relegated to the trashbin of medical history. I piped up: "But the study by X, published eight years ago in *The New England Journal of Medicine*, demonstrated that, on the contrary . . ." The *primario* stared at me in silence. The flock of hangers-on stared at me in silence. Everybody moved on to the next bed as though nothing had happened. I was bewildered—in the United States, hospital rounds are run by the rules of one-upmanship, and the lowliest medical student is applauded for talking back to her attending physician if she can cite the right evidence. Too dumb to realize that I was in a stadium built for an entirely different ball game, I repeated my error a few patients later; the *primario* swept off while I was in mid-sentence.

At the time I didn't yet understand that everything in Italy runs on personal relations and diplomacy, that overt challenge to authority gets you nowhere. At the spot where two egos meet, Americans spar publicly while Italians exchange smiling ambassadorial communiques. The humblest stamp-seller is king behind his post office window, and will find that special issue for you only if he's cajoled rather than bullied.

As I stood there paralyzed between one bed and the next, someone tapped me on the shoulder. I turned and saw a doctor who looked like my idea of a Palestinian, all curly hair and a walrus moustache.* "Don't waste your breath on Dr. B. He's a good jazz bass player but he doesn't know anything about medicine. Come with me, I'll show you a ward more to your taste." He led me off then and there to the Nuovo Regina Margherita Hospital, three miles down the road, and introduced me to the gastroenterology *primario* Dr. Cosimo Prantera, married to an Englishwoman and "lover of all things Anglo-Saxon." We've been working together ever since, thanks to my abortive *tirocinio* and to Dr. Andrea De Arcangelis.

The *Esame di Stato* itself was something of a formality, a sprinkling of holy water before licensure. Similarly, in the States almost no interns fail the third and final portion of their National Boards. The ritual took five mornings for as many examinations, of which the most noteworthy for me was obstetrics. The professor sent us examinees off in groups of four to question and examine a pregnant woman. Vaginal exams were, of course, out of the question. I was the only one in my group to have ever laid a hand on a patient, so I showed them how to listen to lungs and to examine a liver. One poor student had cerebral palsy, and his mother came along not only to push his wheelchair but also to translate his grunts into Italian. He couldn't hold a stethoscope or palpate the patient's abdomen. I asked his mother why he had chosen to study medicine and she said because he wanted to be a doctor.

The *Esame di Stato* climaxed with the granting of a computer-generated medical license or *abilitazione*. Anticlimaxed, rather, since it turned out you couldn't start working without leaping yet another hurdle: membership in the local branch of the *Ordine dei Medici*, the Italian equivalent of the American Medical Association. No membership, no shingle. Yet another stack of certificates to gather.

---

*Not only my idea. Once shortly after a terrorist attack an alert policeman stopped him on the street for questioning. On being told in Roman dialect that he had stopped not a Palestinian but an ophthalmologist, the cop immediately pulled down his lower lid to ask about a spot.

One of the crucial documents for the *Ordine dei Medici*, it turned out, was an Italian passport. Until then nobody had bothered to mention this potentially insurmountable obstacle. It happened I did have a right to citizenship, but since it would be bestowed on me automatically by my Italian husband (Italian husbands are less powerful nowadays), the passport logically hung on Italian recognition of our American marriage, which was in turn predicated on Italian recognition of my husband's American divorce from a prior marriage. The divorce certification, based on various Byzantine legal fictions, was a long time coming. One time there was a false sighting of his Italian divorce, and I optimistically went down to the *Anagrafe* or Central Registry to see whether I could get my citizenship papers. At the end of the forty-five-minute line a small man with slicked-down hair took my documents with a yawn and disappeared into the dark forest of files.

When the clerk emerged, the bored look was gone from his face. He invited me to follow him along the long bank of teller windows, he on his side me on mine, and then pass through a little gate to the employee side. He sat me down, then paced between piled-up dossiers for a minute, no grille window to screen him off, before speaking. "Ms. Levenstein," he said kindly, "You have applied for Italian citizenship on the grounds of being married to a certain Andrea Di Vecchia." I admitted that was true. He paced a little more, lit a cigarette. "Ms. Levenstein," he said again, even more gently, and I should have caught on from the way he repeated it. "I must tell you something. This Mr. Di Vecchia—he is already married to another woman!" His hand was already out to give a comforting squeeze to my shoulder, but it dropped when I laughed and explained that the problem was red tape, not bigamy. I thought later, high drama must be rare behind the certificate window, and he had risen to its call. How many American file clerks would have been so ready for their unexpected moment of glory?

Another problem involved my residence papers, a crucial component in any pile of documents. All residents in Italy must communicate changes of address to the State within three months, and when we left my mother-in-law's for our own place eight months earlier we had duly registered the move. But when I went to pick up an identity document I was told it couldn't be issued because I was still listed at my old address.

I slyly told the clerk in the cage to hold on, scurried over from his Identity Card window to the Certificate window three paces away, had the printer spit out a Residence Certificate bearing my name and the new address, and carried it back in triumph. He wasn't impressed. "Oh, that certificate. That's from the computer, it's not worth anything. Your address has been changed in the computer, but the computerized part of the system doesn't count. What I need is something handwritten by the man who *really* registers changes of address." The pen-and-ink certificate that counted could only be obtained by my penetrating, in person, deep into the bowels of the *Anagrafe*, to cajole a hunched and ancient employee into hand-copying my new address from one tattered ten-pound volume to another, and into scrawling proof of the transaction on a slip of paper. In 1979 Italians adored technology, but didn't trust it.

When I finally thought I had gotten all my documents together for the *Ordine dei Medici*—including a *Certificato di Buona Condotta* (Good Conduct) from the police, two certificates of *Capacità Civile* from the courts (swearing that no criminal charges were pending against me to sully my Civic Capacity), and a *Certificato di Diritti Politici* (attesting to my Political Rights, which would have fallen into limbo had I FAILED TO VOTE DESPITE HAVING BEEN ELIGIBLE during two out of the three last Italian elections)—a last monster lurked in the bushes at the end of the queue: my middle name, Beth. My parents had snuck it past my grandmother Bessie in the first place, since Jewish tradition forbade my getting her name while she was still alive, so some of my documents carried it and others did not. Unacceptable, I was told. In Italy you have one and only one version of your name. But *fatta la legge, trovato l'inganno*, for every law there's a way to foil it, and Italian bureaucracy generally provides the solution once it's created a problem. I had to make another trip to the *Anagrafe*, to swear on my honor before an official of the Italian State that "Susan Levenstein, born on 21 January 1948 in New York City" and "Susan Beth Levenstein, born on 21 January 1948 in New York City" were "one and the same person." Then I had to get the resulting certificate back to the *Ordine dei Medici* toot sweet, since after three months it would no longer be valid and Susan Levenstein and Susan Beth Levenstein would revert to being total strangers.

Within sniffing range of my Italian license, I arranged an appointment with the head of the *Ordine dei Medici* to discuss what I saw as the next step, getting recognition of my internal medicine specialization. He didn't hesitate with his answer: "There's no way for you to get recognized as a specialist." Ha. By now I had learned that in Italy there was a way around any problem. "No, *collega*," he explained, "it's absolutely impossible. Tell me again, what year did you graduate from medical school?" "1975," I said. "No, I mean your Italian *Laurea*." "1979." "And when did you finish your specialization?" "In 1978," I had to answer. "Well, *Dottoressa*, how could you have possibly qualified for a specialization before graduating from medical school?" He leaned back, looking rather pleased with himself.

It came time to decide what kind of doctoring I would do. My original intention had been to work as a salaried generalist in a public clinic, as I would have in the States: the thankless front lines of medicine. But by now I had learned that there were no such clinics in Italy, only individual National Health Service docs, each in his own office. The simplest way to become one was to poison your predecessor. A riotous Italian film from 1968, *Il Medico Della Mutua* ("Be Sick . . . It's Free"), stars Alberto Sordi as one of a gaggle of young docs gathered like jackals around the deathbed of a colleague, jostling to grab his practice once he kicks off. Sordi wins, by seducing the not-quite widow.

Then there was hospital work. But it turned out that Rome public hospitals never hired their staff fresh out of training, even if my residency had been recognized. Young physicians would work on the wards gratis for five or ten years, freeloading off *mamma*, in hopes of eventually landing a paid job. Yes, I was willing to work for low wages, but zero was out of my range. Reluctantly, contrary to my philosophical principles and to my natural professional subservience, I realized it would have to be private practice or nothing.

Shortly before Hang-Shingle Day, I began effusing at a dinner table to an Italian doctor about how excited I was to start practicing at last. He opted for brutal frankness: "But Susan, my dear, you must understand that there's no point in spending your good money to rent an office. No Italian will go privately to a young doctor—in Italy a doctor isn't expected to know anything unless he has twenty years of experience and is a *primario*." Thank God we hadn't met when I first arrived in Rome, or I might have thrown in the sponge long before.

When I finally did get set up in an office in February 1980, business was slow. I saw one patient my first month, four patients my second month, ten patients my third month—a geometric growth curve, as an optimistic mathematical friend pointed out. I felt like a real doc when, after six months, I first saw three patients in one afternoon. Fortunately Dr. Prantera found a way to award me a half-year paid internship; the $180 I earned each month (not week, month) nearly paid the office rent. All in all it was three years between the Big Move and solvency.

As any expatriate will tell you, the joy when success—usually embodied in an insignificant-looking scrap of paper—crowns a protracted war with Italian bureaucracy is so intense that it wipes out the memory of all tribulations faced along the way. Sort of like childbirth. And the saga of my year cleaning those Augean stables, in hopes that my personal medical niche would emerge from under the muck, has long since been demoted to the status of amusing stories. What is the reaction of Italians when I tell them these tales of my Herculean labors? "Unbelievable! You managed to get your license in only a year and a half! You were earning a living after only three years! The efficiency of you *americani* is really amazing!"

2

Wet Paint on My Shingle

By rotten luck, when I consummated my love affair with Italy by moving to Rome the bottom had just dropped out of the lifestyle. In late 1978, the Middle East oil crisis was forcing restaurants to close at 9:00, the normal hour to sit down for dinner; inflation was pushing twenty percent; terrorist groups from both extremes of the political spectrum, and police overreactions to the same, added a fillip of danger to city life. Former Prime Minister Aldo Moro had recently been abducted and murdered by the Red Brigades, plain-clothes cops would flag down motorists to check their documents, and if you mistook the cops for terrorists and didn't stop you'd be shot dead. The bustle had disappeared from the streets, and Italians of my own hypersocial generation, who had their broken sixties dreams to nurse besides the rest of the misery, just sat home and moped. They called it *il riflusso*—literally, the ebbing tide, figuratively, the return to private life.

Andrea at least had his job, while I had nothing but two thumbs to twiddle. What kept me from going nuts during my year plus of forced unemployment was wandering from church to museum to ruin clutching a ragged copy of Georgina Masson's Companion Guide. If an Italian tour guide license hadn't been even harder to obtain than a medical license, I could have earned my keep taking groups around.

A perk was getting to know my *suocera* (mother-in-law) during the five months we camped at her place. Mariada was born in Terracina, halfway down the coast to Naples, and had never set foot in a school; a tutor came to her family's palace. I found her flexibility astonishing. At forty her sons persuaded her to transfer her political loyalties from Christian Democrat to Communist, at fifty after her husband died she learned to drive on medieval Rome streets that I found scary after fifteen years behind the wheel, and at sixty she opened her arms to a foreign daughter-in-law without a trace of bossiness. My worst problem living in her home was having to hide my dirty underwear so she wouldn't give it to her maid to hand wash.

My husband and I could survive on one salary—we were young and could *campare d'aria*, live on air—but it was harder to forfeit the professional identity I had painfully forged in seven years of medical training, that secret pride of riding home on the subway bleary-eyed, stethoscope-cum-identity-badge dangling from my white coat like a Phi Beta Kappa key. In Rome I went from being a hundred-hour-a-week doctor to being a tag-along in my husband's world.

Back in the States I'd have at least kept my dignity as a physician, though temporarily on furlough, but I soon learned that in my adoptive homeland, for better or for worse, you are not defined by your profession. Where New Yorkers pigeonhole you within ten minutes of being introduced, Italians consider it faintly rude to enquire—you might hate your job and prefer not hearing it mentioned, and besides, in their scheme of things work is a minor element. I spent whole evenings without anyone finding out I was a doctor. Not to mention that in Italian you don't say, "I am a doctor," you say, "I *do* doctoring," and for what seemed an eternity I was *doing* nothing of the sort.

Sometimes no other conversation was directed at me either. Andrea tried to convince me that the cold-shoulder was another form of Italian courtesy, it being considered harassment to bombard a new acquaintance with questions. They think it eases a newcomer's vulnerability to let her observe mute and invisible until the others have revealed enough of themselves to orient her. Not me, it just made me feel insignificant.

Not that it helped much when my hypothetical profession did get mentioned. Unemployed Italian doctors were a dime a dozen, and even working docs didn't wear the halo they do in the States. Caption for a 1979 newspaper photo of a picket line: "Like all workers, these physicians demand paid vacations, sick leave, and maternity leave." I was floundering around with no professional role to shore up my ego, just when that forlorn ego needed all the shoring it could get.

By the time I was armed with a license and an office I'd been away from medicine for nearly two years and felt like an imposter. Every case threw me into a torment of indecision: I had lost my nerve. To build my self-confidence as much as to build my practice, I set out to get connected.

For starters I went around introducing myself to all the docs who catered to the English-speaking community. Dr. Jeans, a Scotswoman on the far side of seventy. Dr. Stoppani, a kindly soul and good GP who gave me some tips and once even let me cover for him. (Better-established docs would have tried to steal his patients.) Dr. S., an internist who looked at me and saw visions of a plummeting earnings curve. Dr. Lollini, who boasted not just a twelve-month tan but a past life as a baritone, and had sewn up the top-level referrals from the American Embassy in part by investing in a box at the opera for the Health Unit staff. Dr. Renzulli, a Calabrian nobleman whose pediatric practice supplemented the income from what I ingenuously imagined as vast land holdings. Dr. Lewin, a German-American pediatrician whose piercing eyes never left me as she said, "Italian doctors are so bad you can get sloppy and still be the best around. Don't let it happen." Dr. De Feo, a Canadian-trained cardiologist who patiently answered my nocturnal cries for help, confabbed with me once a week over lunch, and led me by the hand through the booby-trapped maze of Roman medicine . . . So sad to list their names, every one now departed from this world.

Step two was looking into private hospitals—private usually meaning, for hospitals as for schools, run by the Catholic Church.

Obtaining admitting privileges wasn't easy. Nobody was interested in a 30-year-old attending physician, especially foreign, female, and with a distinctly non-Catholic name. My letters went unanswered, and I was too cowardly to make cold calls. One Medical Director in a floor-length nun's habit did grant a brief audience before standing up and saying, "We'll be in touch." In the end, fortunately, the Salvator Mundi International Hospital felt obliged to honor its putative cosmopolitan creds and give me a chance.

Minor medical issues in the family set the rusty doctor cogs in my brain to turning again. Once Mariada twisted her ankle and I told her to keep it elevated all day under an icepack. She was impressed at the outcome and told me that evening that American medicine was marvelous. I thought she was joking, but no—she said any Italian doctor would have prescribed two creams and three pills but no rest, elevation, or ice.

Meanwhile my waiting room stayed empty. I wrote to ninety-odd English-speaking embassies, schools, cultural institutions, international organizations, and companies, letting them know I had opened a practice and enclosing my Curriculum Vitae. There were no computers back then, so my letters were individually hand-typed, hand-stamped, and dropped in the mailbox. The number of patients that effort yielded: zero.

Eventually the US Embassy Health Unit took me under their wing, keeping me in pin money by sending around staff for colds, vaginitis, and periodic physicals, while other customers began to trickle in. My very first paying client, the Neapolitan wife of one of Andrea's colleagues, who came complaining of painful ovulation, has remained my patient to this day. English nannies, college kids from junior year abroad programs, backpackers, and other youngsters were easy draws and said seeing me wasn't like going to the doctor.

Anglophone nuns, monks, and priests passed my name around their grapevine—memorably Sister Anne, whose abdominal pain I could never diagnose properly because she only let me examine her through a whalebone corset. Brother Charles had an ulcer. "I know what gave it to me, doc, it's those damned chapel bells at the monastery. Every fifteen minutes, day and night, they're driving me crazy." Brother Andrew was the only patient who has ever walked out of my office with the advice to lose thirty pounds and walked back in six months later thirty pounds lighter—long live those vows of obedience!

Reinventing doctoring was both glorious and frightening. During medical residency my ambition had been getting my specialty diploma with my sanity intact. Now, plunged into private practice, my main goal was just as primitive: don't screw up. When a patient moved away before I did anything to wreck her fond image of me, my main emotion was relief.

All my life I was scared of other people and terrified of public speaking. When I was invited to speak about my research on stress and peptic ulcer to the Academy of Behavioral Medicine Research, the crème de la crème of psychosomatic medicine, 150 granite-faced academics who had written all the textbooks, my legs shook so much I had to clutch the podium with two hands to keep from falling down.

Starting in practice I was afraid of my patients too, experiencing each visit as a performance in front of a new audience. I secretly missed the aged and half-gaga victims we'd had at Morrisania and Montefiore Hospitals in the Bronx, whose judgment never fazed me. Patients my own age were scary because I thought they'd see through me, brand-new patients because first impressions last, repeat customers because they had higher expectations. At a certain point I noticed that fear would make me leave the ends of my sentences dangling, and with superhuman will power I started to force myself to complete all the sentences I began. Instead of letting "Put your feet . . ." trail off into silence, I'd add "in the stirrups," and "I'm just going to . . ." might finish with "test your reflexes." The sky did not fall.

One of my first Italian patients had a thyroid nodule so large you could see it across the desk. She was a painted doll of a woman, accompanied by an older man in a three-piece suit who did all the talking and put up resistance when I invited him to leave the room during the examination. I insisted, greenhorn that I was, oblivious to the risks involved in making a guy lose face in front of his moll. I told her the lump could be cancerous and advised a needle biopsy, a recent innovation even in the United States. When she didn't show up for her return appointment I called, and he picked up the phone: "How dare you call us, shit American feminist? I took her to a real doctor, who told me the nodule is totally insignificant, you damn lesbian whore!" I do hope it was benign.

My early professional life was short on patients but long on learning experiences.

Over dinner one night I asked an anesthesiologist friend of the family what anesthetic was preferred in Italy for childbirth. *"Il grido,"* he replied, "The scream." As though it were an explanation he continued, "Remember that the book of Genesis says women shall bring forth children in pain." Even today, many public obstetrical wards don't offer either epidurals or painkillers.

I learned from patients' horror stories that Italian surgeons didn't use local anesthesia when they sewed up lacerations, or prescribe strong painkillers after surgery; cancer patients were given opiates only when death was days away. Patient activist movements have improved things a bit by now, and since the turn of the millennium I can even prescribe the equivalent of Percocet. But most of those ER docs are *still* doing their stitching without lidocaine.

I learned from personal experience that in Italy a physician who goes to a drugstore to buy morphine to keep in the office for emergencies is looked at like a drug addict. The first time I filled in a triplicate prescription for four vials and handed it to a pharmacist along with my medical license he looked at me crosswise and said they were out of it. So was a second, a third, and a fourth. Being treated as a criminal makes you feel like one, and for years whenever it came time to replace my expired vials I would put on my best clothes, as I would to go shopping on Via Borgognona, and even so my heart would pound. I can only imagine how hard it must be for Italian cancer patients who need to buy the stuff for personal use.

I learned from the newspapers too. Shortly after I moved to Rome, Giovanni Agnelli, CEO of Fiat, nicknamed "Rake of the Riviera," fell and broke his hip. His personal physician, according to the front-page story in *La Repubblica*, was treating him at home with the leg under traction. I was floored—according to my training, bed rest with traction had been ditched years earlier in favor of immediate surgery, which had patients up and around in days with fewer complications. What I found astonishing was not that an Italian doctor might be behind the times, but that the richest man in Italy would be under the care of an ignoramus. Lesson: loyalty trumps competence. (P.S. A week later, buried on page seventeen, was a one-line report that Agnelli had been flown to New York for surgery.)

Once I had a cold and my voice stayed hoarse for months. The word cancer started creeping into my mind, so I asked an ear-nose-and-throat man to take a look at my vocal cords. He said they just looked a little red and I said great, that's all I wanted to know. As I rose to leave he said, "Wait, I'll write you a prescription." He scribbled the name of a pill, a suppository, and a nose spray. I protested with a smile but he kept going. He added something to gargle with, something to stir into water and drink, and something to inject. Lesson: the longer the prescription the more powerful the prescriber. Whenever I order more than two medications for a single illness I remember that visit.

Old-fashioned Italians assign a hierarchy to routes of administration. Pills are one step down in magic-bullet power from suppositories, two steps down from an intramuscular injection, three from a shot into the vein. The jackpot is a half-hour's intravenous infusion, called by the unsophisticated a *lavaggio del sangue*, getting your blood washed, which cures whatever ails you, at least it did back when I first hit town. I've assimilated some Italian eclecticism by now—pills can be hard on the stomach—and can tell you that even Americans can learn to ease in a suppository. Most, anyway.

I would make house calls then for situations that nowadays I'd triage over the phone straight to the emergency room. Once at three in the morning I raced with my toaster-sized ECG machine to the bedside of an American coed with chest pain. The tracing that rolled off the machine looked like . . . a heart attack, though at her age it was more likely a viral infection of the heart muscle. I packed her into my car and drove madly across Rome to a major hospital, whizzing through dozens of red lights. I never got stopped and never received a ticket, a practical lesson in why Italians don't bother to obey the law.

I learned about Italians' horror of iatrogenesis, damage caused by doctors, when one of our patients at the Nuovo Regina Margherita Hospital went briefly into shock after an infusion of glucagon, standard procedure at the time to relax the stomach for a high-quality x-ray. I wrote up this interesting case and added the names of all the other colleagues involved. To my amazement, even though they'd ordinarily sell their grandmother to get published in an international medical journal, not one of them would sign this report—as though the side effect had been their personal fault. It wound up printed as a letter in the prestigious *Journal of the American Medical Association* with me as sole author.

(American physicians, on the contrary, are terrified by risking sins of omission. This Anglophone/Continental divide goes back a ways, if Queen Victoria's Prime Minister William Lamb could quip, "English physicians kill you. The French let you die." My beloved teacher Dr. Robert Matz used to counter with, "Don't just do something, stand there.")

An Italian colleague asked me how they selected among applicants for medical school in the States. "College grades, mostly," I answered, "But also scores on a Medical College Admission Test, a personal interview, recommendations . . ." He chortled and said, *"Allora tutto il mondo è paese!* So the world is just a small village— even in the great America you have to know somebody." I was mystified, not realizing that when I had translated recommendations as *raccomandazioni* I had produced the Italian word for having someone powerful pull strings in your favor. Case in point: a breast cancer patient called Milan's famous Tumor Institute and was given an appointment a month later. Then she discovered she knew someone who knew someone who knew its Chief, Professor Veronesi, and was squeezed in the next day.

Glossary: *raccomandazione*

A nudge from friends in high places that helps you land a job, a telephone line, a boot camp close to *mamma*. Traditionally offered by a politician in return for votes or support. *La Repubblica* editorial: "Italy is based on the *raccomandazione*, you need one even to get what's yours by right." A *raccomandazione* has no pretense of being based on merit, and is never put into writing.

According to Roberto Saviano, author of *Gomorrah*, the protagonists of one major scandal in Naples sincerely had no idea they were doing anything wrong because no money had changed hands, only favors such as giving someone's brother-in-law a job. The idea that the innocuous and ubiquitous *raccomandazione* is a form of corruption was greeted by many, says Saviano, "with genuine stupor and indignation."

As an examining physician for the Social Security Administration, I once experienced the *frisson* of being the object of a genuine *raccomandazione*: an under-minister phoned to let me know how displeased the Minister would be if a certain Signora was not given a pension. It was slightly disappointing to find on examination that the Signora in question was morbidly obese and diabetic, thus actually meeting the criteria for disability. Pension applicants devoid of connections sometimes offered small gifts, which I would gently push back across the desk. Once I made an exception, when an elderly woman brought six eggs her chickens had laid two hours earlier. The crime of her bribe paled before the crime of leaving those fresh eggs uneaten. I reprimanded the patient but accepted the loot and handed it around to my staff, who proceeded to stick pinholes in both ends and suck 'em raw.

I used pull once myself, to fix a traffic ticket. I had entered a freeway by mistake, asked the guys at both toll booths what to do, made a U-turn and drove off as they instructed, and a month later got socked with a fine for half a million lire (more than $500). I called a politician friend, he must have called somebody, and . . . the fine dropped into a black hole. What a perverse pleasure sprouted in my bosom from this tiny dabble in Italian-style transgression! Italians sometimes try these tricks in other countries, irritating the hell out of people.

Being somebody is even more important than knowing somebody. One friend happens to share a name with a star soccer player, and when cops see his license they tear up the speeding ticket. When a patient of mine got admitted to the San Giovanni Hospital for coughing up blood, I had a gastroenterologist friend who works there stop by to chat up the docs, so they'd know she wasn't just a random carcass.

A musicologist pal in the States once wrote asking me to go to the Museo Braschi, near Piazza Navona, and buy a postcard of a particular painting that featured a small orchestra. I walked over, saw they didn't sell postcards . . . and when I tell the story to an Italian that's as far as I get. "You should have gotten in touch with me," one interrupted, "My sister-in-law works in the Art Ministry!" Another: "I have a friend who knows the director of the Villa Giulia Museum, she could have made a phone call!" What actually ensued was that I asked a guard, he opened the door to the administrative wing, and I knocked at the office of the museum Director. When she heard my request she complained about the trashy exhibit that was hiding my painting behind a panel, searched unsuccessfully through her personal lecture slides for one that would do, and finally arranged for a museum photographer to come in the next week and take the picture that is now reproduced in my friend's book. Despite what Italians think, you don't always need a *raccomandazione*.

The recommendation as we understand it, where a competent person of judgment tells a school or an employer that the candidate is high caliber, is an un-Italian concept. If you insist, your Chief of Service may write more or less, "So-and-so is an upstanding person and has performed adequately during his years under my supervision." Like a reference for a maid: she does her job and doesn't steal.

Giuseppe, an unusually bright and conscientious medical student applying for a residency in the US, once asked me to compose a letter of recommendation in English for his *primario* to sign. I wrote that Giuseppe was one of the five best medical students the signer had seen in the last ten years. The *primario* refused, shocked: "I can't say he's better than other students, that would be unfair to everybody else." I was reminded of how Italian students always study in groups, and how a children's book from Communist China once amused me by its emphasis on cooperation—maybe it's individualistic America that's the odd man out.

In the Italy where I landed, men were men, women were women, and grownups didn't dress like kids. On Via del Corso gaggles of bright-clad girls drifted like so many posies from store to store, old women plodded past in black, wealthy shoppers wore silks and heavy jewelry, guys wore three-piece suits and housewives conservative dresses, and they were all, without pause and without exception, giving each other the once-over. For Italians your looks project your inner self, and being dressed is a far cry from merely being covered. Two women heading in opposite directions scan each other from coiffure to pumps within four paces, clocking every detail. For them the street is not the shortest path between two points but a theater for seeing and being seen. If you skulk along in the shadows trying to avoid attention, they tinge their appraising stare with a smirk.

Trying to emulate impeccable Italian professional women, I felt like a Bigfoot stepsister attempting to squeeze her pedal extremity into Cinderella's shoe. In New York I'd worn corduroy slacks and Clarks Wallabees inside the hospital, blue jeans elsewhere, but in the Italy of 1980 no woman over twenty wore either pants or flat shoes. It was bad enough to be American, which by definition meant devoid of fashion sense, but I was a particularly androgynous member of a particularly style-scorning subculture, and as a doctor it wasn't enough to pass—I had to impress.

No help from shop personnel. Their mission was less to sell clothes than to cultivate a stable of good customers and drive away any new entries whose inelegance would detract from the store's panache. In a boutique above my station, I once referred to the one-inch heels on a chi-chi sandal as comfortably low. "Low?" sneered the salesgirl, "They're not low, they're high, extremely high." The harem atmosphere, the mirrors outside rather than inside the fitting rooms, the girls adjusting the folds on my body . . . for an ex-hippie seeking acculturation it was all one blur of embarrassment.

I found it a mystery how Italians managed so effortlessly to ooze natural style and graceful self-assurance. If it became too hot for a sweater they'd drape it over their shoulders with the sleeves dangling artistically, their sunglasses were tucked decoratively into the neckline when they went indoors, the cloth they sunbathed on at the beach got knotted over one shoulder and voilà a spiffy cover-up. How could I ever match them? I pored over fashion magazines. I learned to go shopping dressed to the nines. I got coached by my husband and his mother on what goes with what— *"marrone e celeste, cafone veste,"* only a hick wears brown with light blue—and on fixing the slouch and bull-in-a-china-shop mannerisms that screamed *"americana."* You usually can tag a tourist on a Rome street on the basis of their peachy Polish complexion, dog-eared English shag cuts, or grammatically correct college T-shirts stretched across all-American pectorals. When you can't, their stride gives them away—window-shoppers may dress convincingly Italian, but as soon as they walk off, a heavy-footed gait spells German, a marshmallow skitter English.

One day I felt confident enough to brave the salesgirls on Corso Vittorio Emmanuele and came home with a pastel green linen suit, two-inch beige heels, and a matching purse. I'll never forget that outfit's first airing in the hospital: nurses, docs, and wheelchair pushers alike complimented me on finally dressing right.

At first I would get dolled up to see patients but otherwise stick to American sloppy, until one day I went in dungarees to a private hospital to look at an x-ray. I ran into the Director in the hall, who glared over his glasses: "Next time you come here, you'll come dressed like a physician!"

That encounter had me living in sartorial purgatory for years, keeping my blue jeans stashed away even on weekends for fear I might run into a patient on the street. Well-dressed patients cowed me—once I was so impressed by the sight of a woman's white blouse, its fine silk hidden under a sweater except the collar tips and an inch of cuff, that I couldn't stop stammering.

In the deeper Italian philosophy of appearance, though, clothes are only a prop. I caught on one Saturday when a friend invited me to meet him at an art opening. Under the illusion that you went to art shows to look at pictures, I showed up in my jeans and workshirt, only to find the gallery filled with a spike-heeled emerald-necklace crowd, including film star Monica Vitti in the flesh. I tried to run away but Silvio insisted on steering me inside by the elbow, whispering instructions. I obediently meditated on the Essence of Enigmatic Woman, drew my backbone up straight, and circumnavigated the room casting a cool neutral gaze straight through each of my fellow guests. Silvio, the prince of flattery, claimed afterward that everybody must have taken me for a foreign celebrity so innately chic she didn't need to dress up.

In the United States nobody drops out of medical school. Here's how it works: you spend your first year consorting with cadavers and test tubes, so of course you stick around the next year to learn physiology, history-taking, and physical examination. But that's just a prelude to the grueling but glorious year three when you play doctor on the wards. Once you've survived the basic clerkships it would be foolish to quit, since in your final year you can choose your own rotations and even loaf a little. The degree you get after four years is useless by itself, so you'd be silly not to endure the internship that's required to get your medical license. *Da cosa nasce cosa*, one thing leads to another . . .

It was a little like that with my move to Italy. I came to try working here for a year, and though after twice that time and prodigious effort I had barely even set up shop, still every advance felt like a triumph. Each new barrier promised to be the last, the joys of living like an Italian always waiting just around the corner. Nothing could weaken my adoration of the country. Even the end of my Italian marriage after nine years didn't drive me away, though it did prompt me to invent a second career as a researcher in psychosomatic medicine to fill all those empty evenings. When I later took up with Alvin Curran, an American composer who's lived in Rome longer than I have, what followed wasn't repatriation but a crash course in contemporary music and the addition of another sideline, as Artist's Wife. It never occurred to me to head home.

3

Seven Hills, Seven Offices

1. Via Savoia 1980

Finding my first Rome office was easy as pie. In late 1979, closing in on my medical license, I met an American doc who had semi-retired to Rome two years earlier. He sublet a room in an accountant's office in a posh neighborhood near Villa Borghese and generously offered it to me two mornings a week, giving me a key and some tips. I had prescriptions printed up, and as soon as the day in January arrived when I was finally licensed to write one, I put on my best clothes and carried a pad over to Via Savoia, along with my stethoscope and blood pressure cuff. The room breathed old-world elegance and sobriety, with a huge oak desk, massive walnut bookshelves lining the walls, and an exam table half screened off in the corner. On the desk was a scribbled note: "The landlord changed his mind. Please leave the key."

Easy come, easy go. I was out before I'd seen a single patient.

2. Via Scialoja 1980–82

My mother-in-law came to the rescue. Her dermatologist neighbor, Dr. Lupi, owned his basement office on nearby Via Scialoja, a couple of blocks outside the monumental Piazza del Popolo gate— after Queen Christina of Sweden converted to Catholicism and renounced her throne, she entered Rome here in 1655—and was willing to let me, for a fee, use a spare room twice a week when he wasn't there. It was dank, it was dim, it was long overdue for a paint job, but it had a desk and a waiting room and I was happy.

Beyond my stethoscope and blood pressure machine I needed an exam table. This was a nontrivial problem: the Italian ones were so flimsy they would tip over if you sat on them wrong, and I knew my American patients would sit on them wrong. I was in luck—the Embassy's Health Unit happened to have an old table to give away. Its red paint was chipping, its back squealed when you cranked it up, and there was a dent in the side, but it had drawers and gynecological stirrups and you couldn't push it over if you tried. I jerry-rigged my unused Via Savoia prescriptions one by one, using a rubber stamp to cross out the old address and print the new one, and I had a batch of business cards run off, declaring in an uneven nineteenth-century type font that on Monday and Thursday mornings the doctor was in.

The office came with a household god named Luigina who was dark, round, bustling, and good at propelling the patients from door to waiting room to exam room and out. When Dr. Lupi was there she took their money as well, but since her only language was a sharp-tongued *Romanaccio* I had to awkwardly collect my own fees from any patient who spoke only English. Every young professional should be forced do this for a while—it forces you to decide your labor is actually worth paying for. Much of the time I had doubts. Medical training in the United States is a blind headlong dash, and when mine culminated unexpectedly in unemployment it was like running full tilt into a brick wall. After more than a year and a half away I could barely remember what doctoring meant, much less actually do it.

In off hours Luigina would be found sitting at a little desk on the fourth floor landing, selling tickets for an avant-garde theater troupe that mingled inside apartment 11, naked, with the spectators. In her day job she protected me fiercely. Once an Italian patient complained she shouldn't have to pay because I had only talked with her—for forty-five minutes—without doing a physical examination. Luigina shot back, "Tell me, when you see your lawyer, do you strip?"

After two years in bargain-basement purgatory my practice had reached subsistence level and I was ready to take up Professor Rossi, my thesis benefactor, on his invitation to join the group practice where he worked afternoons. Financially risky, but a quantum leap forward status-wise.

3. Via del Tritone 1982–91
The Medical Diagnostic Center

I sat in a circle with Signora O. and the ten physicians of the Medical Diagnostic Center, near the foot of Via Veneto on the Quirinal hill, fielding an interview in my one suit and one pair of heels, trying to approximate a flawless smile and aura of professionalism and keep my ankles crossed under the chair. Professor Rossi had talked up my competence, but his colleagues mainly wanted to know how much business I'd bring. I told them I was in with the Embassy and had gone around and introduced myself to some of the main actors on the expat medical scene. But when Signora O. asked me about Professor So-and-so, I had to admit I'd never heard of him: *"Mai coperto,"* I said using my husband's habitual phrase. The shadow of a giggle emerged from her direction, and I heard stifled snorts elsewhere in the room before we hastily moved on. I got home to Andrea and demanded, "What does *'mai coperto'* mean, exactly?" He was alarmed: "You didn't say it to anybody, did you? What it literally means is 'I've never fucked him.'"

The group wanted me, even if my language gave reason to suspect I kept bad company. As a genuine American doc, I'd add to their international cachet and eventually, they hoped, lure in masses of foreign patients. The only holdout was the internist Dr. S., who had already met me and smelled competition. In the end he was strong-armed into letting me in, on one condition: none of the docs in the office would ever refer a patient to me. And, in the nine years I was there, no one ever did.

Like most large medical offices in Rome, the Medical Diagnostic Center was designed to fuel a diagnostic testing laboratory, the physicians mere appendages imported to funnel work to the blood-letters down the hall. Three owners shared its paltry profits: one ran the laboratory, the second was the ophthalmologist, and Signora O. did the administration. She was a good enough egg, but had an incorrigible habit of beating around the bush. Flailing about to get straight answers out of her made it harder for me to settle in.

The classy location on one of the city's top shopping streets had drawbacks—you don't really grasp how loud background noise is until you try to use a stethoscope. The waiting room was dark as Hades, and the only magazines it offered were *Famiglia Cristiana* and *Polizia Moderna*. But my examining room was large verging on cavernous, the in-house lab testing and x-rays were convenient, and the group's specialists covered all the bases. Even not getting patients from my colleagues had its advantages; that way nobody expected a kickback.

I shared my room with a dermatologist whom I will call Dr. M. After hearing that one of the UN agencies had stopped referring to him because he had the habit of seducing his patients, Dottoressa Goody-Two-Shoes sat Dr. M. down for interrogation. "Absolutely untrue," he said, "I've never had sexual relations with a patient . . . inside this office." At least he drew the line somewhere—offered the right sum, I could name several Rome docs who do use their examining rooms for trysting.

A new secretary, Mariateresa Barbieri, was hired while I was off in Jamaica on vacation. People talk, and when I got back she was curious to meet the *dottoressa americana* who swore like a truck driver. What I noticed was mainly that she was blonde and spoke five languages, and I called her by the polite *Lei*.

Until June, that is, when Jimmy Cliff came to town to sing a concert in a huge tent near Mussolini's EUR district. His timing couldn't have been worse—that night Italy was playing Argentina in the World Cup. Everybody in Rome preferred being glued to their television sets to listening to reggae, except my husband, me, and another few score hard-core fans who included Mariateresa. As she tells it, she pointed me out to her friend. "There's the Dottoressa Levenstein sitting across the way." "Look, the Dottoressa Levenstein is clapping her hands." "Look, the Dottoressa is standing on her seat and dancing!" It was the beginning of a friendship and a working relationship that has become reciprocally indispensable—I couldn't work without her, and she claims if I quit she'd throw over the medical world and open a bed-and-breakfast.

After three decades, I still work with Medical Diagnostic Center physicians—endocrinologist Vincenzo Bacci, radiologist Plinio Rossi, surgeon Virgilio Ciampa—but my most important inheritance from Via del Tritone was definitely Mariateresa. Office business aside, we're great friends and have traveled together to Tanzania, Thailand, Turkey, the Soviet Union, and, once, San Francisco, where we spent a free afternoon in Marin County visiting a lesbian couple who had been patients when they lived in Rome. Admiring a panorama, one of them asked us whether we had a view over Rome from our bedroom. Mariateresa and I looked at each other and choked with laughter, it having never occurred to us that we could be thought to be, much less actually be, a couple. But it made sense—why else would a doctor and her secretary be so close?

Nothing lasts forever. The ophthalmologist died, and his heirs, not unreasonably, preferred cash in hand to one-third interest in an unprofitable business. So the apartment was put on the market, and I was back on the street.

4. Via Cesare Balbo 1991–97
The Balbo Medical Associates

The demise of the Medical Diagnostic Center was a blessing in disguise—a chance for two of my American-trained colleagues, Mariateresa, and me to embark on our own medical start-up, free of alternative facts and the *Christian Family* magazine. We found a place on another of the hills of Rome, the Viminale, between Santa Maria Maggiore and the opera house, with one examining room per doc. My two male Italian partners trooped off to a condominium meeting to get our neighbors' grudging OK for a medical office in the building, prudently leaving their unsettlingly foreign female colleague behind.

The place had been a fashion showroom in its previous incarnation, so there were bright lights and lots of mirrors, but the rest was up to us. Mariateresa decided to reign from the end of a long welcoming corridor, and designed a custom-built desk. We carved out a tiny waiting room, sound-proofed a door, ripped out some carpeting, laid down terracotta in one room and doussié parquet in another, printed up an "Introduction to the Balbo Medical Associates" brochure, and were ready to roll.

There was one small hitch: no patients. It turned out that when word came down that the Medical Diagnostic Center was going to fold, the internist and the dermatologist had quietly called the phone company and stolen one of the lines, ordering it transferred to their newly-rented office nearby. Then they instructed their receptionist to tell anyone who innocently phoned for an appointment with other MDC docs, "He (or she) doesn't work with us any more"—which was the literal truth—"and we don't have his (her) telephone number"—which was a lie. In my case they had the receptionist add: "We hear she may have gone back to America." A year later I was pleased to hear that these two gentlemanly ex-colleagues had come to blows over money, sending each other to the emergency room.

I'm not big on change, and when the move was compounded with that lesson in Italian collegiality and a case of the flu with every complication in the book, I was thrown off balance. I assumed my daily migraine was psychosomatic; it took me a year to realize it was those damned halogen showroom lights.

In the end the patients came straggling back, and it became a pleasure to work with my buddies in that cozy office, subletting afternoons to several colleagues and making our collective administrative decisions over a weekly trattoria lunch. Outside the window birds chirped in place of the Via del Tritone traffic, and when the Suore Oblate Agostiniane around the corner pulled the rope on their chapel bell every evening at six, they sent such beautiful harmonics into the surrounding air that I'd take the stethoscope out of my ears to listen.

This good thing, too, came to an end. After six years one of the docs in the office was finding business slow and convinced himself the problem was our location in central Rome, across the street from the Ministry of the Interior. No matter that we were near numerous bus lines, within reach of the Metro, and surrounded by parking spaces—all right, they *were* all illegal, but nobody ever got a ticket, and if once a year a team of tow trucks came round and hauled off all the cars I'd call that good odds. Maybe eventually City Hall would close off the neighborhood to private automobiles, but for the moment its principal drawback for motorists was being a favorite spot for thieves—the challenge of working literally in the shadow of cop central seemed to give them a kick. Virtually every morning there'd be a new little splatter of bluish glass morsels somewhere on the block, where one more car window had bitten the dust.

My colleague laid down an ultimatum in January 1997: in three months he'd leave, with or without the rest of us. We scrambled to find a replacement, but History was against us. The Clean Hands corruption investigation was in the process of bringing down all the reigning political parties, and the trickle-down effect decimated Italians' discretionary spending, emptying out fancy restaurants and private doctors' waiting rooms as though all the money that had kept them full originated in bribes or blackmail. Maybe it did. In any case, private Italian medical clienteles melted away all over town, and none of the colleagues we called were willing to gamble on taking over a share of the expenses at Via Balbo. We were castaways again.

5. Pinciano District 1997–2003

The Rome International Clinic

Dr. Bacci managed to find a large multispecialty office just outside Porta Pia, a city gate designed by Michelangelo, that reminded him of our old Medical Diagnostic Center and was eager to have us. The other colleagues jumped at the chance, I hesitated. The joint called itself "Rome International Clinic" when nobody spoke anything but Italian, the women behind the front desk were poured into hokey little identical green miniskirts, and I thought I recalled rumors impugning the business ethics of its physician owner, whom I will call Dr. C. But majority rules, and my memories were vague, so I threw my lot in with the rest of the gang.

We met with Dr. C. around plates of pasta to discuss the imminent merging of the Balbo Medical Associates into the Rome International Clinic. Or rather, the guys discussed it; Mariateresa and I were neither seen nor heard. At least Dr. C. was a democratic sexist, ignoring a physician alongside her secretary. I'd often had an Italian accountant or carpenter talk with my husband over the head of the Invisible Woman, but in professional settings physician usually trumped female. This meeting did not bode well.

We moved to the RIC lock, stock, and barrel, having arranged to have complete autonomy as a group and maintain exclusive access to our secretary. My room was large, pleasant, quiet, and comfortable, and my total expenses were a third less than at Via Balbo. The location was near buses, close to parking lots, and a stone's throw from a department store as well stocked as Macy's. It might have been the best place ever . . .

. . . except that once we had signed our contracts the gloves came off. Dr. C. refused our every request, down to putting sinks in the examination rooms. I guess the other docs never washed their hands. Far from exclusive access, he tossed Mariateresa into the secretarial pool, at starvation wages that we had to top up under the table, and watched like a hawk to make sure she didn't do anything special for us. And what a pool it was! The secretaries answered the phone but didn't take messages ("He's busy, call back in fifteen minutes," "No, he's with another patient now, try in another ten minutes"), didn't even have pens or paper. When it was a patient's turn a secretary would holler the name so everyone could hear it in the waiting room across the hall, without bothering to come out from behind the reception desk.

Dr. C. was not stupid. One of the secretaries, who lived outside town, started skimming off the docs' daily take. She was found out and proven guilty but couldn't be fired because of arcane twists in the labor law. So Dr. C. got rid of her by studying the railway schedules and reassigning her to work hours that would have made her miss the last train home.

Like the old Medical Diagnostic Center, the RIC had a laboratory. But here the referrals were not just encouraged, but obligatory. A patient who lived in Capalbio, two hours north of Rome, was to be ordered to make the trek to the Pinciano any time she needed tests done. When Dr. C. found out I was sending patients to labs closer to their homes, a knock-down battle ensued. In the end he gave me permission to give out other names as long as I wrote them down in my own room, behind closed doors.

The guiding principle of the Rome International Clinic was obscure to me. It didn't seem to be excellence, but it wasn't greed either—our suggestions of how to collect more bills or get more outside referrals went unheeded. There was something there about power, that much I figured out, but exactly what remained a mystery. Its administrative style was typically Roman, half rigidity and half chaos, a mix of petty dictatorship with muddling along.

Mariateresa spent those years in hell, underpaid, undervalued, and overworked, but she did manage to leave one legacy behind the front desk after we flew the coop: pens and paper for taking phone messages.

From the moment we moved into the Rome International Clinic I was plotting my escape. After five years the number of co-conspirators reached a critical mass, so we went public, gave our six months' notice, and were off office-hunting once more . . .

6. Circus Maximus Area 2003–2009

The Aventino Medical Group

The place was gorgeous, *alla romana*. It was on the Aventino, the most elegant of Rome's seven hills, and boasted inlaid travertine floors, faux porphyry bathrooms, cherrywood shelving, push-button electric blinds, recessed lighting, a distressed paint job, a wisteria-shaded terrace, and a curved wall of top-of-the-line glass bricks embellishing the foyer. Not my style—the television production company that had rented it two tenants back was a better fit—but guaranteed to awe our patients.

Three hours after the ad first appeared online I had seen the apartment, decided it was right, and obtained a promise from the landlord, whom I'll call Signor R., that he would hold it until I could bring my partners around at ten the next morning. We came on time, approved, and signed a preliminary agreement. R. tossed off an aside: we were lucky the people with a 9:30 appointment had come late, otherwise he'd have given the apartment to them. We were so blinded by the beauty of the office that this peculiar comment set off no alarm bells.

This time, remembering the internist's treachery, I'd mailed every patient I'd seen in the previous year a change-of-address card, damn the expense. Good thing too—as it turned out, Dr. C. ordered the secretaries not to give out my new telephone number to anyone if they valued their jobs. Prospective patients would plead with them in tears, as I heard from one who tracked me down via the White Pages (those were pre-Google days). Less enterprising long-time patients who didn't happen to have come recently lost track of me forever, notably a whole community of Filipina maids whose patronage I had particularly prized.

Bullying my patients wasn't enough of a vendetta for Dr. C., so he invented an excuse to ask me for money. A lawyer would send dunning letters twice a year, with increasingly threatening language. Three years on, Mariateresa passed me a phone call. The caller identified himself in a would-be intimidating voice as a lawyer for the Rome International Clinic—and was clearly astonished by my reply: "Thank heavens, finally there's a normal person I can talk to!" I presented my case, he listened, I never heard from Dr. C. or the RIC again.

In the meantime, our newborn Aventino Medical Group had filled its examining rooms with eleven physicians and four psychotherapists, created a website, and become a booming business. It was a terrific bunch of co-workers and a terrific place, and though I'd have preferred a clientele less top-heavy with international civil servants from the nearby Food and Agricultural Organization, all those well-paid, well-insured United Nations patients were great for the household finances. The only problem was that the rent was so high we had to locate our secretaries in the waiting room so as not to waste precious floor space.

The bubble burst in the first months of 2009, when one of the doctors in the group decided to leave the office. What followed would have been no more than a tempest in a teapot if the land-lord hadn't decided to take the occasion to move into harassment mode. He sent a series of faxes to me and my partner, French dermatologist Alain Duval, exploring various possible lines of attack, from a perennially defective lock on the gate to our office insurance policy. This last seemed the most promising, and Signor R. summoned us to discuss it. We had, he told us sternly, failed to give him a copy of a proper policy within six weeks of renting the office seven years earlier, as called for by the contract. He would be within his rights in terminating our rental contract. But he liked us, he said, so he would offer us a way out: present him with an acceptable policy within five days and he would let us stay on in return for a small fine, three months' rent.

He incidentally suggested we expand our office into an apartment he owned in the building next door. Alain asked, "But isn't there a tenant there already?" R. shrugged: "They're wastrels—leave lights on in all the rooms. I'd kick 'em out."

We scurried to send a copy of our insurance policy the next day, not realizing the game was already over. There was a reason R. hadn't asked to see the policy seven years earlier: the requirements he had laid out were impossible for any insurance company to meet, and the contract clause was intended less as a safeguard to his property than as what is known in Italy as a *clausola abusiva*, a condition inserted in the contract with the sole purpose of enabling the landlord to expel a tenant whenever he feels like it.

After five years' abstinence, I started bumming cigarettes.

The rest was theater. R. in his office yelling for a lackey to come stand in the doorway, reel off a list of a dozen defects in our insurance policy, and hightail it without giving us anything in writing. Colleagues storming and sneaking in and out. Alain and I scurrying around trying to placate the unplacatable, hiring a lawyer who declared, "You'll win if I have to take it all the way to the Supreme Court."

We were babes in the woods. When Alain once ventured a mild Gallic protest R. glared at him: "I could throw you out on the street tomorrow." I saw Alain's face deflate, the vitality falling out of it as he recognized this was no normal interlocutor. In 1943 the Nazi occupiers demanded fifty kilograms of gold from the Roman Jews in return for their lives. The community scraped together the ransom and historians say that their leaders, on consigning it to the Nazis, politely requested a receipt. When the Nazis laughed, the leaders suddenly understood who they were dealing with. In its own tiny way, ours was a similar moment.

I stepped up to buying packs of Camel Lights.

In May a fax rolled off the machine saying we had four weeks to leave. It took much longer, of course, but by New Year's we had indeed moved out, restored the apartment to better than new, and made a date to give back the keys. Instead, more theater: R. appearing on the threshold, pointing at a scratch in the floor, screaming he would go no further, turning on his heel, and walking away in feigned fury. (The *portiere* heard him whistling a jaunty tune as he strolled out of the building.) Our welterweight lawyer putting his dukes up when R. tossed off a demand for 240,000 euros in return for leaving us in peace: "That sounds perilously like extortion. Are you going to force me to start acting like a lawyer?" A judge ruling R. was within his rights to refuse to take the apartment back and could drag the state of limbo out indefinitely if he so chose.

This was the last straw. I started taking sleeping pills.

The sole moment of respite came in August 2010, when an appeals court ruled in our favor and sent a bored bailiff to press the keys personally into R.'s unwilling hands.

Long afterward, in March 2012, we trooped to the courthouse in good spirits to hear the final verdict, assured by our lawyer that the judge would give an even-handed Solomonic ruling. Nope, nothing even-handed about it: R. was pronounced in the right up and down the line, and we owed him 80,000 euros. At least this fell to 40,000, about $55,000, once you deducted our deposit and the rent we'd continued to fork out after the eviction. R. generously allowed us a year to pay. Our lawyer's words about the Supreme Court evaporated like dew in the sun.

Was the judge bought off? Angry with us for having made an appeal over his head to force R. to take the keys back? If you remove all the *Commedia dell'Arte*, the answer was probably simpler: when it came to drafting or defending a rental contract, Signor R. hired the best lawyers in the business.

A better question is, why did R. want us out in the first place? With the corollary, if he wanted it so badly why did he refuse to take the apartment back? It wasn't because we were bad tenants, on the contrary. It wasn't to get more money from the next victim—at that moment rental prices were in free fall. No, we eventually decided, it was for fun. According to neighborhood scuttlebutt, his business was landlording, but his passion was torturing tenants. They all supposedly got fined, evicted, or both, and invariably lost in court. An army of sharp attorneys made sure his contracts were both vicious and iron-clad, apparently so he could indulge safely in the pleasure of making innocents like Alain and me bristle, scramble, and squirm.

It was my first encounter with anything resembling sadism, my first experience of High Anxiety, and further demonstration that in Italy power considerations—trifling in Dr. C.'s case, possibly sociopathic in R.'s—trump economic self-interest. After thirty years in Rome, I was still learning.

7. Via Sant'Alberto Magno 2010–
The Aventino Medical Group Redux

The German bishop Alberto Magno, Albert the Great, died in 1280 but had his day in the twentieth century: in 1929 a street was named after him, then in 1931 he was canonized. Rather than waste marble on a new street sign, the city kept the old one but had a sculptor chisel a miniature "S." for Saint into the corner.

This *pentimento* (artist's afterthought) perfectly suited that two-block street higher up the Aventine, genteel but slightly down-at-heel, where my group and I found haven after escaping from R.'s clutches. Again, I was the first prospective renter to answer the ad. I told the owner over the phone that I wouldn't bother coming to see it if there was any possibility our neighbors would object to a medical office in the building; she reassured me emphatically.

The apartment was all dark wood and matte glazing, in a quiet low-rise building immersed in green, a hundred yards from Piranesi's famous keyhole with its surprise view of St. Peter's. It would have been a lovely place to live. Not so easy to camouflage as a medical office, but beggars can't be choosers. Between the indefatigable Mariateresa, a terrific Polish contractor, and Levenstein-Duval legwork, we got the rooms soundproofed and equipped with running water, desks, designer lamps, and air conditioning, and at New Year's 2010 the Aventino Medical Group occupied its new digs without missing a beat.

Two weeks after we opened for business, Mariateresa knocked on a door downstairs to ask where the electric meter was. The neighbor replied pleasantly, "It's in the basement. But don't bother to go looking, you won't be here long enough to need it—the building rules don't allow medical offices and we'll soon be kicking you out." The owner's verbal reassurance, her email claiming she had gotten the approval of the condominium, and our lawyers' benign interpretation of the archaic language of the rules, had all been wishful thinking. I had made it to age sixty without needing an attorney, but I was making up for lost time.

The theater was relatively tame this time—just a few accusations that we were strewing cigarette butts in the elevator, plugging the toilets with diapers, and bringing down property values—and we won the case, so I'll spare you the details. As of this writing, the Aventino Medical Group is keeping four secretaries busy, its website gets two thousand visitors a month, and at least for now we're breathing easy.

Through the retrospectoscope, my first group office looks pretty damn good. I didn't see it that way at the time. Its aura gave me the creeps, I was shocked by the fee-splitting and the tax evasion, repulsed by the dermatologist's roving hands, irritated by the lack of collegiality. I laughed at the magazines in the waiting room, sneered at the ENT's ten-point prescription for laryngitis. I was a thirty-two-year-old with attitude and a 1968 mentality; they were a bunch of well-off grownups whom I feared and looked down on in equal measure. But the docs knew their stuff. Plinio Rossi was one of the pioneers of interventionist radiology in New York, Dr. S. was a sterling internist, Amleto Gliosci's facelifts showed artistry and judgment, Virgilio Ciampa could remove an appendix blindfolded and never had a complication. (One elderly monk bashfully peeled off shoe and sock to show me a black, gangrenous toe; down the hall to Ciampa's room and a half-hour later the monk who had hobbled in on ten toes strode out on nine.) Decision-making was, if not entirely collective, at least not dictatorial. The secretaries took phone messages. Now I can see that the Medical Diagnostic Center had been, relatively speaking, a class act. How four decades of exposure to Roman medicine have lowered my expectations!

Quo Vadis, Doc?

July, 1995. At 8:00 a.m. I'm filling my Moka Express with water for my morning coffee. My mind's eye follows the overflow down the drain, through pipes dating back to Caesar, out the 2,600-year-old *Cloaca Massima* a stone's throw away, down the Tiber River to the modern town of Ostia erected on the silt that landlocked the ancient Roman port. Its final destination is the on-again-off-again wastewater treatment plant that is supposed to clean it up before any unwitting beachgoers take a dip in my swill.

Out my kitchen window is the Isola Tiberina, Rome's only island, where in 291 B.C., according to legend, a seasick snake leapt off a ship bearing a Greek sculpture of Aesculapius. Since snakes happened to be sacred to the healing god, the statue was unloaded on the spot and a temple built; its priests' stethoscoped descendants are there to this day. A Jewish outpatient clinic and a Catholic hospital (the Fatebenefratelli, "Do-Good Brothers") face off across a minuscule piazza, both looking like the convents they once were. I see a patient toss bread crumbs out his window to a swirl of seagulls, a few yards above an open Roman-era drain pouring ominously red effluvium into the river below.

Glossary: *il passato*

The past. Whether you feel comforted or suffocated by their enclosing arms, Rome's three millennia of history have you in their embrace. Decadence was old hat in this city before Jesus was born. An atmosphere heavy with the weight of centuries gone by is what we foreigners crave on our tours and thrive on as rookie émigrés, and an albatross around the necks of reformers and many young Italians.

By ten I'm in my car, headed for a wasteland of furniture factories and car dealers seven miles away on the outskirts of town, to check on a post-op cancer patient in the private Rome American Hospital, which opened a year earlier. It's a mud-colored former old folks' home—in Rome's age-old pastiche tradition, each generation builds on the wreckage of the last. The renovators had to custom order narrow hospital beds to make them fit into the existing elevators.

Back in central Rome at 12:30, after two hours' driving for thirty minutes' doctoring, I abandon my car in Trastevere under a no-parking sign next to a cart piled with black eggplant, green chicory, and yellow peppers, and enter the public Nuovo Regina Margherita Hospital where I do research into the influence of stress on ulcers. In New York, a forty-year-old hospital is up for demolition; the cornerstone of the NRM was laid a thousand years ago. After huddling with my collaborators I grab a chestnut and egg custard *gelato* for lunch, drive home across the Garibaldi bridge with a glance over to the distant dome of Saint Peter's, park under the fig tree in my condo garden, and head off on foot past the Renaissance turtle fountain in Piazza Mattei, between the nineteenth-century headquarters of the ex-Communist and ex-Christian Democratic Parties, down the baroque Via del Gesù, around the Marble Foot from a lost statue of the Egyptian goddess Isis, through the fin-de-siècle Palazzo Sciarra Gallery, past the tourists snapping shots of the Trevi Fountain, to the heavyset 1910 building near Piazza Barberini where my 2:30 patient awaits.

He's an Irish diplomat with bronchitis, who is followed by an Italian teacher with painful periods, a Mozambique-Dutch United Nations wife with fatigue, an American woman with anxiety, a car mechanic with heart disease, a Senegalese fisheries expert

Dottoressa

with memory loss, a *liceo* student with migraine, an English tour guide with an unwanted pregnancy, a French artist with a breast lump. Nine patients, eight nationalities, six hours, home at nine, par for the course.

moto perpetuo
ad libitum

4

Joining the Club

After France, Italy has the best system of specialization and medical training in the world.
—Stefania Giannini, Italian Minister of Education, 2014

The daily papers report a terrifying sequence of deaths in hospitals and emergency rooms, deaths that shouldn't have happened. A first reconstruction of the facts says the cause is poorly trained physicians. It's natural to ask: are Italian physicians well trained?
—Dr. Arnaldo D'Amico, "Why the Mistakes,"
Repubblica Salute, March 2008

I must have done well at my first interview for the Stanford University School of Medicine back in 1970, because they called me back a second time. On the other side of a large desk sat a tall, soft-around-the-middle biochemistry professor with a wispy blonde bun who wormed her way into my brain by inches, wielding a motherly smile, until I heard myself yelling, of all things, "No, my brother is *not* an alcoholic!" At that point I paused, appalled at having gotten so flustered and not understanding how the conversation had swerved from here to there. Then a little bulb lit up in my head: "This is a stress interview, isn't it?" She nodded. "Guess I flunked." She nodded again.

When it came time to interview for the Mount Sinai School of Medicine, I was determined I'd be the one doing the manipulation. The interviewer, towering and to my callow eyes ancient, looked as ill at ease in his horn-rimmed glasses as I was myself, wearing my only skirt and clutching a purse freshly stripped of its Equality and Stop the War buttons. I delicately psyched him out, and when under gentle prodding he admitted he felt uncomfortable talking to women, my posture and manner underwent such a sex change that at the end he shook my hand, saying, "See, I'm shaking your hand just as though you were a man." My acceptance was in the bag.

My first month in Rome, in 1978, I felt a breast lump, checked into a small private hospital for a biopsy, and got to chatting with the young doctor who recorded my history and my blood pressure. Not having yet faced the training equivalency officer at the Foreign Ministry, and therefore still under the optimistic illusion that the Italian Consulate in New York was already arranging my medical license, I told her I was looking for work. In the morning she came in with news: she had found me a job! I was thrilled. She went on to explain the job wasn't taking care of patients but . . . drawing blood in a laboratory. Lesson number one in Italian medical economics: doctors were a glut on the market.

The reason was Open Admissions, that is, anybody who wanted to go to med school could. Since 1923 a graduate of an élite *liceo* could study whatever university subject he or she chose, including medicine, and in the 1970s that privilege was extended to regular high schools. In post-war Italy, where genteel twenty-year-olds had little better to do than kick around a soccer ball like the characters of Fellini's *Vitelloni*, and university courses cost next to nothing, why not sign up? It was more respectable than being unemployed, warded off boredom, made *mamma* happy, and let you fiddle low-risk with the fantasy of becoming a doctor.

And sign up they did, in droves. During the 1980s 1,200 medical students would be crammed into lecture halls built for 400, without counting those who were on the books but never bothered to show up for class. Only one in three ever graduated, but even that was way too many—Italy, population fifty-six million, granted as many medical degrees every year as the United States, population 236 million. By 1994, the head of the *Ordine dei Medici* was pleading with young people not to choose a medical career. When I got to Italy, one in four of *all* licensed physicians was out of work, so the default position after med school was unemployment. I hadn't picked the best time to immigrate.

It was obvious that open admissions had to go and that the number of new doctors spawned every year should match the number the country really needed. How to pick the elite legionnaires out of the army of aspirants? A conundrum. In the US, where most applicants have straight A's and ace the MCATs, schools rely heavily on face-to-face conversations to separate the wheat from the chaff. In Italy interviews were out of the question—they'd be perfect smokescreens for favoring the son or daughter of a hospital Chief. So would personal essays. Recommendations? Don't make me laugh.

In the end, it was decided to make the selection process hang on a single multiple choice examination, and by 1999 open admissions was history.

What's on the exam? I checked out the 2012–13 edition online, and saw that high school student candidates were expected, for example, to know which vaccine was optional under Italian law: mumps, diphtheria, polio, hepatitis B, or tetanus (mumps—not being a pediatrician, I had to google it).

Cheating schemes pop up and mutate like so many whacked moles. The son of a Bologna physician hid a mic in a fake plaster cast on his arm and an earbud in a wig so Daddy could help out—he was caught when his neighbors were distracted by his muttering. In Bari, sixty students paid $65,000 each for a subtler scam, devised by their exam-preparation teacher. Accomplices signed up for the test, chose seats close to the wall, and whispered the questions through Bluetooth devices to a group of physicians who huddled in the entry hall of a nearby hospital building, agreed on the answers, and texted them to nanosized cell phones hidden in the students' underwear.

> To study the phenomenon of disease without books is to sail an uncharted sea, while to study books without patients is not to go to sea at all.
> —Sir William Osler

We started on the back. Philosophies differ, and I was glad Professor Levitan, the chief of anatomy at Mount Sinai, belonged to the prone rather than the supine school. No risk of ruining delicate structures with our first uncertain stabs, or of having to look our victim in the face.

In theory, the first cut into our cadaver was unforgettable, but I can't actually recall which of the four in my group made it. Everything about the first year of medical school is initiation into the guild, including distinctive use of language—"gross" means visible to the naked eye, "bland" means uninfected, um*bili*cus is pronounced umbi*lie*cus and *cen*timeter is *sahn*timeter—which is to doctors what a secret handshake is to Freemasonry. The crucial rite of passage, though, is gross anatomy class, where you break the deepest of taboos by defiling a corpse with your own hands. After the initial shock, cadaver dissection was mostly drudgework, with a soundtrack of dark student humor, but it was studded with small epiphanies. I remember catching on to some deeper meaning of the circulatory system while fumbling to tease out the mandibular branch of the facial artery as it curled around the jaw, and grasping the finality of death when I held a brain in my hand. Nowadays the cadavers' humanity is treated with more respect than in my time—surviving relatives are invited to thanking ceremonies at the end of the year—but whether students' discomfort is handled through jokes or memorial rituals, that first tremulous scalpel incision marks leaving life as a layperson behind.

For Italian medical students, all this is but legend. Their knowledge of anatomy comes from books, unless you count the daring few who, like one childhood friend of my ex, rustle up a gang of classmates to raid a graveyard for bones. Students are forbidden to touch a cadaver, so they never do hands-on dissections, and few even see one performed. Historically, anatomy professors would perform demonstrations on bodies abandoned by families too poor to bury them. When this practice went by the boards as ethically dubious, dissection simply disappeared. Today, enterprising students may fly to medical schools in France, Hungary, even the US, for the privilege of watching anatomical dissections and the hope of participating.

> My son is working in England, in an emergency room, so he can learn to be a doctor . . . in Italy he didn't learn anything. In our hospitals the trainees never see a patient.
> —Dr. Francesco De Lorenzo, Italian Minister
> of Health, 1990

One of the patients I saw as a third-year medical student in New York was a Hasidic man who had come to the emergency room after passing black, tarry stool. It was scary being the first person to face him one-on-one—find the right questions to ask, apply my stethoscope to his chest, do a rectal exam—and thrilling when the stool on my glove streaked blue, positive, on the paper strip testing it for blood. I felt confident presenting the patient to my team—my very own bleeding ulcer! The next morning we got word that his wife had given birth to a baby boy during the night and I stuck out my hand to congratulate him. He looked at it but didn't move. As a religious Jew he could submit to a woman doing whatever was medically necessary, including putting her finger up his butt, but could not voluntarily touch her.

This was the American sink-or-swim apprenticeship system. First-year anatomy class may be baptism under fire, but it's those hospital specialty rotations that make you into a doctor.

In Italy's jam-packed Open Admissions era individualized teaching was out of the question, but overcrowding wasn't the only problem. Italian medical training ossified centuries ago as a university discipline, like medieval history or physics, to be learned by rote and polished off with a scholarly dissertation, with hardly any hands-on training even in taking a medical history or listening to the heart, much less giving an injection. Practical learning used to depend entirely on individual initiative—some medical students volunteered sixty hours a week on hospital wards, others literally never laid a finger on a patient.

In the late 1990s, egged on by the European Union, epochal reforms began moving medical students from the lecture halls onto the wards. By 2008, the head of the reform commission could boast that Italy had reached European norms, with 1,500 obligatory hours at the bedside in hospital rotations or *tirocini*. But in 2015, students were still complaining in online forums that in *tirocini* "you're wallpaper," and that they "get stuffed with facts for six years but never learn how to hold a scalpel."

That doesn't mean Italian medical school is a cinch. Students have always spent long hours poring over books, preparing for exams that require regurgitation of vast numbers of facts. Years ago, one of my friends wowed his interrogators in Clinical Medicine by knowing all about torsade de pointes, a heart arrhythmia so rare I've never seen a case. Then they asked about one of the most common medical problems, congestive heart failure, and he didn't know a thing.

The entrance quiz can be the last time Italian med students have to answer a question with pen on paper. As I've mentioned, in Italy grades are mostly determined by oral exams, from first grade on. This means that students learn to game "interrogations" just as well as Americans game multiple-choice tests. Name any political subject, and you're more likely to hear a lucid, fluent, off-the-cuff speech from a Rome taxi driver than from a US senator.

Oral exams also offer a university instructor the chance to exorcise his bad moods. In the sixties, according to my Italian ex, an infamous Rome anatomy professor—I'll call him Professor Lucifero—took a drill to a human skull hidden in his personal stash and added a phony hole to the dozens of real foramens that the various nerves and arteries pass through. He amused himself that year at exam time by asking student after miserable student to name the mystery opening, flunking them when they couldn't, until he finally reached one who was sure enough of himself to answer, "The foramen of Lucifero."

Before moving to Italy I had taken exactly one oral exam, as part of my specialty certification. The US Board of Internal Medicine sent you to examine a hospitalized patient solo and then present the case in front of a three-person commission. The word on the street was that they chose classic cases of common diseases, so my stomach sank when I found myself faced with a groggy woman who was nearly mute and had a bewildering set of physical findings; I had no idea what was wrong with her. I dragged my heels into the interrogation room, prepared to be flunked after three residency years of hard labor, and couldn't keep my voice from shaking as I described what I had observed, and presented diagnostic possibilities that seemed one more outlandish than the next. There was a moment of dreadful silence until the head examiner said, "Well, you've done as well as the ward staff. After three days in the hospital they still haven't figured her out." The bastards. Deep down I suspected they were getting back at me for having joined the hospital workers' picket line a year earlier . . .

The norm for Italian medical students is to straggle to the finish line a year or more behind schedule, and one in three still drops out altogether. Italian universities let you proceed at your own pace, so as your interest fades you can let the exams you sit dwindle year by year, from eight to four to none. Those who fall by the wayside do, however, eventually have to face Mom and Dad. One medical student I knew didn't take any exams after his second year, finding it suited him better to DJ at a local radio station. He managed to keep his lack of progress a secret from his parents for three years, following which all hell broke loose. Another med school dropout got into the papers by going a step further: he kept up the pretense all the way to what would have been graduation time and then, to spare his parents the shame of discovering his perfidy, shot them. When his case came to trial he threw himself on the mercy of the court on the grounds of being an orphan, thereby fulfilling the traditional definition of the Yiddish word chutzpah.

In the 1970s, Italian specialty trainees had an even-steven deal: they didn't get paid, and they didn't do any work. After graduating from med school you could go off and sell ladies' underwear or sail the South Seas, and you'd get certified as a urologist after five years as long as you showed up for oral examinations every spring; you could get authorized to perform surgery without having ever set foot in an operating room. Ambitious souls would collect five or six specialty certificates in their spare time, a typical prescription pad reading "Specialist in Pulmonology, Sports Medicine, and Angiology."

The residency I'd just completed in the Bronx was another story altogether: sleepless nights, unremitting labor, weighty responsibility, the daily visceral terror that you might make a mistake and kill someone. I spent my first day of internship scurrying back and forth to the bathroom with the runs. It took a jibe from a senior resident for me to realize it came from nerves. A girlfriend who'd started a year earlier gave me one of the most vital bits of time management advice: when you have to piss, piss.

During my internship year, I remembered a survey of Radcliffe graduates in medicine I had helped analyze as a college senior, when I had no thought of becoming a physician. On reading from one woman, "I managed to produce two daughters and a son during medical school and residency," I thought sleet ran in her veins instead of blood. Now, seeing how grueling and rigorous a residency was even without children to care for, I understood what she was talking about.

Italy, on the other hand, is a country of improvisers: "A people of poets, artists, heroes, saints, thinkers, scientists, sailors, and migrants," as Mussolini emblazoned on the building that dominates Rome's EUR district, so even in the days of exams-only residencies, many trainees would invent top-rate medical training for themselves. A budding internist might volunteer on the wards, a budding surgeon apprentice himself to his father, a budding orthopedist skip off to a London hospital for a year. My office-mate Vincenzo Bacci, after two years of frustration with Italian specialty training, cleverly signed up for a simultaneous residency in the United States, hopping back to Italy every May to sit his exams. That way he got to have his cake, becoming an excellent internist and endocrinologist, and eat it too—avoiding ostracism by a jealous Italian medical guild that might otherwise have punished him for jumping ship.

In 1981, the European Union decreed that specialist certification in any one country would be valid in all. A death blow to Italian training programs—French or German patients might possibly balk at having their gallbladder removed by someone who was holding a scalpel for the first time. Italy promised a radical overhaul, to avoid the humiliation of being the only country excluded from the reciprocity agreements. But *siamo in Italia*, "we're in Italy," as Italians say ironically. Ten years later, on a bus, I ran into a former research assistant who told me she had just finished her specialty training in gastrointestinal endoscopy. After my congratulations she said the course had involved 400 hours of instruction, and then asked, "Can you guess how many of those hours were spent with my hands physically holding a gastroscope or a colonoscope?" It took me a while to work my way down to the correct answer: zero.

When Italy started paying trainees salaries in 1992, the practical side of specialty training began inching toward predominance over the academic side. Graduating surgeons are now certified as having performed a certain number of appendectomies, cholecystectomies, etc., and specialty training conveys some degree of clinical competence. But, again, we're in Italy. According to my inside sources, a surgical Chief may testify in three books of three trainees that each was the surgeon removing a single patient's gallbladder, when actually all three had merely held the incision open. And *caveat emptor*: the surgeons now at the tops of their careers got certified in the bad old days.

Newly-hatched physicians are far better off now than in 1980—with med school enrollment down by more than ninety percent, a doctor shortage may even be in the making—but Italy still leads Europe in unemployed and underemployed doctors. They compete to cover nights in private hospitals, man the medical tent at soccer games, examine insurance claimants, ride ambulances, accompany student groups on study vacations, and administer cellulite-melting "mesotherapy" injections at massage parlors. Some take up acupuncture or homeopathy, hoping the world of alternative medicine will be less saturated. Almost all still spend years skipping from one temporary contract to the next while praying for a full-time permanent job.

Like all Italian civil service jobs, hospital posts are, by law, filled on the basis of nationwide competitions or *concorsi*. And like all Italian civil service jobs, in actuality many positions are "wired" for a hometown candidate. Getting around the mechanisms designed to guarantee fair competition can take ingenuity, but Italians are famously ingenious. Problem: the applicants sit an essay exam that gets scored anonymously. Solution: the preselected winner is instructed to insert a specific phrase into her answer so a clued-in reader can pick her out of the crowd.

> Bari: Rigged Competition in Medicine, Blitz During
> Oral Exam
>
> Florence: Medicine, Competition Halted, Two Professors
> Under Investigation
>
> Rome: She Wins the Job in Medicine But Her Degree Is
> in Literature
> —*La Repubblica* headlines, 2002–2008
>
> She performed so well it will be extremely difficult for us to
> find a way to eliminate her.
> —A commission member about a physician candidate
> slated for blackballing. *Nature*, 1992

In the United States, university professors get tenure and promotions on the publish or perish principle. In Italy, that holds for hospital physicians as well; clinical competence counts a little, scientific publications a lot. In 1991 a pair of Italian researchers, their brains long since drained to the United Kingdom, revealed in a letter to the prestigious journal *Nature* how one typical *concorso* had been run. Using standard objective measures to rate the candidates' publication lists, the authors showed that the candidates with the most glittering bibliographies were eliminated on the first round. On only one parameter did the ones on the short list stand out: the number of articles they had co-authored with members of the search commission. The ultimate winner had one or more commissioners as co-authors on seventy percent of his publications.

A few years back, a hospital in Sicily assigned an open job to the daughter of a local *primario*. Nothing new there. But in this case the job was as a high-level associate professor, and the daughter was fresh out of medical school. This was too much for the other applicants, who sued, and lost.

Glossary: *lottizzazione*

From the fall of Fascism until the early nineties, Italian political parties sliced up every pie, however small, into segments or "lots" proportionate to the importance of the parties. The lion's share of public television money went to the Christian Democrats' RAI 1 station, a smaller cut to the Socialists' RAI 2, and the dregs to the Communists' RAI 3.

Nearly as important as having the right parents is political party affiliation, though which party varies with the institution and the times. Back in the day at the Nuovo Regina Margherita Hospital where I did my internship and research, it was the Communists. Lately the parties have changed but not the principle: in 2007 a *cupola* of medical *baroni* from all over Italy was caught having mini-Apalachin Meetings, Cosa Nostra style, to choose the next generation of Chiefs on the basis of friendships, family ties, and affiliation with Berlusconi's *Forza Italia*.

It would be surprising if medicine were the only field where training is unpredictable. Take stamp makers. By law, Italian doctors need a practice stamp for every office: name, address, registration numbers. The last time I moved office I went to a hole-in-the-wall "Stamps and Plaques" shop and handed my five lines of text to the tall, pleasant, long-haired young man who was owner and sole employee. A week later, I went to pick up the self-inking stamp. When pressed down on a piece of paper, it printed only the first and last letters of every line. The owner was suitably embarrassed and said come back in another week. The refurbished stamp printed . . . the first and last lines, not the three in between.

Yes, I have a world-class medical secretary, my composer husband has a world-class sound engineer, and our AC technician can beat any comer, but sometimes it seems no one else knows what they're doing. Piano technicians leave my piano out of tune, clothes come home from the dry cleaners stinking, my office is blessed with no-stick Band-Aids, splintering tongue depressors, and fall-over stools.

Sometimes a sloppy job—one that's done, in the Italian phrase, *a cazzo di cane*, like a dog's penis—merely represents the path of least resistance. When I needed to renew my driver's license in 2012, the examiner pointed at two random letters on the chart per eye, for me to read with glasses on. Only when I got home did I notice that his certificate also included my uncorrected vision score, which he had never tested, and my glasses prescription, invented wholecloth.

Professional certificates are little better. When I first met radiology professor Plinio Rossi, he proposed that I come work for him once I got my Italian credentials. I was honored but puzzled—not only was I not a radiologist, I said, but how could he know I was any good? When he answered that my American Board certification was plenty enough qualification I shrugged, thinking of all the Board-certified internists I'd never want as my own doctor. It took me years to appreciate how much those credentials do guarantee: the specialist has spent years of tough supervised work with real patient responsibility, has been declared qualified by the head of his specialty department, and has passed a challenging set of examinations. Board certification is no guarantee of excellence, and it's compatible with being superficial, alcoholic, money-grubbing, or utterly lacking in empathy, but it does mean a certain minimum level of competence. An Italian *laurea* or specialty certification doesn't quite, not yet. For every great clinician, there's a doc who never learned which side of the patient is up.

5

ItalyCare

Comprehensive health insurance is an idea whose time has
come in America. There has long been a need to assure every
American financial access to high quality health care. As
medical costs go up, that need grows more pressing. Now, for
the first time, we have not just the need but the will to get this
job done.

—Richard Nixon, 1974

Early in the AIDS epidemic I went to Rome's Gemelli Hospital
to visit a patient of mine with Cryptococcus infection, a sweet
skinny African-American guy who taught English and always
wore a suit one size too big. I asked if they were treating him all
right. He said, "All right? Doc, anything they do is all right with
me. Back in Detroit I'd have been dead on the street long ago."

My uninsured American husband was doing leg presses on a
Nautilus machine near Largo Argentina when his thigh got smashed
by a neighbor's flying barbell. He hobbled to the Fatebenefratelli
ER on the Isola Tiberina, where they gave him x-rays and good advice and never asked for his address, much less payment.

An elderly patient with kidney failure came over from Ken-
tucky to a small Italian town to live with his daughter, and was
immediately enrolled free in a dialysis center he swore was cleaner

and more efficient than the one back home, plus it sent a driver to take him there and back.

Mary Beth, an American college student abroad, had fainting spells from a potentially fatal irregular heartbeat. I arranged for her to sign up with the *Servizio Sanitario Nazionale* (which I'll abbreviate as NHS for National Health Service) for the student rate of $300, after which she got cardiac catheterization, studies of her heart's electrical system, and curative ablation free in a public hospital.

Italians don't have to look over their pills every morning—as my mother, a distinguished psychologist, did in California—to decide which to take and which to skip so the supply will last longer. Kidney transplant patients don't have to fall back on community fundraising campaigns to pay for medical follow-up after Medicare bows out, as many do in the land of stars and stripes. Nobody in Italy dies because they can't afford their chemotherapy.

The Italian NHS is a universal-access system on the British model, with general practitioner visits, hospital stays, and generic medications entirely free at the point of care. Outpatient specialist visits, diagnostic tests, brand-name drugs, and ER visits for non-emergencies entail small co-pays, but some or all are waived if you're impoverished, unemployed, disabled, or have a chronic disease, as well as for the very young and the elderly if their family income is under $40,000. (Italians soften the blow of co-pays by using the foreign term "*il ticket*," just as they make life's overload less painful by calling it "*lo stress*.") In 2000, the World Health Organization rated the Italian health system second-best on the planet, after France, and Italians live longer than anyone except the Japanese.

Glossary: *lo Stato*

The Italian State has always been top-heavy. Through the 1980s the country, while putatively Christian Democrat, was co-run by the Communist Party, and the economy was wannabe Soviet. Stores closed at one p.m. for a synchronized siesta, utility companies were all public. It freed up whole chunks of your mind—when you needed gas you could just pull up to the nearest pump, prices all being equal. Even now Italian doctors, train conductors, university professors, and opera house ushers remain civil servants, and you still have to notify the Registry Office every time you move.

So why is this terrific health care system an object of derision among expats and of despair for the locals, especially from Rome southward? The answer hides in the mixed on-the-ground reality that lies between the world-class organizational charts and the gold stars for life expectancy.

To start with, the NHS is grossly impoverished. The US is notoriously the world's biggest health care spender: $9,892 per capita in 2016. France weighed in at $4,600, the stingy UK at $4,192, Italy a mere $3,391 per person. Always strapped for dough, Italy's budget has now been slashed to the bone by European Union-dictated austerity. The system is nationally regulated but depends ever more on local funding, which has led to widening discrepancies between the wealthy North and the barely-scraping-by South; in February 2018 the percentage of Italians satisfied with the National Health Service was twenty-one percent in Sicily, sixty percent (still not much) near Venice.

Every aspect of medical care is hamstrung by underfunding. Disabled Italians supposedly have the right to home-based physical therapy, but the waiting list is so long they often die in the interim. A surgical colleague told me, "We can't even get pathology exams anymore because they ran out of microscope slides."

Add in a dollop of corruption and inefficiency, plus Italy's wildly uneven training programs for doctors, and you have a recipe for mayhem that would surely push the country down in terms of life expectancy (which, together with universal health care coverage, is what drives those WHO ratings) if it weren't for societal saving graces such as low income inequality and a sterling lifestyle.

Everybody in Rome concocts personal schemes for navigating an overloaded, unreliable public system. Mine hinges on cultivating acquaintances inside the NHS and keeping up with which is the best hospital for which disease. My patients depend on friends with connections, brother-in-law Chiefs of Service or next-door-neighbor lab techs, to help them sidestep co-pays or jump the waiting lists (eight months for a non-emergency abdominal sonogram). One said of a relative who'd had a heart attack, hopefully exaggerating, "If she hadn't called a friend who knew a senator, she'd never have gotten into the hospital."

When the system flops, the blow is softened by Italy's one highly functional, all-encompassing institution: the family. Drug addicts go home for lasagna at *mamma*'s on Sunday, carrying their dirty laundry. Schizophrenics are allowed to keep sleeping in their childhood bedrooms even after they set the apartment on fire. Elderly Romans expect to live out their years at home.

Glossary: *mamma*

Mamma serves to stand and wait. Good thing utility bills started being automatically paid by your bank instead of in person at the post office at about the time Italian women joined the labor market en masse, otherwise the country would have gone into meltdown. Early in my Roman life, my mother would get on my case for depending too much on my mother-in-law. Once, visiting from the States, she was keeping me company on a line in the Registry Office to get one certificate or another, when the clock hands reached 12:30 and the clerk drew the blinds down over her window. As the line meekly dispersed, an employee who saw my frown said, *"Pazienza,* you can come back tomorrow morning." I protested: "I work, I can't take every morning off." He gestured toward my companion: "But you don't have to come yourself, you can always send *la mamma.*" In that moment, my mother achieved enlightenment.

From my time as an intern in the Morrisania Emergency Room in the South Bronx, one young Hispanic woman stands out in my memory. In the middle of all the bedlam, surrounded by screaming patients and shouting doctors and rattling crash carts, she looked into my eyes and asked quietly how her husband could bring her to orgasm. People came in all the time with such less-than-life-threatening problems, exasperating the staff. Emergency room physicians in Italy see fewer bullets to the heart than we did, but because everyone has free primary care on the National Health Service they see less of the small stuff too.

For Italian doctors looking for work, the NHS is the dream job, the setup for life, worth whatever you have to go through to worm your way in. Private medicine is a separate kingdom, clutched tightly in the hands of high-level moonlighters. Only a handful of physicians who have special selling points—such as my American nationality and training—can make a stab at supporting themselves by private practice alone.* And who needs the headache? Nowadays a full-time public hospitalist or GP may earn $150,000 a year in straight salary, plus overtime, permanent tenure, great retirement benefits, bottomless sick leave, five months' paid maternity leave, and six weeks' vacation. As a private practitioner my benefits are nonexistent, and after thirty-eight years of paying into the system my pension is a measly $2,000 a month, fully taxable.

Glossary: *sistemazione*

Getting settled, or *sistemato*. The city planner Le Valadier has *sistemato* the Trịnità dei Monti hill by digging the Spanish Steps out of its slope, and your children are *sistemati* when they're set up with a spouse and a career. The Italian quirkiness we variously call freedom or sloppiness, according to whether it's presently charming or maddening us, is just a descant over a plodding tune that goes: find your niche and nestle in. Better unhappily married than a bachelor, better to earn $40,000 a year in a State sinecure than $60,000 from a private company that might fold tomorrow. Once an Italian has been *sistemato* his future is mapped out for him, and he can safely indulge in being capricious, impulsive, or eccentric. The writing is on the wall, though: *sistemazione* is going obsolete, even in medicine, in favor of a blossoming Italian "gig economy."

---

*Advice from the head of a university medical department in Rome: "Susan, I have only one lesson for you. If you have a unique skill, don't teach it to anyone."

The NHS revolves around an army of general practitioners who divvy up the population at 1,500 patients max for each doc and receive so much per head (between $80 and $120 a year, as of 2018) in return for guaranteeing office access within twenty-four hours and, theoretically, house calls within forty-eight. Unlike the unfortunate clients of the tottering British National Health Service, Italians can still expect to see the same GP at every visit.

Your GP is your central reference point, uniquely empowered to refer you for a specialist appointment, get your disability pension started, and certify that you're sick enough to take time off or healthy enough to drive. When I order medications, lab tests, or x-rays for someone with NHS coverage, the patient will bring the request to their GP for rewriting on an official prescription form, so as to shrink out-of-pocket costs. GPs are used to this relationship with private docs and usually submit quietly, relegating the task of recopying prescriptions to their secretaries.

Italian general practitioners tend to be those left behind in the selection for specialty training, and their ignorance used to be the stuff of legend: "Little Andrea Mancino, three months old, is referred to the children's hospital because of incontinence." (Supposed GP emergency room referral note in Antonio Di Stefano's book *Stupidario Medico*.)

Lately, though, they've been polishing their image. In 1998 a mere thirteen percent of Italians said their GP was their main source of medical information (trailing television medical shows), but ten years later sixty-seven percent did.

They still certainly don't splurge on supplies. In 2012, when my Aventino Medical Group's neighbors sued unsuccessfully to get us kicked out of the building, one of their sillier accusations was that our patients scatter bits of bloody cotton wool on the stairs. Called as a witness, my secretary explained this was impossible because there *is* no cotton wool in the office. The judge replied, "Impossible—when my GP gives my daughter a shot he always gives her some cotton wool to press on the site." She couldn't believe a doctor would buy Band-Aids (the thermometer covers and foil-wrapped alcohol pads I import are admired as exotica).

The job of an NHS general practitioner is heavy on certification, light on examination. I've had patients tell me that when they asked their GP to measure their blood pressure they were sent to the pharmacy. My most disturbing personal corroboration came when the Social Security Administration had me examine a widow who had lived in Indianapolis years earlier with her bricklayer husband. After returning to her Italian mountain village she had managed to be assigned an SSA disability pension, on the basis of some trumped-up heart disease, and came to me in hopes of renewing it. As per American routine I put her in an examining gown, and when I opened it to apply my stethoscope I saw a giant cancer that had eaten its way through the skin of her left breast. It had remained her secret for three years, undetected by the GP who saw her two or three times a month, or the cardiologist who had backed up her disability claim, neither of whom had ever examined her with her shirt off. I gently urged her to seek treatment, and wrote a report that would at least keep her paltry disability checks coming.

Some physician subspecies peculiar to the NHS:

- The *Guardia Medica*, or emergency medical service: young doctors hired to make telephone consultations or, in a pinch, house calls after 8:00 p.m. and on weekends for patients not quite sick enough to call an ambulance. *Guardia Medica* jobs are so grueling—twelve-hour shifts at twenty-two euros an hour—that they go begging even in the current recession.
- The *Medico Turistico*: hired June through October to offer tourists walk-in clinics, hotel visits, and night coverage.
- The *Medico Prelevatore*, or doctor phlebotomist: due to Byzantine regulations, the person who draws your blood in a lab is usually a physician.
- The *Medico Fiscale*, or medical cop: a linchpin of the Italian welfare state. Sick leave is generous, and public employees can spend an additional two weeks a year at a spa for "water therapy," but even in Italy they try to curb some abuses, and phony

sick leave is one. You never know when a Fiscal Physician will drop in unannounced to check that you're not spending your sick days sunning on the beach.

- The *Barone*, or Super Chief: You've already met the *primario*; important ones at academic medical centers get sarcastically dubbed barons for the near-princely power they wield and because the simplest way to become one is to be born to one. A *barone* is a Big Cheese whose entourage of subordinates will indulge his (almost never her) whims, down to picking him up at the airport. The status of a *barone* is diminished not a whit if his microfiefdom contains only two hospital beds or, like one oncology *primario* who made the Rome papers in 2012, never sets foot on the ward but leaves packets of pre-signed prescriptions for his subordinates to fill in the blanks.

Because of the National Health Service, Pharma isn't quite so Big in Italy. Sure, "detail men" peddle their wares door-to-door in doctors' offices just like in New York, and they push the same blockbuster drugs, but pricing is another story. In 2013 colchicine, a gout remedy that dates back to the pharaohs, jumped from a dime a pill to five bucks in the US. Two years later the price of a tube of Carac cream, for treating precancerous skin lesions, got hiked from $159 to $2,865. Self-proclaimed robber baron Martin Shkreli was dubbed "the most hated man in America" for raising the price of Daraprim, a time-honored lifesaving drug for parasitic infections, from $13.50 per tablet to $750, and in 2016 when Mylan raised the price on the much-used allergy rescue Epi-Pen by a mere 300 percent all hell broke loose. The justification, according to one drug company CEO, Nirmal Mulye? "It is a moral requirement to make money when you can."

You can't pull those tricks over here, because the government negotiates prices for all medications available through the National Health Service. Price-gougers find their product exiled from the formulary and thus practically unsalable. Colchicine is free on the NHS, and even private customers pay only three bucks a month; Daraprim and Epi-Pen are distributed without charge in hospital pharmacies. If your doctor thinks your adrenal glands need stimulating, an injection of corticotropin will set you back sixteen dollars in Italy, $7,000 in the US. The same international drug companies that charge obscene prices in the States meekly accept government price controls in Italy, fighting tooth and nail to get included on the NHS formulary. Gilead Sciences insisted on sticking to its $1000-per-pill price for its hepatitis C drug Solvadi, so the Italian authorities retaliated, first by making it unavailable except for patients at death's door and then by threatening to ignore the patent and manufacture a generic equivalent themselves. In mid-2017 the NHS declared victory, with Gilead agreeing to accept barely ten percent of what it had originally demanded for a course of treatment.

I help my patients game the system by trying to keep track of which drugs are covered by the NHS and how long they've been around—older ones cost less. Drug companies can, however, let an unprofitable product lapse altogether, for example penicillin VK, *the* standard oral antibiotic in the 1970s, which disappeared from Italian pharmacies long before I arrived. When a drug goes off patent, dark forces determine whether a cheaper generic version will become available: there's generic amoxicillin but not ampicillin, ciprofloxacin but not tetracycline. Bupropion is free on the NHS as an antidepressant called Wellbutrin, but costs $2.70 a pill if it's sold under the brand name Zyban to help smokers quit.

In Italy prescription drugs don't get marketed straight to customers, by the way—that particular invitation to misprescribing is allowed nowhere in the world except the US and New Zealand.

> Once upon a time there was a country that was based on the illicit . . . Whoever had money to give in exchange for favors had generally made that money through other favors done in the past; thus evolved an economic system that was circular and not without a certain harmony.
>
> —Italo Calvino, "A defense of honesty in the land of the corrupt"

Like the larger Italian universe, the world of medicine is littered with sticky fingers and greasy palms that make the ubiquitous *raccommandazione* seem a quasi-innocent bit of local color . . .

In 2013 I was proud to vote for Ignazio Marino as mayor of Rome, figuring he'd bring a touch of class to City Hall. He wasn't merely a physician but had spent years as a pioneering transplant surgeon at the University of Pittsburgh Medical Center. Later I was chagrined to read reports in the press that he hadn't left Pittsburgh voluntarily, but had departed after being accused by the university of submitting, and cashing in on, some $8,000 in duplicate expense reimbursement requests. In 2009, a UPMC spokesman was quoted in the *Pittsburgh Tribune* as saying, "Dr. Marino was compelled to resign solely as a result of irregularities uncovered by UPMC auditors. Period." It must be said that Dr. Marino strongly disputes this version and has in fact won a defamation suit against Italian newspapers that had promulgated it. Wherever the truth lies, what I personally find most shocking is not the possibility that a well-paid surgeon had put his career at risk for a few thousand bucks, but that most Italians, when they hear the story, shrug.

When faced with, say, an unguarded entrance to a pedestrian-only area, the classic Roman motto is *"tentar non nuoce,"* it never hurts to try. Even if you get caught there's rarely follow-up, so only one in four traffic tickets ever gets paid.

In 2016, *Nature* published a brilliant study confirming the Italian propensity for cheating. University students in twenty-three countries were allowed to roll dice unwatched and report the results to researchers, receiving cash awards according to the number they claimed to have thrown. Aided by the law of averages—in the long run a die comes up six exactly one-sixth of the time—the researchers were able to estimate each country's honesty rates. Italians flunked: when offered the chance to earn money by fibbing a mere twenty-five percent consistently told the truth, far below any other developed country (forty-three percent in Spain, eighty-eight percent in Germany). Tanzanians were the worst at three percent, poor things.

Glossary: *corruzione*

Corruption. For five postwar decades the Christian Democrats ran Italy on bribe-juice, while the Communist Party made the *questione morale* one of their chief banners, more than revolution or even cost-of-living raises, and got elected to run local governments because they were thought less likely to pocket city funds. The Christian Democratic Party eventually collapsed under the weight of corruption scandals, but apparently it's still common for public financing to be misappropriated, promotions made without regard for competence, external audits dodged, and unnecessary positions invented and filled—even in times of economic crisis—because somebody's nephew needs a job.

When the distinguished Neapolitan physician Francesco De Lorenzo was appointed minister of health in 1989, he bragged with Trumpian chutzpah that, being independently wealthy, he had no need to take bribes. Several years later the cops raided his home and caught him burning compromising documents in a frying pan; an overstuffed hassock, slashed open, turned out to be stuffed with millions of dollars in cash.

For thirty years I was the Social Security Administration's point physician in Rome, mostly examining ex-emigrants who had worked long enough in the US to be eligible for a disability pension. Or their widows—Italy had a free hand with disability pensions as a way of topping up low incomes, so one able-bodied black-clad woman after another would hoist herself up onto my examining table in hopes that the Americans would be equally generous. I was hurried into the job after the Social Security people discovered my predecessor had been peddling his endorsements to the highest bidder, and it took me a year to reexamine every person he had certified infirm.* So many of them were from a single mountain village that I fantasized an open-air nurs-

---

*In *Christ Stopped at Eboli*, a memoir of his internal exile in a back-of-beyond village under Fascism, Carlo Levi described an ex-emigrant whose great accomplishment in life was having fooled the American government into giving him a pension. He perfected the art of toppling over backward without moving a muscle

ing home, a latter-day Valley of the Blind, where every last man, woman, and child limped or hobbled or panted his way down the street croaking out feeble greetings. One day I recognized the last name of an examinee as matching that of a fellow I had recently nixed for fabricated ailments, and inquired whether someone in his family had come in to see me. He said no. I was curious, had the secretary dig up the other chart, and saw that not only the names but the addresses were identical. He stood up, said, "Yeah, OK, that's my brother," and had the good grace to walk out rather than going on with the charade.

Italians say *il più pulito ha la rogna*, the cleanest among them is mangy, and the health industry is no exception. The papers never lack tales of contractors who win the tender for a new hospital wing by giving someone a percentage, white-coat laundries who keep their contract by greasing palms, laboratory directors who wangle two payments per test and pocket one, hospital administrators who siphon off money set aside for employee pensions, drug companies that pay off employees of the Italian Drug Agency to get their products listed on NHS formularies or block competition from generics. A 2013 PriceWaterhouseCooper report for the European Union estimated that thirteen percent of Italian health expenditure goes up in smoke because of corruption (which is, to tell the truth, not much more than what American Medicare supposedly loses between upcoded diagnoses and outright fraud).

Glossary: *la legge*

The Law, so rigid it begs to be broken. In Italy even knocking down a plaster wall between two bedrooms requires government authorization, so citizens too upright to resort to bribery bring in workmen on the sly and have them spirit the rubble out to the dump under cover of night. If a malicious neighbor calls the cops you can always hope for one of the periodic blanket amnesties for scofflaws (Confession, followed by Absolution).

---

to break his fall, and then gave a demonstration to one doctor after another until they set him up with a monthly check for the rest of his life.

Innovations are particularly liable to zealous overenforcement. In the first weeks of anti-evasion "intelligent cash registers," cops gave fines to ten-year-olds who bought a lollipop without insisting on a receipt for their nickel. The day Piazza Santa Maria in Trastevere officially became a pedestrian island, a police officer assigned to keep out cars took it as a personal affront that a girl dared to drive past him. While she was backing out, having realized her mistake, he shot her dead.

For one brief moment in the early 1990s it looked as though Italy was about to turn the corner and become what its citizens ironically call *un paese normale,* a normal country. The European Union would force an overhaul of medical training now that Germany had to allow Italian surgeons to operate. Free trade would force Italian companies to start paying their bills on time. The Clean Hands campaign that had brought down most of the old political parties would destroy old habits of everyday corruption. Instead, Silvio Berlusconi stepped in to fill the illegality gap and corruption burst all its buttons, infiltrating areas hitherto untouched.

I got my Italian medical credentials at age thirty-one, too old to hope to be hired by a public hospital—the limit was thirty-five, the average wait five years. A nurse at the Nuovo Regina Margherita Hospital suggested I get a disability certificate to gain an extra five years' leeway. I was floored. "But I'm healthy as a horse." She shrugged: "You're a doctor, your colleagues will certify anything you want."

I didn't have the nerve to plunge that deep into mendacity, and had neither the humility nor the financial cushion for the multi-year unpaid apprenticeship that was the unofficial prerequisite to becoming a National Health Service GP. So, as I've said, I was forced willy-nilly to join the private realm, a ghostly shadow of the NHS, complete with its own doctors, labs, and strictly-for-profit hospitals.

For a red-diaper baby, the daughter of an ex-Communist Party father and an ex-Socialist Party mother, this was a disappointment. I'd figured the chance to work in a National Health Service would be a perk of moving to Italy, and my insecurities—I had always leaned on colleagues for advice—made me a doubly improbable candidate for setting up shop on my own.

Luckily for me, if not for the local population, from Rome on south public medicine is a particular shambles and the private version flourishes. An Italian with private health insurance or money to burn may bypass her GP and go to a private cardiologist for her high blood pressure, a gastroenterologist for her heartburn, an ENT for the sniffles. Even a carpenter, if he's getting up ten times a night to pee, may scrape together his savings and get his prostate Rotor Rooter'd privately. As the public hospitals deteriorate, with ever longer waiting times and such a shortage of beds that a critically ill patient can get shipped twenty miles away if he's admitted at all, the private system picks up some of the slack—forty-five percent of specialist visits are reportedly now for pay.

Private means convenient. To have a lab test done on the public system you have to wait in line three times: for your GP to write the prescription, for the blood to be drawn, and to pick up the results. If you're paying cash you can walk into any private lab, stick out your arm, and name your tests.

Glossary: *fare la fila*

To wait in line, a foreign concept. When I moved to Rome, getting served in a bank or a delicatessen meant braving a throng where you held your own by keeping your eyes peeled. For decades I couldn't pay my light bill without waiting an hour at the post office. Nowadays there are Take-A-Numbers instead of elbows, but waiting still punctuates the rhythms of Rome's daily life. When your car gets nabbed at a no-parking spot, a policeman who could be out catching bad guys is instead assigned to carry the ticket to your door, ring the bell, and hand it over in person. If no one's home he leaves a notice, and you have to endure the line at a post office to pick up the summons before graduating to the line at the central traffic police station to learn how much it comes to and another line back at the post office to hand over your cash.

Private also means boundless ostentation: lavish waiting rooms, marble lobbies, Morandis on the walls, Vivaldi on the telephone. As Christine Smallwood once wrote in the *New York Times*, "Extravagance, of course, is what Italy is all about," and of all Italians, Romans are the fondest of posh—Rome has been Glitz City since the time of the Caesars.

Most private practitioners either own their own office or see patients in multispecialty clinics like the Medical Diagnostic Center and the Rome International Clinic, where docs feed patients to each other and to a laboratory whose director owns the premises. The common American arrangement, several internists or dermatologists or gynecologists who share a space and cover for each other, is almost unheard of—Italian physicians are so scared somebody will steal their patients that when they go on vacation most of them let their office phone ring unanswered, rarely even leaving an out-of-town message, much less the name of a substitute. My own Aventino Medical Group, where docs of the same specialty collaborate with no hidden economic agenda, is *più unico che raro*, so rare as to be unique.

The public system has always been threadbare and economical, the private luxurious and expensive. Lately, though, burgeoning co-pays and waiting lists on the NHS have combined with physician unemployment to breed a new phenomenon: low-cost private medicine. A few ambitious young Italian docs even learn a foreign language or two so they can offer their fresh-out-of-medical-school "expertise" cheap to unsuspecting tourists by peddling 24/7 house calls to hotels. Watch out.

In Rome few high-up public docs limit themselves to their paycheck, most heading off to private practice after mornings in the hospital, which is why the usual time for medical appointments is afternoon-evening. An invitation to corruption—"Sorry, the waiting list for a hip replacement is six months. Of course you could get it done next week if you went to the *primario* privately . . ." The resultant neglect of public structures ranges from the benign (show up late, leave early) to the malignant (pilfering supplies) and the laughable (headline: "Carabinieri Raid Local Health Clinic Number 37 in Naples While Patients Applaud. Four Doctors in Jail for Absenteeism"), while netting bigwigs hundreds of thousands extra a year.

The cozy monopoly of hospital *primari* who skipped out after two hours' work, parasitized the public system for private patients, and charged outrageous fees under the table began breaking down in 1999, when Health Minister Rosy Bindi introduced a carrot-and-stick process to induce hospital *primari* to either be full-time Chiefs or limit their private practice to on-site hospital facilities. In theory she won, but so far the docs have managed to finagle a Newspeak interpretation of "on-site," getting their swanky offices defined as virtual extensions of public institutions. By law, my office neurologist spends his Thursday afternoons seeing patients at the Policlinico Umberto I hospital; what sat behind a desk on the Aventine hill at the other end of Rome last Thursday, using hospital prescription pads and receipts, was merely his avatar.

> Anyone who can't afford a private doctor, a specialist, or a private hospital, falls into a Dantean circle of hell with fate unknown.
>
> —*La Repubblica* editorial

We private docs like to pretend *La Repubblica* is right. One cherished theatrical exercise of the physician who serves an international clientele is to sweep into the chaotic public hospital ward where an innocent foreigner has landed, look around with disgust, and peremptorily order the patient transferred to a *clinica* more like what he expects in a hospital—nurses scuttling in and out of rooms instead of yelling from opposite ends of the hall, no need to bring his own toilet paper or rely on his roommate to get him a glass of water.

But appearances can be deceiving. My initiation came late one

1983 evening when I was called to the boarding students' quarters at an international private school to see Marcy, an eleventh grader with diabetes. She confessed she hadn't been keeping up with her insulin, and I recognized the dehydration and heavy breathing of impending diabetic coma. For the first time I cashed in on the admitting privileges I had arranged at the Ars Medica *clinica*, intending to treat her the way I had been trained: doing lab tests once an hour, and having nurses adjust the treatment on the basis of the results. After she got settled into her room I went to set things up, and learned what a mistake I had made—there was no intensive care unit, a single nurse for forty patients, and the laboratory closed until morning. Marcy was huffing and puffing more than before, and it was midnight. I counted to ten slowly, then decided, OK, I can handle this. I was trained by a world-class, fanatical diabetes specialist, Dr. Robert Matz, so I knew this condition well enough to be able to guess her blood sugar by putting test strips into her urine, her potassium level by doing hourly ECGs, and her acid-base balance from how fast she panted. I spent the night at her side, giving her insulin injections and fluids every hour on the basis of those seat-of-the-pants estimates, and she did fine. (Today I'd no longer have the expertise, or the balls, to pull that feat off . . .)

This baptism by fire taught me that most *cliniche* were hotels with white coats on the bellboys, intended for people to get their fibroids and gallbladders lopped out in comfort. A few have small intensive care units, but in a real emergency you're generally better off at a public hospital—run down and understaffed, perhaps, but complete with night coverage, consultants, emergency equipment, and specialized nurses. The *clinica* Villa Bianca may be a dream place to have your baby, but if he's born with respiratory distress syndrome he'll get transferred to the neonatal ICU in the vast, public San Camillo Hospital.

After public and private there's a third limb to the medical system: other countries. Italians are so sloppily xenophilic that I buy my apples at a store they call Happy Fruit and my skirts at one inventively dubbed Young's Club, and even though Italian medical care has gradually joined the modern world, many locals remain convinced it's better elsewhere. Where we boast of the American way, Italians refer without embarrassment to *"un classico pasticcio all'italiana,"* a classic Italian mess. They take pride in having no pride, get self-ironic Jewish jokes better than most Europeans, and admit their country's medical provincialism with the unruffled gentility of a once-imperial people who now peek in from the world's periphery. Patients commonly believe a 300 mg American aspirin pill is stronger than a 500 mg Italian one, and have been known to ask me the name of the best US hospital to have a hernia fixed, convinced that even the simplest medical procedure is beyond the reach of their countrymen.

(Some Italian physicians, on the contrary, harbor an intense resentful pride of nation and caste. One disability examiner refused to read my supporting letter when he saw from my letterhead that I was American. An Italian doc who goes abroad to specialize may make a triumphant return, only to find himself unemployable, ostracized like a *mafioso* who's broken *omertà*, for having dared to betray his native career ladder. One US-trained hematologist who applied for a hospital job on repatriation swore to me that at his practical examination in blood smear interpretation they switched slides on him mid-stream.)

Switzerland used to be the classic destination for Italians seeking first-class medical care, but its refusal to join the European Union has made it a less popular medical Mecca than countries such as Germany, which offer free reciprocity. And Italian hospitals have improved to the point that the Gustave-Roussy cancer institute outside Paris no longer has an entire ward devoted to Italians on "journeys of hope," as it did in the eighties. These days, it's mostly foreigners I'll ship to London for a brain tumor, or Marseilles for a complicated knee replacement.

Romans have always preferred to stick close to home anyway, where nobody speaks *straniero* ("foreign," slang for any language that's not Italian) and flocks of relatives can bring them noodle soup for supper. In 1995, one of my patients insisted on having his heart surgery at San Camillo Hospital even after I told him that one out of three patients didn't make it home alive and the *primario* had been convicted of manslaughter. Italians say *Mogli e buoi dei paesi tuoi*, choose wives and cattle from your home town.

The Jews? They're just poor Christians like the rest of us.
—Woman-on-the-street interviewed in Rome
  by RAI television, 1982

Catholicism may not be the official state religion any more, but the word "Christian" is still synonymous with human being, a crucified Saviour still presides over public hospital beds and classrooms, and the Church is still a major player in the medical system. When my mother died in Rome we were relieved to find that the hospital kept one of its five *camere ardenti* crucifix-free, so we could hold an atheistic wake.

From San Giovanni (St. John) to the Bambino Gesù (Baby Jesus) and the Santo Spirito (Holy Ghost), each of the major characters in the Catholic panoply has bestowed their name on one Rome public hospital. My Nuovo Regina Margherita Hospital was retrofitted within an old nunnery, and on your way to radiology a spiked clausura gate—the barrier the nuns never crossed—is mounted on the wall to remind you of its previous incarnation. On the gastroenterology ward landing, when I was working there, a Madonna wreathed in bright tiny light bulbs, with flowers at her feet, commanded the staircase.

Glossary: *i preti*

The priests, a synecdoche for the Catholic Church, as in, "The Farnese movie theater belongs to the priests." The black shadows of priestly *tonache*, their long loose gowns, used to pepper Rome streets. Nowadays most go around in mufti, except a few coming from far-flung lands where priests still like to stand out in a crowd. Any long-time Rome resident can pick out a gaggle of seminarians around a restaurant table, though, no matter what clothes they're wearing.

Historically, Popes entrusted themselves to Jewish physicians, whose immunity to Vatican intrigue made them less likely to poison their patient. But until recently there were no Jewish students at the Catholic University medical school, because the required documents included a letter from your parish priest. For years I was refused admitting privileges at one Rome private hospital and, characteristically, blamed my own personal and professional failings. I was gobsmacked when I learned from a "deep throat" that the true reason was my Jewish name. Eventually they relented, but only after a patient who happened to be a nun with Vatican pull put the screws on.

Compared to American Calvinism, Italian Catholic moralism is more goody-goody than fire-breathing, and my patients and I suffer less than you might expect from its omnipresence. Historic precedent: when the Spanish Inquisition expelled the Jews in 1492, many found a safe haven in central Italy, which was at the time ruled by the Pope. And nobody's ever shot an Italian abortionist.

Here in the Pope's back yard, first-trimester abortion has been legal and free on demand in public hospitals ever since the Radical Party rammed through a law in 1978. The Church's rear-guard action has primarily consisted in convincing, cajoling, and strong-arming medical staff to register as conscientious objectors. Here's the syllogism: any public hospital gynecologist worth his or her salt also operates privately in a private hospital or *clinica*, the *cliniche* are overwhelmingly owned by the Church, anyone known to perform or even sanction abortions is barred from Church-run institutions, therefore if a public doc wants to protect his private practice he has to avoid any taint of abortions by registering as a CO. The upshot is that seventy percent of gynecologists and more than sixty percent of paramedical personnel have signed up, skewed toward Italy's South.

Once when I was in a Catholic private hospital to see a patient, an administrator handed me a form to sign swearing I would never give any patient information about abortions, whether inside or outside the *clinica*. By then I had been in Italy long enough to know what *not* to do: refuse, protest, bargain, bribe, or sign. I tossed the piece of paper in the trash and nobody's ever brought up the subject again.

The conscientious objector trick hasn't made abortions completely inaccessible, but in some parts of southern Italy a woman may have to spend weeks trudging from hospital to hospital trying to arrange one, and often her appointment will be more than another two weeks off. Which is why for every five hospital abortions there's supposedly another one done illegally, either by the same grisly practitioners who did them back when or sometimes, it is whispered, in the private offices of certified conscientious objectors. A patient of mine developed complications after one of those illicit procedures and had to throw herself on the mercies of the public hospital emergency room, lying about what happened to her and risking permanent damage, just as in the America of the dark pre–*Roe v. Wade* era I caught the end of in medical school.

Medical abortion using mifepristone or RU 486, which simplifies the procedure by eliminating the need for an operation, is available in some Italian hospitals, and by 2017 was being used in one in six abortions. As a sop to the Church, women who take it are often required to spend three nights in the hospital between the first pill and the second—medically unnecessary, but intended to make the whole procedure seem less of a cakewalk. Most patients, no fools they, just go home and then come back to the hospital when their second hit is due.

Second-trimester therapeutic abortions are theoretically legal in cases of fetal malformation or risk to the mother's life, but in practice they're near-impossible to obtain. One of my most tragic cases was Mariella, who developed aggressive breast cancer at age thirty-nine. Before knowing she was pregnant she had exposed an embryo to chemotherapy, putting it at high risk of malformations. All the Rome hospitals turned her down, and I moved heaven and earth so she could fly to England to terminate the pregnancy at twenty-two weeks, which broke both her heart and her spirit. She died before the baby would have been born.

Rome Professor Severino Antinori's post-menopausal *mammenonne*, mommy-grandmas, made international headlines in 1994 by bearing babies using donor eggs. The Church responded by pushing the Berlusconi government into making it illegal to use donor sperm or eggs, or to use embryo selection to prevent genetic diseases such as sickle cell anemia. Until 2014, when European Union courts forced Italy to strip that law from the books, thousands of well-off couples would cross the border into Spain or France every year for fertility treatments. Surrogate pregnancy, and in vitro fertilization for gay couples or single women, are still illegal in Italy as of 2018.

Male chauvinism can trump theology. I've overheard one fertility specialist saying he refused on principle to do donor sperm insemination because, "You can't have children who don't know who their father is." Yeah, OK. Except I happened to know for a fact that the same guy regularly and illegally performed donor egg IVF, clearly having no scruples about producing children who wouldn't know who their *mother* was.

Medical ethics is a field where the Church has staked out a large claim in Italy. Its all-out campaign against Living Wills failed in late 2017, but it has continued to prevail against assisted suicide, and in favor of maintaining patients similar to Florida's Terri Schiavo in persistent vegetative states. Though I may disagree with specific positions, I often find myself secretly thankful for its dull, unflagging insistence on some kind of natural order in this tricky age of undead organ donors and Rent-A-Wombs.

> The Italian health care system is the best, the most generous, in the world. Its services are the worst and the laziest.
> —Roberto Gervaso

When the refreshment stand at a Fela Kuti concert boasted a "Bacon lettuce and tomato sandwich," I couldn't resist. Great bread, fresh lettuce, sweet tomato and . . . raw bacon. Some Italian dreamer must have heard of the BLT concept without ever having experienced the reality. At least I didn't risk trichinosis, because, unlike the US, Italy inspects its pork.

Italians are great at winging it, and consider inconsistency not a vice but a virtue. So without inside dope there's no predicting whether a given ward, a given physician, a given remedy will belong in the twenty-first century, the nineteenth, or the timeless realm of imbecilic improvisation. Is the cabbie who won't turn on his AC in August environmentally aware or just tightfisted? When I first came to Italy, every patient on antibiotics was knocking back little vials of Entero-Germina, a benign bacterium intended to rebuild your body's defenses. At the time the idea seemed to me like giving with one hand and taking away with the other. Thirty-five years later and rebranded as probiotics, it's the latest and greatest. But then there was the *La Repubblica* report of a woman who lay down trustingly on a gynecologist's exam table to have an IUD inserted. He took his tongs and his speculum, immersed them in a bowl of alcohol between her legs, and— apparently hoping to kill even more germs—set the bowl on fire, causing third-degree burns over half her body.

Brain infection, take one. At a cheap *pensione* I examined a young American tourist with glazed-over eyes who complained of headache and didn't answer my questions quite right. Suspecting meningitis, I rushed her by ambulance to the infectious disease emergency room of the Policlinico Umberto I. Within fifteen minutes the doc had performed a spinal tap, seen pus cells under the microscope which confirmed the diagnosis, and administered the first, life-saving dose of intravenous penicillin. No American hospital could have been more efficient, and she went home in perfect health after three days.

Brain infection, take two. At another *pensione*, deep into August, an English nun refused to get out of bed. The head of her pilgrim group called me in to "give her a shot of Valium" so they could all fly home that day, on schedule. She was lying there looking into space and reciting numbers—"thirteen, seventy-two, twenty-nine, forty-four . . ." (A lottery-obsessed Italian colleague asked eagerly, "Did you write them down?") The problem was clearly not nerves. Another ambulance, to another institute in the same Policlinico. There the staff hurried around and proceeded to do . . . nothing whatever. No spinal taps, no blood cultures. I would go to the ward every morning, watch the patient drift into an ever more profound coma, and plead impotently with my colleagues to try to figure out what was going on, while a pair of her sisters in Christ lurked in the hallway demanding I tell them exactly when she was going to die so they could arrange their plane tickets. She hung on until day five, and never had a diagnosis.

Blood cancer, take one. A junior year abroad student phoned from Sardinia, saying his roommate had been turned away from the local hospital barely able to walk because "the white blood cell count was too high." I made him count out the zeros on the lab report twice over: two-oh-oh oh-oh-oh, 200,000. Having grasped that the boy had acute leukemia, I phoned the hospital myself and, aghast, heard from a colleague's lips that they had indeed kicked him out, because they had no hematology ward and felt no obligation to help him reach one. I managed to arrange for a private plane to fly him that night to the mainland and for a private ambulance to deposit him on the doorstep of a world-class Hematology Institute in Rome. Knowing the lay of the land, I didn't warn the hematologists he was coming until I figured the ambulance was about to arrive. Then I called and when they said, as expected, "Sorry, we're full up" I replied, "Too bad, the ambulance is pulling in." They did the right thing, admitted him, gave him his first dose of chemotherapy before dawn, and in four weeks he was back in Iowa convalescing. In retrospect it's a great story, my chance of a lifetime to act the hero riding in on a white charger, but during those hours fighting over the phone with everyone from the head of the university program to two sets of colleagues I was sweating bullets.

Blood cancer, take two. A friend called one August asking me to check on her brother Ennio, who was languishing in the Spallanzani infectious disease hospital with a high fever. I walked in past monumental columns flanked by palm trees, through a vast atrium, up a marble grand staircase worthy of a Busby Berkeley movie musical. Ennio was cheerful and energetic, despite water on his lungs and hugely swollen liver and spleen, and said that that morning, after five weeks of futile antibiotics, they had finally removed a lump in his groin for study. Two days later he was diagnosed with Hodgkin's disease, an eminently curable lymph node cancer, and was transferred to the above-mentioned Hematology Institute. My supposed diagnostic acumen now unnecessary, I went off on a carefree holiday. When I got back four weeks later, I found Ennio moribund, too weak to raise his head from the pillow. Why? Because the Institute's protocol called for a liver biopsy as part of tumor staging, and the one doctor who did their liver biopsies was on vacation, so they had allowed Ennio to drift toward death instead of treating him. This absurd story had a happy ending, and I consider myself privileged to be one of the few physicians to have seen end-stage Hodgkin's disease respond, within days, to cancer chemotherapy.

The unreliability of the system doesn't affect my own practice as much as it might, because my patients are mostly foreign, of working age, and fit. For acute illnesses I usually treat them as outpatients or ship them to their home country, and serious chronic diseases tend to bring expats' Italian adventure to a close, so I largely succeed in steering clear of hospitals. And *piano piano*, slowly slowly, the European Union's drive for continent-wide standardization is making inroads even here in the *bel paese*. But in the meantime, there's only one thing a foreigner absolutely needs to understand about Italian medicine: it's a crapshoot.

6

In the Crunch

When I was doing my internship on the gastroenterology ward of the Nuovo Regina Margherita Hospital in 1980, at 9:00 a.m. all the patients would be in bed for morning rounds, awaiting the ceremonial laying on of hands. By noon, most of them were hanging out with their families and the resident cats in the hospital's thirteenth-century cloister, feeding the goldfish in the ancient Roman bathtub fountain in the tenth-century cloister, or standing at the bar in their bathrobes enjoying an espresso and a smoke. The sixteenth-century cloister was less popular—no benches.

The Nuovo Regina Margherita's emergency room entrance was built in the sixties, but the brick archway leading to Piazza San Cosimato, Trastevere's market square, supported by marble columns with Corinthian capitals, had been there since the building began its life as a monastery in the Middle Ages. The wards stank of cigarettes, the dingy green walls were half-lit by forty-watt bulbs, and the only hospital trappings were the ubiquitous white coats. No American hustle and bustle, no patient-laden gurneys crossing paths, no PA system obsessively "paging Doctor X." At mealtime, servers walked down the hall doling out plates of *pasta e fagioli* from deep metal bins yelling, "Who wants some?" Some days you couldn't take a deep breath without coughing, because outside the open windows they were spraying the rosebushes.

Patients could be off wandering the grounds because most of them weren't very sick. In that golden age of fiscal irresponsibility, an Italian GP would send a headache sufferer to a neurologist in the public system, who without insurance companies breathing down his neck might pop her into the hospital just to get a few tests done. Dr. Prantera admitted each of his inflammatory bowel disease patients once a year for a four-day checkup.

Gastroenterology ward rounds at the Nuovo Regina Margherita Hospital, as at San Camillo, meant the entire coterie swarming from one bed to the next, discussing each case in obfuscating medical jargon, while the patients in the room strained to catch every word for later collective exegesis. Bedside censorship of medical facts involves verbal gymnastics—cancer becomes "mitoses" or "neoangiogenesis"—that mystified this hapless foreign observer as much as the patients. Only once did I hear a patient speak out of turn during the solemn ritual. Dr. Prantera had shifted into what the Italians call macaroni English, to portray the dire impending fate of an elderly sailor with cirrhosis of the liver who lay in the center of our gathering, yellow as a banana peel, his huge fluid-filled belly pushing up the sheets. In one of the long pauses while my colleague hunted for a word, the world-traveled patient looked directly at me and asked, in perfect English, "What part of the States ya come from, Doc?"

The days of patients sunning themselves among the roses are long gone. With the number of hospital beds down by a third for lack of funding, even a broken hip or a heart attack isn't a ticket to instant admission. Patients still bring their own pajamas, though, and run-down is still the norm. Visiting a patient in San Giovanni Hospital recently, I needed to use a public bathroom. No toilet paper, no toilet seat, and no lock—I had to assume a yogic position with one foot wedged against the door. There was a sink, but no soap, disinfectant gel, or way to dry your hands. On the plus side, the doctors' ashtrays are now history, and the lighting is good enough to read by.

Try not to get admitted to a Rome hospital on Friday afternoon; you may get no medical attention until Monday morning. Sometimes a distraught relative, unable to get a physician to tend to a desperately ill patient over the weekend, dials 113—the local equivalent of 911—and enlists a platoon of cops to drag one to the bedside. And remember not to get sick at the wrong time, such as mid-August or World Cup finals. Theory: handicapped access is mandatory, even in the smallest medical office. Reality: in August 2009, a disabled patient of mine was admitted to the Forlanini Hospital, and found there was no accessible bathroom on her ward. The nurses told her there was one on a neighboring private ward, so she wheeled herself over, only to find the entire ward was shut down for the summer holiday. Necessity being the mother of invention, she broke in.

Many hospitalized patients are too sick to use the bathroom, which is why bedpans, urinals, and bedside commodes exist. Rather than stocking any of this equipment, most hospitals in the Eternal City, including at least one of its top stroke units, instead outfit every one of their bedbound patients with diapers. Antitherapeutic, disgusting for the patient, and a setup for bedsores. A nastier cleanup job, too, but the nurses duck it by insisting the patient's family not only buy the diapers, but change them as well.

Sometimes Rome hospitals can be in the vanguard. A friend's mother, hospitalized at the giant Umberto II Hospital, sent her daughter to the phalanx of vending machines just outside the ward entrance to pick up a box of tissues. The machine was all out of Kleenex, but dropping a couple of one-euro coins in the slot and pushing the right button would have bought my friend . . . a condom. Admirably foresighted, hip even, but who exactly is expected to use them? And *where?*

A new patient will sometimes look around my office and say, "Gee, Italian doctors' offices are different from American ones," or comment on the way out, "I see doctors do things differently in Italy." This always gets my goat, since I think of my practice as straight-up New York, with Levenstein spin. Yeah, sure, I tell them, Italian medicine's plenty different from American standard, and so is my own, but they're *different* different. Where they really bang heads is in emergencies . . .

Four in the afternoon. Jeremy R. is sitting on the exam table shaking so hard he has to cling to its sides. He showed up panting for breath and slightly confused, one week back from Africa. Possibly cerebral malaria, definitely very ill. I run through our options. The Salvator Mundi Hospital, my usual private haunt, couldn't handle someone so sick even if they were allowed to try. The private Rome American and Mater Dei hospitals have intensive care units, but they wouldn't take him—by law no private hospital can admit a patient who might be contagious—so he's fated for the public system. I overcome his protests, write a note for the emergency room docs at the Spallanzani infectious disease hospital, and put him in a taxi. My job is over.

Nope. At 7:00 p.m. he calls the office: he still hasn't seen a doctor, and the triage nurse in the ER told his wife he's Code Green— mildly ill—so he'll be waiting a long time. Can he go home? I say no, here's what you do: stagger up personally to the triage window so the nurse can see your condition. At 9:00 my home phone rings: he did what I said and they changed him to Code Orange, but they still haven't called him in. He's exhausted, can he leave now? I say no, hang in there. At midnight his wife phones. He vanished into the inner sanctum an hour earlier, she's had no news, and she's worried. I say take some deep slow breaths. At 1:00 a.m. she calls again: he's been seen by an infectious disease doctor and officially admitted to the hospital, but he's still lying on a stretcher in a hallway for lack of a bed and they won't let her in. I say that's TERRIFIC! Go home and get some rest!

As Italian emergency room stories go, that one was smooth sailing. Jeremy was in a specialized hospital, there was an intensive care unit when he turned out to need one—he had Severe Acute Respiratory Syndrome (SARS)—and he got excellent care.

What happens when the sailing isn't smooth? An Italian patient calls from the island of Elba with a grade ten out of ten headache and a stiff neck: meningitis. I order her to the nearest ER pronto— where the docs send her back to her campsite without any testing or treatment. It must have been viral, because she survived.

An elderly friend tripped and fell into a pothole, fracturing four ribs and filling half her chest with blood. She phoned me in panic after two days on an emergency room stretcher: she still couldn't walk or take a full breath, but in an hour they were planning to put her into a wheelchair and push her out onto the street. I went to the hospital and argued with the staff, to no avail. The only solution I could come up with was to drive her to my place and nurse her myself.

Every emergency is a fresh nightmare. The ambassador who has a convulsion at a diplomatic reception, the artist with a stroke, the writer with labyrinthitis so severe she can't keep any food down, all bring the same series of nail-biting questions: can I get away with treating her at home? If not, can I use a private *clinica* where I stay in charge? If it must be a public hospital, can I recommend a specific one? And if he gets dumped in an odoriferous open ward with an invisible nursing staff, will he be so angry with me I'll never see him again?

In 1983, I drove outside Rome to the bedside of a Catholic monk who said he'd been up all night with chest pain battling the angel of death. My portable ECG machine agreed, and I sped him to the San Giovanni Hospital in my own car. The ER staff rushed him into an empty room and hooked him up for another electrocardiogram. I felt the responsibility lift from my shoulders. When the ECG rolled out of the slot they tore it from the machine, unhooked the patient, and . . . dashed away, the whole crowd of doctors and nurses, ECG and ECG machine in tow, in search of a cardiologist to tell them what to do. My patient was abandoned, alone with his heart attack, at risk for sudden death. No one had even checked his blood pressure, much less given him the then-standard package of intensive care unit, morphine, nitroglycerin, lidocaine, an intravenous line, a cardiac monitor, and a vigilant nurse. I stood helplessly at his bedside figuring if things went downhill I'd start CPR, scream, or both. After forty-five minutes a cardiologist strolled in and signed admission papers—not to an ICU but to a regular medicine ward, where the poor man died two days later.

For years after that experience I would admit heart attack victims to my small private *clinica* instead of sending them to the public hospital. Treatment wasn't cutting-edge, but anything was better than what I had seen at San Giovanni. Times have changed now, and patients deserve a chance at having their clogged coronary artery unblocked pronto even if they live in Rome, so crushing chest pain means "call an ambulance." But even getting to the best cardiac unit in town is no guarantee; in 2017 it sent one of my patients, who had severe, obviously cardiac chest pain, home without testing or treatment. He survived the impending closure of the heart's main artery only because he had insurance that would cover a private hospital, and because he hung on for the four days needed to organize bypass surgery.

Emergencies are the black hole in my professional life. Even during my training I wasn't a whiz at handling them, and in Rome there are all those extra damn decisions. For a given dire case, the best solution may be to meet Professor X and me at a private hospital, fly to Paris tonight, or head for the nearest ER like anywhere else in the civilized world. Sometimes I feel like my whole business is a scam, a medical Potemkin village, with no backup behind the façades. An expat may feel safe under my or my colleague's wing, but if he has a stroke or gets run over we have to shrug our shoulders, open our palms upward in the Italian gesture of "Too bad, but what can I do?" and fling him into the maw of the public hospital system. I followed one patient with multiple sclerosis for years, renewing her medications and having her seen periodically by a trusted neurologist. But when her disease relapsed it happened to be mid-August, the neurologist was off scuba diving, and both of Rome's specialized MS clinics were closed for the month.

If you live in Paris you know you can trust the hospitals, and if you live in Yangon you know you need to escape to Bangkok at the first sign of trouble. Simpler choices, clearer consciences. The problem with Rome lies in the gamble: the medical system works just fine except when suddenly, inexplicably, it doesn't. As the years go by, I feel ever more weighed down by the responsibility for my patients' lives, and more anxious at having to juggle unreliable options.

I've seen spectacular saves—a woman with a ruptured ectopic pregnancy who was on the operating table ten minutes after she hit the ER, my American tourist with meningitis who received instant diagnosis and antibiotics—but too often the Roman concept of emergency lacks any sense of crisis. Even the usual Italian word for it, *urgenza*, is wimpy. In 1980 my Nuovo Regina Margherita Hospital had no crash carts; death being brought by God or kismet, cardio-pulmonary resuscitation would be presumptuous. A cancer originally diagnosed as curable may no longer be so four months later when the patient reaches the top of the queue for surgery or radiotherapy.

One day in 1985 my patient James started hallucinating the smell of coffee, a classic early symptom of herpes encephalitis. Just a year earlier the disease had been uniformly fatal, but at the time James started wandering around his apartment searching for the coffee an effective drug, Zovirax, had come on the market. I felt huge relief when at eight p.m., after a CAT scan had confirmed the diagnosis, I managed to get him transferred from a back-burner hospital to the Policlinico Gemelli, which had the best neurology ward in Rome. There the rescue operation sputtered to a stall: the on-call neurologist balked at doing anything more active than putting James between two sheets, intending to await his *primario*'s OK at morning rounds before prescribing any medication. James would likely have died if I hadn't bludgeoned my colleague into sending the patient's wife out to scour the all-night pharmacies until she found one stocked with the new miracle drug. The *primario* did grouse, and the patient did slip briefly into coma, but he recovered, returned to full-time work, and sees me twice a year to this day.

Caring for the desperately ill is what US hospitals do best. An American who comes in for bronchitis may mention only on questioning that, oh yeah, he's had four brain tumor operations, or spent six months in coma after a car accident, or was defibrillated out of a cardiac arrest. American medical personnel are emergency addicts, Superdocs and Supernurses who really feel their oats only when they're dragging someone back from death's door. I once escorted a comatose patient home to the States on a Pan Am stretcher, suspended astride nine seats in the rear of the plane, and landed to discover the ambulance we'd arranged wasn't waiting— not grasping how sick the patient was, her family had cancelled it. They sent a wheelchair pusher instead, who sized up her unconscious form and said, "Sorry, this is not my job." Next came the Pan Am service rep who said the same, then the police, and then the fire department, none of whom could help, but all of whom stayed. While they milled around the aisles, airline staff cleaned the headrests and emptied the ashtrays and a crowd of fresh passengers clamored on the skyway. Pure Marx Brothers. Finally two ambulance attendants burst in through the front door and charged full tilt down the aisle clutching their emergency kits and shouting, "Where's the victim?" They were so miffed that their Ambu breathing bags and adrenalin-loaded syringes weren't needed that they nearly refused to roll my poor patient off the plane and deliver her to her hand-wringing relatives.

The rare Italian who's survived weeks in an intensive care unit may say, along with her family, that she was *miracolata*, saved not by the medical staff but by a miracle. Italy generally shows its worst colors with tasks that require organization, vigilance, scrupulously-followed protocols, and attention to detail, such as creating web sites and running ICUs. How Italians become world-class air traffic controllers and Formula 1 pit mechanics is a mystery.

One October morning in 1982, sitting at my desk at home, across the street from Rome's main synagogue, I looked up and saw an explosion. It was not altogether unexpected: Israel was bombing the hell out of Lebanon, and the Jewish community in Rome had begged the city administration, in vain, for police protection against possible blowback. Having already been awakened twice by bombs since moving to Rome, I thought I was used to terrorism, but eyewitness was different. I froze, watched the smoke climb, and thought calmly, "There's the Palestinian attack we've all been waiting for," when a second and larger bomb shook my building and I threw myself on the floor. I had seen three inert bodies on the sidewalk and called the ambulance emergency number, which rang five agonizing minutes by the clock before I gave up and phoned the police. I then went down and cradled the head of one bleeding victim until an ambulance arrived . . . twenty minutes later.

At that time, a Rome ambulance was a litter on wheels. The drivers were geniuses at getting patients down the treacherous stairs of medieval buildings and maneuvering frameless canvas stretchers that reminded me of body bags, and they were cool with turning on the sirens and running red lights, but their medical training was zilch. Nowadays the vehicles are manned by trained volunteers, many have physicians on board, and some are even equipped for advanced life support. On a bad day, though, those precious mobile ICUs may all be parked outside overcrowded emergency rooms acting as extra gurneys. And ambulance-riding docs are likely to be recent graduates, meaning their medical knowledge comes from books. In 2006, a house guest of mine had an asthma attack so severe that I helplessly called the emergency number while he sucked at his albuterol inhaler. An ambulance was there in five minutes, complete with a fresh-faced physician who had clearly never seen a person so short of breath and just stood there frozen, clutching another identical inhaler in his hand. He eventually agreed to load up my friend and head for the ER.

In 2013, actor James Gandolfini had a fatal heart attack in his Rome hotel room. The Italian press boasted that an ambulance had reached him in a mere eight minutes. Only one problem: there was no defibrillator on board, the one piece of equipment that might have saved his life.

But even the best equipment can be trumped by incompetence. In 2012, when soccer player Piermario Morosini collapsed on the field with a cardiac arrest an ambulance was present and its crew leapt into action. This being Italy, a police car was blocking their escape route—empty, because the cops were off watching the game. Undaunted, the ambulance team were at Morosini's side and had already switched on their defibrillator when the physicians of both teams dashed onto the field and for some mysterious reason, likely pure ignorance, forbade them to use it. Not surprisingly, Morosini was dead on arrival at the hospital.

Physician Makes a Mistake, Is Killed by Mafia

Wife Dies During Hysterectomy, Grieving Husband Shoots Surgeon

—*La Repubblica* headlines

By some measures, Italy is the most litigious country in Europe. Since there are plenty of medical errors, you'd think generations of lawyers would have had a field day. Think again: in the eighties direct action—a urologist kneecapped here, a surgeon's hand smashed there—seemed more frequent than lawsuits. One reason was the notorious snail's pace of Italian courts. The family of one woman who died in 2003 from an undiagnosed rip in her aorta was paid a million euros in damages, but not until 2013. During my first fifteen years working in Rome, I followed my colleagues' example and went bare, not bothering to take out malpractice insurance. Only when the Salvator Mundi International Hospital demanded it, in 1995, did I buy my first policy, for the annual pittance of $200.

Times have changed, and Italians now bring 30,000 malpractice suits every year, enough to breed an Association of Physicians Unjustly Accused of Malpractice, but it's not obvious what's driven the boom. Other kinds of lawsuits haven't increased, nor, from what I see, have medical errors, quite the contrary. My theory is that the suits reflect the gradual creep of the Italian physician-patient relationship into the modern age, the paradoxical flip side of an increased faith in doctors. You don't sue a shaman if her spells don't work.

The stakes are piddling by American standards, plaintiffs rarely scoring more than $40,000, so my insurance premium has gone up only to $550 a year compared with the $35,000 I'd be paying on Long Island, where I went to high school.

In Italy, medical errors can theoretically be a criminal as well as civil offence, but you can count the guilty verdicts on your fingers and toes. The team doctors in the Morosini case were eventually convicted of manslaughter and spent time in prison. Another case hit the news in 2013: a urologist condemned to eight months in prison when his patient bled to death after bladder surgery. He had noticed that the patient's blood pressure was falling over three days, and had the nurses put a pillow under his legs, but didn't check the blood count or notice—nor did the nurses, apparently—that the man was lying in a pool of blood.

In the late 1980s, a northern Italian couple noticed strange bruises around their two-year-old's buttocks and brought her to an emergency room. Instead of running any medical tests, the ER docs grabbed their fifteen minutes of fame by turning Dad in for rape and calling the papers, who obliged with eight-column headlines. The child was removed promptly from her parents' custody and it took a month of tears and pleading before they managed to get her back, during which time she was never once examined by a physician. The poor child's discoloration actually turned out to have been due to leukemia, which killed her within a year. What most impressed me was that there was post hoc breast-beating by journalists for the way they had jumped the gun and by magistrates for being so quick to join the lynch mob, but not by the hospital doctors, who came out of it unapologetic and scot-free. Not only did their arrogant and possibly lethal malpractice hardly come up for comment, but the family gently turned away suggestions to sue.

The ills of Italian medicine sell more newspapers than yet another public official caught taking bribes (yawn). In every year I've been in Italy, the papers have featured at least one scandal of *malasanità*, sickness of the health care system:

- "Bari, *Malasanità* Strikes Again, Woman Dies of Stroke Misdiagnosed as Gastritis."
- "A Call from the Hospital: 'Help, Police!'—No Nurses. A Patient Is Saved by the State Police." A male nurse from the men's surgery ward and a female nurse from the women's ward, the en-

tire night staff, had gone off for an hour's tryst, locking the wards behind them.

- "Death by Hospital: A Voyage to the Bari Policlinico Where Life Is Worth Nothing." After a car accident, a journalist's father died of an undiagnosed ruptured aorta in a hospital bed. One *primario* from another ward was quoted as saying, "If you get out of here alive you're just lucky."

The Chief who had mistaken a stroke for gastritis did get suspended from his job, but a Rome heart surgeon convicted of voluntary manslaughter in the deaths of several patients managed to keep operating for another two years, until a journalist smelled a rat. The surgeon's *primario* apparently thought suspending him would be unsporting.

Then there's the private wing of the system. One June morning, an English expatriate has a baby in a Rome private hospital. As her obstetrician is heading home for pasta and a glass of wine, a nurse corners him to report that the mother is bleeding heavily. But lunch is sacrosanct, and off he goes. His meal is disturbed by increasingly frantic phone calls from the patient's husband. When the doctor has spit out his last cherry pit and arrived back at the *clinica*, the patient is dead. This particular case made headlines, and the obstetrician was disbarred for several years.

A patient of mine hospitalized in a *clinica* for hernia surgery shared a room with a fellow-sufferer who boasted, without ironic intent, "My *Professore* is a real expert on hernias. I should know, he's fixed mine five times!"

One large private facility in Rome is notorious for drawing patients into a consultant vortex. Consult a GP for bronchitis and you're likely to be referred in series to a pulmonary specialist, a cardiologist, an endocrinologist, an hematologist, a gastroenterologist . . . until the trivial test abnormalities have been exhausted, the daisy chain of appointments draws to a close, and the gang moves on to the next sucker.

That kind of racket has many variations. One foreign doctor kept an appendectomy scam going, in cahoots with a surgeon, for forty years. Abdominal pain? Chronic appendicitis, lop it out. Headache? Chronic appendicitis, lop it out. One of her last gestures before she was carried back to her native land to die, at ninety-five, was getting her claws on a patient of mine who had the misfortune to develop rheumatoid arthritis while I was on vacation—yet another appendix in the trash.

The medical guild does not welcome public airing of its dirty linen. Paolo Cornaglia-Ferraris, an NHS physician who, under the pseudonym of Medicus Medicorum, broke ranks in a best-seller called *White Coats and Pajamas: Physicians' Faults in the Italian Health Care Disaster*, got fired.* When Berlusconi's TV empire produced a drama series on medical errors, *White Crimes*, organized medicine hit back hard, saying the program was trying to "stir up the population against doctors and the health care system, like 1940s–50s American Westerns against the Indians." The show was axed.

In my experience, it takes vigilance to practice medicine in Rome, but it's just a special case of the vigilance required for daily life. You need to keep an eagle eye on your place in line while pretending to concentrate on a neighborly conversation about the electric bill. You need to be ready to catch out the market woman when she slips a rotting tomato into the bag. Italians intersect each other like so many amoebas intermingling at their edges, their lives a constant bumping of pseudopods and jostling for position. I always find it a bit of a relief, on a trip back home, to slip back into my American force field bubble and readjust, temporarily, to steering through life on automatic pilot.

It took me years of trying to become Italian to realize you can't. Once a *straniera* (foreigner) always a *straniera*, no matter how nicely my phrases were turned, how often I'd sat down to Sunday family dinners, how well I'd learned to crank the wine press, or how long I'd held an Italian passport. Though now the *tratto-*

---

*Four years later the Supreme Court ordered him rehired, with back pay and big bucks in damages.

ria kitchens are manned by immigrants from Bolivia and Bangladesh, Italy has held on to its self-image as a country that people run away from rather than toward, and its conviction that Italian is born, not made. Foreigners' children are *stranieri* too, even if they were born in Italy and speak nothing but Roman dialect.

But expats can increase the amount of happiness in the world if they absorb the grand Italian virtues that the locals summarize, with a whiff of irony, as *"Italiani brava gente,"* Italians are nice guys: authenticity, tolerance, flexibility, resourcefulness, patience, modesty, friendship, generosity, graciousness, aesthetic sensibility. My perfect secretary and best friend, Mariateresa, exemplifies them all. She hasn't performed enough miracles for Catholic sainthood but is my personal candidate for a secular version, as the only person I have encountered who genuinely considers every other soul on earth to be as valuable, as worthy of consideration, as completely human, as she is.

My mother once made a tourist hop from Rome to Assisi by bus. Midway through the three hours an elderly fellow made his way to the front, spoke with the driver, and the bus pulled over for an unscheduled pit stop. What amazed my mother was the lack of grumbling. All those notoriously hot-tempered Italians commiserated with the old guy and sat patiently while he dribbled against a tree. "What would have happened in the States?" I asked. "The passengers would have been infuriated with the old man for getting on when he knew he couldn't hold it, the driver for indulging him, and the bus company for not having a bathroom on board," she said. Italian society treats the ill and the handicapped with charity and compassion, though it's predictably weak on such details as architectural accessibility.

It's easy to sneer at Rome medicine; my patients do it all the time. One American doesn't consider a visit complete until she's lodged a half-dozen complaints: she had to pick up her own lab results, the hospital assigned a man instead of a woman to remove the Holter monitor that had been strapped on her breast, the orthopedist gave her pills instead of the injection she thought she needed. A local told me after a visit to one of the city's best emergency rooms, "It's worse than Burundi." But a touch of humanity can bring redemption. My dentist, who thinks I'm a sissy for wanting to be able to bite down on both sides of my mouth at once, has been known to come into his office on a holiday just to drill into an abscessed tooth. All *clinica* rooms include a couch-bed for a companion, and even public hospitals let parents stay on the ward with their kids. In 1986, after writer Francis Steegmuller was mugged in Naples, he described in *The New Yorker* how much better he was treated in the local hospital, by physicians who treated him like a member of the family and took real interest in his life, than after he arrived home in New York.

Italian docs may be sloppy, impatient, or paternalistic, but they offer their patients a sense of shared humanity. Not so the hospital docs in the Bronx trenches of my training years, who might refer to a patient as a GOMER (Get Out of My Emergency Room) or even a SHPOS (Sub Human Piece Of Shit). I trained with an intern whose efficiency in keeping his patient population down—he'd have ten when everyone else had seventeen—was universally admired until someone found out how he did it: he was spied brandishing a six-inch long spinal tap needle in front of a new admission and saying, "Now I'm going to shove this straight into your spinal cord." When the patient replied, "No way," the intern whipped a leave-against-medical-advice form out from behind his back saying, "Sign here on the dotted line." Until a series of scandals forced new legislation in 1986, an ambulance carrying an uninsured dying patient could be turned away from a private New York hospital without ever seeing a doctor; I heard emergency room interns boast of punting heart attack patients to the public hospital down the road.

When my favorite Rome travel clinic developed some quirks in 2013, I fired off an irritated email, never expecting a reply. The next morning a nurse called my office phone number, apologized in a calming baritone for their unanswered phone line, and reassured me that if patients did show up unannounced they wouldn't get turned away. Life in Italy is like that. Twice I've been awakened by bombs set by home-grown Italian terrorists, but both times it was at 3:00 in the morning when nobody would be hurt. My wallet was once stolen on a packed bus by a world-class pickpocket—you've got to be good to catch a native Manhattanite with her hand off her purse—and at the police station I complained about the trouble it would take to replace my driver's license: "I spent two weeks standing on lines to get my documents together for it." The cop looked at me with surprise, and asked, "Was the wallet itself valuable, crocodile skin or something? No? Then don't worry, you'll get everything back, they'll drop it in a mailbox or leave it where someone will find it and bring it to you. They understand how hard it is to get a new driver's license." Sure enough, two days later there was my wallet, delivered to my office minus the cash but complete with checks and driver's license. In New York, when I lived there, robbers not only didn't try to spare you waiting on line, but would razor-blade your face out of spite.

One key to Italian edge is that racism is not a founding principle of society, though its culture of tolerance has been sorely strained of late by right-wing political parties. During the German Occupation in World War II the Nazis only managed to ship off twenty percent of Italian Jews to the camps—the rest were saved by their Christian neighbors. American medicine is tarnished by the dark side of American history. When I took the written part of the American Board of Internal Medicine Certifying Examination, exactly three of the imaginary patients read as non-white, all blatantly stereotyped: a Puerto Rican woman with anxiety, a Native American man with alcoholic liver disease, and an "inner-city" woman with gonorrhea. The surgeon in charge of one outpatient clinic called us medical students in to see a woman who was complaining of severe stomach pain, and showed how if you distracted her with chit-chat she'd let you examine her abdomen without complaining—"A typical hysterical Puerto Rican, nothing wrong with her." Five days later, I learned by chance that she had died of intestinal gangrene.

Despite the daily uncertainties of practicing medicine in Rome, I can't complain. It hasn't hurt to share the Italian lifestyle, make friends with fascinating people, or get to view the Sistine Chapel ceiling from atop the restorers' scaffolding. But the professional side hasn't been pure sacrifice either. Losses: I have neither the peace of mind that comes from reliably high-quality hospitals, nor a substantial nest egg. Gains: a fascinating clientele with widely varied health problems; long, deep patient relationships; backup (however uneven) from a public National Health Service; a research career finagled with barely a dime of funding; freedom from bosses, insurance companies, and Electronic Medical Records. I can get a patient to a physical therapist or a psychiatrist within a day. And I've never needed to learn to counsel patients on gun safety.

7

La Dolce Lifestyle

Health spending per capita: United States $9,892, Italy $3,391
Life expectancy at birth: United States 78.8, Italy 83.2
—Organisation for Economic Co-operation
and Development, 2017

How do Italians get so much health bang for their healthcare buck? One reason: the famed lifestyle that has lured foreigners from Goethe to George Clooney, and keeps us expats hanging in there even when everything from mailing a letter to renovating an apartment is a potential minefield.

Food

Dr. Black: We all know that you should eat a healthy diet. We all know what that healthy diet is. But what that document doesn't seem to address is how one should do that. That's hard.

Dr. Weber: I think it's worse than hard. It borders on impossible. Let me just recall a very successful trial called the DASH diet. That was a diet with a lot of fresh fruits, vegetables, and low-fat foods. It was a very good, very healthy diet. People's blood pressures came down and it looked very, very desirable. The problem was that if you went home and tried to create that diet at home, it would be your life's work to go shopping for this, shopping for that, cooking it this way, cooking it that way.

—Prominent US cardiologists discussing American Heart Association guidelines, 2013

Like all doctors, I spend lots of time trying to cajole my patients into eating right. But I have it easier, because expats' Italian friends and neighbors serve as living models—the DASH diet is more or less Italian traditional, and if you tell Romans it borders on impossible they'll laugh.

Eating for Italians is like sex for a tantric practitioner: the fundamental sacrament, the polar opposite to Protestants à la *Babette's Feast*, who eat tasteless food to mortify the flesh and ask God's forgiveness for any hint of overindulgence. The Italian equivalent of saying grace—a housewife's, "Don't wait for me to start, the food will get cold," as she scurries back and forth from the kitchen—is a paean to the pleasures of the table, which take precedence over any rules of etiquette that might demand the hostess be the first to lift her fork. (The authentic *casalinga* never sits down at all, but nibbles factory seconds by the stove: burnt toast, clams that failed to open in the frying pan.)

A truly good person is *un pezzo di pane* (a piece of bread), a highfalutin' intellectual is deflated with *parla come mangi* (talk like you eat), the core of any celebration is a feast—weddings are short on dancing, long on dining. Italians can and do spend a whole dinner party hashing over the quality of the wine, the garlic, and the brand of spaghetti with no offense to the hostess.

Of all foods, the holiest is pasta, whose power can sanctify the most foreign of soils. I have seen a Rome film crew take over a Moscow restaurant, in Soviet times, to boil up a vat of De Cecco linguine brought over for the occasion. I have seen a Neapolitan arrive at a Zanzibar beach village, the kind of place where huge furry bugs would fall from the rafters onto your sleeping face at night, bearing a backpack full of spaghetti, and set off a collective rush to score a camp stove, a giant pot, and tomatoes.

Traditionally, southern Italians ate mostly fruit, vegetables, grains, wine, and olive oil. The he-man snack peasants carried into the fields might be two slabs of bread separated by spinach, plus a small jug of *vino*. A diet without vegetables is no sweat for most Americans, whose idea of greens is slime Popeye squeezes out of a can, but for Italians it's akin to torture. As part of a research project in the 1980s, I allowed patients with inflammatory bowel disease to eat fruit and vegetables after years of deprivation, and they packed in four generous helpings a day.

That traditional diet was subverted by 1950s America-mania, when war-starved Italians dreamed their children would grow up gigantic as the GI's they'd seen breakfasting on steak and eggs. Meat became fashionable. By the time I first traveled to Rome, most Italians started the day with bread dipped in *caffelatte*, had their big meal at one p.m. with a pasta or rice first course, vegetables, a protein main course, wine, and fruit, and supped lightly on vegetable soup, bread, wine, and fruit. This pattern survives as an ideal despite the pace of modern life and the death of the extended lunch hour. Rossi: "Did you have lunch?" Bianchi: "No, I just had a couple of sandwiches."

But Italians' undying gastronomic love affair is with the vegetable world and with their platefuls of boiled-up little strings (spaghetti) of flour and water, so by now many have amputated the "main course" and returned with relief to their traditional low-meat Mediterranean diet, which is locavore *ante litteram*. Virtually all the produce my husband and I eat grows within thirty miles of our apartment, including herbs, hot peppers, and lemons from pots on our own terrace. We've visited the Umbrian farm that produces our evening glass of wine and the oil we pour on our salad. Friends even more intimately involved with their ingredients gather their own wild asparagus, harvest wild chicory in the fall, or scatter into the woods after a rain to hunt furtively for *porcini* and *ovuli* mushrooms, each hiding the tracks to his or her secret treasure spot.

A few years back Consumer Reports researchers looked at their highest-rated brand of pasta under the microscope and saw . . . insect parts. They immediately stripped De Cecco of its title, failing to understand that hygiene is the nemesis of taste. Water buffalo mozzarella, king of fresh cheeses, is traditionally produced in fly-ridden, dung-stained, chicken-pecked shacks scattered around the former swamp area between Rome and Naples. In the 1970s, the Italian health authorities decided to clean up the mozzarella factories by decreeing a set of rigorous modern hygienic standards, which defanged the intoxicating animal flavor. For years my favorite supplier, a few steps from the Pantheon, put legal, sanitary mozzarella on display out front, but kept a secret stash of the delicious grungy kind in the back room to sell to customers in the know.

How miraculous that the blissful Italian way of eating happens to be good for you—researchers report a new health benefit every week. The mid-century American diet was part of why our coronary disease death rate was three times Italians'. Even now, though Americans smoke less and have superior emergency services, they are still nearly twice as likely as Italians to have a fatal heart attack.

One reason is the difference in heft. Italians eat when they're hungry and stop when they're full, three squares plus maybe a few crackers at five to tide them over until a late dinner. No grazing, no raiding the refrigerator, no using food as a psychotropic drug, less bingeing when they're in need of consolation. So they may be ample, but are less often obese (one in five Italians, one in three Americans), and half as likely to be diabetic. American expats who adopt the local diet are often amazed to find themselves *losing* weight.

People often wonder how Italians stay thin eating all that pasta. Well, in living memory they didn't. I remember my awed first glimpses of G-string bikinis on the beach at Ostia in 1970, and the size of the hips and breasts they were stretched around. But the flesh came from eating big meals, not from noshing, so when ideals of feminine beauty shifted from harem to Twiggy it was a relatively minor sacrifice to halve the portions and the number of courses. Overnight, Italian women slimmed down—to under 140 pounds on average at last call, the thinnest in Europe, compared to Americans' 166 and climbing. It can be tough for American women to find large enough sizes in Rome boutiques.

Kids here are less likely to acquire a sweets addiction, because bread and toothpaste aren't spiked with sugar and meals still end with fresh fruit—each season's fruit is greeted by making a wish on first eating. *Gelato* is a category of its own, a way to keep your spirits up and your temperature down on a dog day afternoon, the only food an Italian matron will let herself be seen eating while walking down the street (their antidrip secret is in the tongue work).

In 1981 I traveled home after three uninterrupted years in Italy. On the airplane, the economy section was dominated by a tour group from Cleveland who were so fat they had to edge down the aisles sideways and passed the time handing around candy and potato chips. I felt like I was in a school of beached whales. Visiting friends on that trip I suffered constant hunger, since what was set in front of me at the table never required more than a few bites. I was baffled by the combination of tiny meals and large waistlines, until one Berkeley evening, halfway through a pleasant dinner, I noticed the adolescent kids were picking restlessly at their salmon. When I asked what was going on, I found out it was the first time they had all sat down together at supper for a year. The penny dropped: my various hosts were dipping into the icebox all day when I wasn't looking, our skimpy collective meals a mere nod to tradition.

The Italian edge on heart disease is due not just to being slimmer but to eating fewer animal fats. When I started out in a Rome hospital I figured the lab used a different technique for measuring cholesterol, since patients usually had 180–200 as compared with the 250–300 I was used to in the States. I learned otherwise when I started treating bacon-and-eggs Americans in my office: sky-high values again.

In the seventies and eighties olive oil was barely given a passing grade by American cardiologists, because as a merely *mono*-unsaturated oil it was thought inferior to the *poly*-unsaturated varieties such as corn oil. This last was marketed in Italy under the brand name "*Cuore*" (Heart), with ads featuring the great soccer goalie Zoff leaping cheerfully over fences. It never made much headway, though, good olive oil being as addictive as good wine. Traveling Italians will wrap a couple of special bottles in newspaper to bring friends trapped in New York or London; one of the reasons they love vegetables is as an excuse for pouring on the oil. Happily, the scientific rug has now been pulled out from under the corn-oil mongers, and olive oil gets not just a pass but an A+.

Forty-five percent of American adults and a whopping ninety-one percent of children eat truly awful diets, according to the American Heart Association, but once upon a time we too were into vegetables. Mark Twain quipped that the only way to eat corn was out in the field: pick with the right hand, husk with the left, and toss immediately into a pot of boiling water set up between the rows. In Italy that venerable food culture has blessedly persisted. True, Monsanto tomatoes are starting to nose out those sweet local varieties, the middle schoolers who giggle past on their way home look a bit plumper, and teenagers don't gobble fruit and vegetables as they used to. But Romans still adore their produce and their pasta, and still cook from scratch, season with olive oil, and wash it all down with wine. Here where it was born, the Mediterranean diet is alive and well.

Booze

> There are more old drunkards than old doctors.
>
> —French proverb

On a bright June afternoon in 1979, I sat on my couch listening to our friend Antonio, perched on one of those rock-hard Italian armchairs, pour his heart out. His wife's distance, his suspicions . . . I asked sympathetically if I could get him a glass of wine. He was so astonished that he stopped crying. "No—why on earth would I want wine?" I had to consult a native informant to discover what an Italian would offer in similar circumstances: coffee, brewed expressly for him (the meaning of *espresso*) as a sign of affectionate support. In Italian, "You look like you need a drink" is a nonsense sentence.

After two years here I was watching an American film on TV

where the hero heard bad news and immediately strode over to the liquor cabinet to pour himself a double whiskey. For a split second I was baffled.

Most Italians consume alcohol every day, but it's not what we call drinking. For Americans and northern Europeans alcoholic beverages are mind-altering drugs, used as tranquilizers, sleeping potions, inhibition-looseners ("Candy is dandy but liquor is quicker"—Ogden Nash), or roads to inebriation. That is to say, to getting tipsy, high, drunk, plastered, smashed, sloshed, sozzled, soused, crocked, wrecked, juiced, stinko, tight, pie-eyed, cross-eyed, shit-faced, blitzed, fried, wasted, gassed, polluted, pissed, tanked up, ripped, loaded, pickled, bombed, blasted, blooey, blotto, blind drunk, roaring drunk, dead drunk, falling down drunk, drunk as a lord, stewed to the gills, or feeling no pain—and that's just my own personal vocabulary. Italians reach that state so infrequently that their language provides only a few tame options—*ubriaco* (drunk), *brillo* (tipsy), *alticcio* (high), *sbronzo* (drunk)—with at most *perso* (lost) or *fradicio* (rotten) tacked on for a touch of color. They don't even have a proper word for a hangover, though if pressed they'll come up with the stately *postumi della sbornia*, aftereffects of overindulgence.

For Italians, wine and beer are foods. If they provide a little buzz that's just a pleasant side benefit, improving the sparkle of the conversation. When I first traveled in Italy, parents regularly fed wine-laced water to their kids (*"acquavino"*), vaccinating them against later dipsomania. And at lunchtime in the cafeteria of my Nuovo Regina Margherita Hospital the docs would jostle to sit at the chaplain's table, because he'd always bring a bottle of good country wine. Even the harder stuff fits into a culinary protocol: a seven p.m. Campari is meant to whet the appetite, and the cognac or *amaro* at the end of a large meal to aid digestion. Which is why, in proportion, Italy has one-tenth as many problem drinkers as America.

When I trained in the Bronx, half our General Medicine admissions were due to alcoholism. In the Nuovo Regina Margherita Hospital, not so much. My gastroenterology ward did have occasional patients with cirrhosis, but almost none with pancreatitis. This shows Romans aren't lushes—the liter of wine consumed by a *padre di famiglia* over lunch may subvert his liver, but it won't burn out his pancreas like Wild Irish Rose on an empty stomach. And since the Italian family continues to nurture even its most aberrant members, hopeless alcoholics are unlikely to wind up sleeping on the street, meaning hospital wards aren't stuffed with winos suffering from fractures and malnutrition.

Even the few Italians who drink to get drunk are unlikely to show it. In England, I'm told, partiers start dancing around with lampshades on their heads the moment they take their first sip. Whereas if you walk in on one of those endless Italian dinners the only way to tell whether the invitees are on their first glass of wine or their fourth is by which course is on the plates. An Italian who finds herself getting tipsy may mutter, with slight distaste, "Seems I've had too much to drink," and stick to water until she sobers up. The lack of a cultural norm of drunkenness gives the Saturday night streets here a different look, even now that some young people are experimenting with boozing it up: those roving crowds are cheerful, but they walk straight and act straight. The rare pugnacious drunks on the streets of Rome are almost always foreigners.

Some wind up in my office. Billy B., an Irish expat, was brought in by his wife shaky and wild-eyed. After three years working in inner-city New York hospitals I instantly recognized impending delirium tremens, a stage just before the pink elephants. I asked how much he drank every day. "A couple of beers with my pals," he said. Sure his wife would tell a different story, I turned to her with a conspiratorial smile, "Just a couple of beers, eh?" "Yes, doctor, it's like he says, a couple of beers." For a moment I thought my diagnosis could be wrong, then it occurred to me to ask, "What do you mean by a beer?" "One of those Italian bottles," his hands framing the shape of a one liter bottle, nearly a quart. "And how many is a couple?" "Oh, six or seven." It was the DTs all right.

Moderate drinking gives another boost to Italian health. As far back as the 1970s, the medical profession knew that alcohol (not just red wine) prevents heart attacks, but for years, unimaginable as this may seem in the age of the internet, they deliberately kept it secret from the general population. I remember the medical journals debating whether to go public with the news, one prominent cardiologist warning in 1979 that we doctors "have a message for which this country is not yet ready."

When I first visited Italy, in 1970, wine consumption averaged out to 114 liters per year per person, and Italians drank twice as much pure alcohol per year as Americans. By 2013 the wine had plummeted to forty liters, about the glass or two a day doctors recommend, and total alcohol consumption was lower than in the States. One reason was the demise of the traditional one to four p.m. lunch break, which had been long enough to go home, consume a big meal with wine, sleep it off, and head back to work. Universal motorization delivered a one-two punch: first it allowed masses of people to get jobs farther from home, then it clogged the roads so nobody could make it home and back, much less fit in a nap.

Some young Italians choose the mild rebellion of refusing to drink wine at all, accompanying their food with water or Coke in the winter and beer in summer. But Italians drink fewer sugary beverages than almost any other country in the world, and one of their four Coca-Cola factories closed in 2013, so all is not lost.

If food is a sacrament and wine is a food, it follows that wine-drinking is a sacrament as well—perhaps, historians say, predating Christians' Holy Communion. Certainly the basic recipe for wine-making is as close as I know to proof of divine creation of the universe: smash some grapes, and wait.

Exercise

> Walking makes for a long life.
>
> —Hindu proverb
>
> Bodily exercise profiteth little.
>
> —The Bible

Ride up the escalator at Rome's Fiumicino airport and see who's climbing the stairs next to you: American yuppies in Nikes and hunched-over Italian biddies in black. Group one does it to stay healthy, group two because that's what they've always done. The disabled pensioners I examined for the Social Security Administration would hobble up the stairs to my office rather than take the elevator, and when my mother-in-law Mariada came for a visit she always covered the two and a half miles on foot. Italians aren't far enough from their country roots to be couch potatoes, and don't yet need medical goading to use their legs rather than their cars.

One place they *didn't* learn those habits was phys ed class. In the seventies, a friend who rotated among Naples high schools teaching gym told me her students mostly spent the hour seated at desks. In the rare building equipped with a gymnasium, she would preside in a skirt and heels, cigarette in hand. As recently as the nineties, Italians would ridicule my advice to take up jogging as an *americanata*. Nowadays they're crowding the gyms, but exercising while female entails special constraints—practice what Italians perversely insist on calling *footing* and you still attract catcalls.

Walking an hour a day, like Mariada doing her shopping, is yet another way they reduce their risk of heart attacks, and more isn't necessarily better. Do you know how the classic long-distance run got its name? In 490 b.c., an Athenian runner named Philippides, dispatched to announce the glorious defeat of the Persians, ran the twenty-six miles from Marathon to Athens, gasped out his message to the sitting magistrates, and dropped dead.

Smoking

In the ointment of the healthy Italian lifestyle, cigarettes are the fly. When I moved to Italy in 1978 about one in three adults in both my countries smoked, but Americans have done better at kicking the habit—the latest figures are 24.4% here, 16.8% in the US. In compensation, Italian smokers average fewer cigarettes a day than Americans, quit while they're pregnant, and have been uncharacteristically docile in obeying smoking bans in bars and restaurants.

Earlier phases in the tectonic shift away from tobacco weren't so easy. My assistant Mariateresa still reminisces nostalgically about sitting in movie theater balconies watching her smoke drift into the beam of light from the projector. That was before my time, but I have personally been kicked out of a taxi for trying to make the cabbie put out his cigarette, seen discreet little piles of butts on the floor under No Smoking signs, and lauded the courtesy of an Italian soldier who agreed to extinguish his cigarette in a non-smoking compartment after I claimed it was giving me asthma.

Dope

An American ex-junkie who came over to help organize a therapeutic community near Rome confided to me that he couldn't relate to the pampered Italian heroin addicts: "When I was fourteen I was on the streets and living off my gun. These kids are twenty-five and still living off mommy." Not only do respectable Italian *mamme* nurse their offspring through cold turkey, but most (according to one study) confess to having scored drugs for them. I had a pang when I learned of this loving though not necessarily constructive solidarity, remembering the isolation of a strikingly beautiful teenage girl I admitted to North Central Bronx Hospital, at death's door from an infected needle track in her arm. She had lain in a coma on the bed in her lonely studio apartment for three days before someone happened to come by and find her.

Heroin didn't hit Italy until the mid-seventies. Before then the Mafia pumped drugs into the American ghettos but deliberately kept them away from their own kids. There have always been far fewer users than in the States, even before the current opioid crisis, and there's strangely little abuse of opiate painkillers, considering that any doc can now prescribe them free of paperwork. Italy may simply be a less addictive society.

A third of Italian adults have smoked cannabis, usually in the form of hashish. Is it legal? Maybe. You used to be allowed to possess a little for personal use, then you couldn't, now you can again.

I think. A Legalize It referendum passed handily years ago, but nothing changed. It might be legal to smoke a joint but not to pass it to your friend. It's legal to grow some for personal use, or it's not, or perhaps it's legal until the plants are fully grown. A friend's son was once arrested while tending his three-bush roadside plantation and held overnight in jail, only to be released in the morning with apologies because the policeman who took over on the day shift, unlike the one running the night shift, considered cultivation to be lawful.

Since 2010 medical marijuana is authorized in some regions, but pharmacy prices are so exorbitant that patients prefer to get their supply on the street. You can also buy "Cannabis Light" online or in "grow shops"—it's so low in THC it can't get you high.

Cocaine is relatively big in Italy, and has trickled down from stockbrokers to working stiffs. Especially cabbies. I remember one so obviously and terrifyingly coked up—running off at the mouth, leaning on both his horn and the gas pedal—that when he stopped at a light I jumped out and fled. Hallucinogens and amphetamines never made headway; Italians are impressed when I tell them I was at Woodstock, but what really overawes them is that I spent day two flying on mescaline.

Many of the sharpest memories I have of my training in New York involved drugs. The gangrenous arm one teenager gave herself by injecting amphetamine into an artery instead of a vein. The strapping young men who, after a shot of naloxone, woke up combative from their overdoses and swung at anyone within reach. The addict delirious with meningitis from a dirty needle, who, after thirty milligrams of intravenous Valium (five milligrams would knock you or me out for a day), had to be held down by three nurse's aides so I could give him a spinal tap.

I see no such drama in my Italian practice. There are fewer dope fiends here, they can duck infections by buying clean needles over the counter without a prescription, their long-suffering families keep them off the streets, and supposedly half of Italy's heroin addicts are holding down a job despite the recession. The forgiving Italian way wins again.

Rhythms of Life

"You need to have a cystoscopy every three months for the next year. Let's see, it's May now, I'll give you an appointment in September." "But May to September is four months, not three." "Oh, August doesn't count, everybody's on vacation."
—Urologist to patient following treatment of early bladder cancer

"When I said we were open every day of the week of course I didn't include *Monday*. You can't buy tickets on Monday anywhere in the world."
—Employee at the Rome Opera House box office, on a Tuesday

I've been told the reason monastery bells ring every fifteen minutes is to remind the monks they are a quarter of an hour closer to their deaths. That sense of time passing, the great rotation of wheels within wheels in nature's cycles, gets intensified in Italy by a cultural emphasis that highlights all its subdivisions.

The day: Romans set their watches by the noonday boom of a cannon on the Janiculum hill, wear dull colors in the morning and bright ones in the afternoon, avoid eggplant in the evening because it brings bad dreams. Neighborhood markets close at two, and many stores are still shuttered from one to four.

The week: on Sunday, the one day everybody has off, Rome's Botanical Garden is closed. So are state museums on Monday, city museums on Tuesday, mom-and-pop grocery stores on Thursday afternoon, and carpenters on Saturday. Bus strikes are Fridays, you lunch with the folks on Sunday, restaurants serve *gnocchi* on Thursday and *trippa* on Saturday.

The month: You harvest peas when the moon is waxing, grapes when it's waning. Menstruating women shouldn't swim, touch flowers, have sex, or get blood tests. The last day of each calendar month, the post office closes early.

The year: Women exchange their sandals for closed shoes at the fall equinox whatever the thermometer reads, and everybody plays games of chance—*tombola*, blackjack, *Mercante In Fiera*—during the twelve days of Christmas. Summer brings beer and banishes ricotta, sausage, raisins, and polenta. You eat lentils on New Year's Eve to bring wealth, fava beans and sheep cheese on May Day to bring luck, lemon juice and artichokes in winter to purify your liver, panettone at Christmas, and chocolate at Easter. Anyone foolish enough to eat an orange in July or a peach in December, imported from the ends of the earth, deserves whatever he or she gets.

From an Italian point of view, summer and winter, the two true seasons, are born from the labor pains of the "changes of season," when body and spirit temporarily lose their way. In those treacherous spring and fall months Italians are prone to indigestion, bad breath, ulcers, joint pain, headache, back pain, cystitis, insomnia, and fatigue. All to be warded off, traditionally, by detoxifying courses of vitamins, supplemented in the spring by laxatives and in the fall by the *cura dell'uva*, three weeks of eating nothing but grapes. One young mother reported her pediatrician's instructions in a 2007 online forum: serve her toddler a breakfast cookie dipped in castor oil, followed by a chamomile enema, "at least twice a year."

In November 1820, when John Keats's tuberculosis was going downhill, he was sent to Rome to be cured by the legendary warm winter; he died before spring. A century and a half later, when I moved here, many Romans still pretended their climate was so mild they needed no heating at all, and any radiators that did turn on for a few hours a day were so feeble that the only way I could play the piano was wearing gloves with the finger tips cut off. My first December in Rome my toes turned red, swelled up, and itched unbearably, stumping my Stateside medical knowledge. My mother-in-law Mariada instantly diagnosed *geloni*: chilblains, the first stage of frostbite. The cause is never getting properly warmed through, which explains why I'd never seen them in overheated New York.

Summer is the lung that allows the Italian year to breathe. Ferragosto, August 15th, a holiday the Church stole from the Romans when they needed a day to celebrate the Madonna's Assumption, is the one day when nobody works, more sacred than Christmas or Easter, the still point around which the year revolves. Life slows in August, even for those who don't scatter to the beaches, the city and all its inhabitants paralyzed for a month like a lizard on its rock as the old year is burnt out of them. In the first days of September you stir by degrees into a fresh start, like a yoga practitioner reviving after the corpse pose.

Summer nights mean sweating into limp sheets, if you're one of the many Italians who believe air conditioning spawns everything from backache to bronchitis. A GP told a patient of mine with Bell's palsy that her facial paralysis was caused by having gone straight from an air-conditioned room into the summer air. Another bit of folk wisdom is so off-base as to be astounding: I've heard numerous Italians say you shouldn't drink liquids during the summer because they make you sweat.

Natural Perils

> *"Aria di fessura, aria di sepoltura,"* "Air from a chink is air for a burial."
>
> *"Dove entra il sole non entra il medico,"* "Where the sun comes in, the doctor stays out."
>
> —Italian proverbs

Ever been in a Rome taxi where the rear windows are missing their handles? Unscrewed by the driver, because a draft from behind would give him a stiff neck. A draft on the abdomen causes diarrhea, going outside with wet hair in the winter causes fever. Sweat is dangerous ("I perspire too much, my doctor says that's why I get bronchitis all the time"), especially if allowed to dry on the skin. Their marvelous weather isn't good enough for Romans: at sixty-five degrees they complain of the cold, at seventy-five of the heat. When the *scirocco* wind blows up from the Sahara they wilt—turning, in Luigi Barzini's words, "weak, impotent, irascible, their heads filled with cotton wool." Italians act so fragile you'd think they were shtetl-bound Talmudic scholars rather than a generation or two away from tilling the earth.

As a stickler for honesty, I must have told thousands of patients no, their sniffles didn't come from a chill. That hoary theory, as all American medical students are taught, was scientifically disproven on army recruits in the 1950s. Cold virus was spritzed directly into their noses during a freezing rain and then, according to the luck of the draw, half of them spent the night shivering outdoors naked, the other half tucked in under the blankets in a toasty infirmary. Both groups got cold symptoms at exactly the same rate.

One day, a retired British colonel with bronchitis asked me why I thought he had gotten sick. I was tired that afternoon, for once I didn't feel up to squaring off against a patient's preconceptions, and I said, "Well, maybe you caught a chill . . ." He drew himself up and said sternly, "Now doctor, that is certainly *not* why. When I was a young soldier I participated in a study where they squirted cold virus up my nose . . ." You can't win.

In the Italian folk pharmacopoeia the sun is a panacea, and a tan a sign of health. They disdain sunscreen. But the demon Sea is first cousin to the devil Draft, in that any contact with water within range of a meal will distract the circulation from the digestive organs and lead to "congestion," with potential loss of consciousness and thus, if you're swimming, death. In 2014 Professor Antonino Reale, Chief of the emergency room at Rome's top pediatric hospital, the Bambino Gesù, posted a helpful schedule of how long to make children wait before bathing ("Ham sandwich: three hours"). Overheard at the seashore: "Dry your feet and put your shoes on. Wet feet will give you a tummy ache." At least they're no longer forced to swim in woolen bathing suits to avoid a chill, as some of my Italian friends were as kids.

The dangers of the sea are nothing compared to the menace lurking in lakes. Many Italians don't consider them fit for swimming, and with 5,000 miles of seacoast they don't have to. Even when fresh water isn't cursed by pollution or a local deity it might contain treacherous currents, unexpected whirlpools, and algae that entangle your legs and drag you farther under the more you struggle, like one of those Chinese finger traps.

Safety

Helmet laws for motorcyclists proved surprisingly acceptable here, a source of civic pride slightly marred by cynics who pointed out that head coverings can be useful in a heist. They've never been able to hack seatbelts, though. Seatbelts are for sissies. I once got pulled over by the police for wearing one—a woman driving a convertible with a seatbelt on was so unlikely as to be in itself a suspicious act. When seatbelts became mandatory, one enterprising Neapolitan came out with a driver's T-shirt, white with a black diagonal stripe painted across the chest, to make it look from a distance as though you had buckled up. Modern cars, rigged to scream at unbelted drivers, challenge Italian ingenuity but don't defeat it.

Italians drive fast, they drive crazy, they'll head the wrong way down a one-way street without compunction, but they rarely drive drunk. That's why sixty percent more Americans, proportionately, die in traffic accidents.

How about at home? Italian gas heaters explode all the time, and buildings collapse under their own weight. Put a plug in the wall and sparks fly, pull it out and the socket pops out with it (complete, in my apartment, with a blind third hole intended to fool you into thinking the system is grounded). Some old-style electrical transformers we American expats used for our 110 volt equipment looked the same on both sides, so a distracted person could easily grab a live plug. That once happened to me. By the time I managed to drop it I'd felt the 220 volts zip up my arm to a few inches short of my heart.

I've never understood why one of the world's most industrialized countries, with a proud history of artisanry, can't get those small things right.

In compensation, outside the Mafia, violent crime isn't their style. A woman walking alone at night in Rome risks merciless verbal harassment but not rape, pickpocketing far outstrips armed robbery, Italy has one-quarter the murder rate and one-eighth the incarceration rate of the US. Schoolchildren have never even heard of lockdowns.

Stress

Most Italians still live relatively stable lives, embedded in strong social networks. They form a circle of lifelong friends when young, usually stick close to home for college and work, and wouldn't dream of moving away when they retire. All of which has health benefits—if nothing else you have people you can count on to feed you if you're hungry, check up if you don't phone, drag you to the doctor if you're sick.

Does their web of relationships shield them from mental suffering? Is the time wasted going to the *latteria* for your milk and the *forno* for your bread and the *norcineria* for your salami—in enclaves as yet not strangled by the tentacles of the supermarket moguls—offset by the calming power of the friendly interchanges in all three, daily confirmation of your intimate nestling into your neighborhood-village-within-a-city where everybody is *somebody*?

Italians, running away from the very aspects of their country we consider so endearing, find an opposite but equal freedom in the anonymity of New York or Chicago.

Some of the ways Italians handle stressors may also lighten the burden. Fatalism takes the edge off both anger and frustration, and their notorious tempers quickly defuse—*se ti incazzi ti scazzi*, they say, you blow up and then it blows over. There's no Italian for "guilt trip" or "judgmental." If you are horrified by somebody's act of reckless endangerment that by sheer luck ended well they'll say, puzzled and dismissive, *"Ma non è morto nessuno!"*—"Nobody died!"

In the end, it may be that Italians' best protection against stress isn't their habits or character, but their welfare state. Nothing like five weeks' vacation, six months' sick leave, and five months' maternity leave to boost your health, serenity, and longevity.

8

Down There

Sex: Talking the Talk

> It's normal for a very young child to see his whatsit as a plaything from time to time
>
> —Amazon forum

> I don't know how to say this—I'm English, you know!
>
> —A patient with gynecological symptoms

Once upon a time I was in a Trastevere apartment enjoying a bowl of *spaghetti all'amatriciana* with a tableful of displaced Manhattanite intellectuals when our host started to tell an embarrassed-teenage-daughter story. The girl had been jeans shopping in a hip clothing emporium strewn with life-sized plaster copies of Roman statues in the buff. "There were some boys looking at her, so she was already self-conscious and didn't notice how she was turning around next to this statue, and her hand landed right on his . . . his . . ." His illustrative gesture stopped in mid-air and hovered while he hunted for a word. We howled.

What choices did he have? *The Sopranos* hadn't yet brought four-letter words to prime time. Dennis, the well-mannered four-year-old son of visiting American friends, when taken to see the naked gods and goddesses who alternate along the walls of the Palazzo Spada's courtyard, pointed out the important parts: "Penis, vulva, penis, vulva, penis, vulva . . ." No good—too Sex Ed. Genitals would be even worse, weiner is wimpy, pecker is past its use-by date. Cock and prick mean one that's erect and ready to roll, dick is only marginally less sexual.

While the English language has little to offer between the clinical and the obscene, Italian offers a whole gamut: for starters *pisello* (pea), *uccello* (bird), *pistolino* (little pistol), *fava* (as in bean), *pesce* (fish), or *mazza* (bat, as in baseball), without counting dialect terms from *bicio* in Venice down to *minchia* in Sicily, or the crude, pan-Italian *cazzo*. A little boy has a little *pisellino*, just as his leg is not a *"gamba"* but a *"gambina."*

Proud young mother to friend: "Just look at his cute *pisellino!"* What does her American cousin say? Maybe she'd call it a "thingy," a term I first heard from a Midwestern coed who permitted examination only through her armored bra.

Proud young mother to friend: "And look at her adorable *patatina!"* Here the American cousin is speechless, it's never even occurred to her to have a way to refer fondly to what the Italian calls *patatina* (little potato), *topa* (from *topo*, mouse), *passera* (from *passero*, sparrow), *gnocco* (think of potato *gnocchi*), *papera* (duck), or *fichetta* (diminutive for the coarser *fica*). A friend says when she was a baby her grandmother affectionately called her *"boccuccia di fregna"* (little pussy-mouth).

At Christmas, Italians dust off their *tombola* sets to play a kind of bingo. In the version played in Naples every numbered square on the board has a name assigned to it, and a game can go from beginning to end without the corresponding numbers ever being called. If the MC announces, *"Anni di Cristo!"* (The Years of Christ), everybody knows to put their chips on number thirty-three, the number of years between Nativity and Crucifixion—one of the few names that make any sense. Number six is *"Chella ca guarda 'nterra!"* (The Thing That Looks Down), and twenty-nine is *"O pate d' 'e criature!"* (The Father of Children), which my own bilingual *tombola* board helpfully glosses from Neapolitan dialect straight into English as "cunt" and "cock."

The Rome area is foul-mouthed by tradition. I did one double-take when I first heard a friend greet Andrea with an affectionate "*A stronzo,*" "Hi turd," and another when an old peasant woman in widow's black, whom we had just met, told us she had recently sent a building inspector to *fanculo,* go fuck himself. I eventually picked up enough of the local habit to get myself in trouble on visits home by sprinkling apparent insults into English-language conversations with friends.

The toughest separatists of the Northern League party were dubbed *celoduristi* by journalists: the "mine is harder faction." Would that fly in American papers?

On Pompeian wall paintings the penis may be gigantic, but in spoken Italian it usually means something insignificant. He's stupid? He doesn't understand a *cazzo.* Something that's not worth a *cazzo* ain't worth shit, *incazzato* means pissed off, and a *cazzata* is a silly action. The 1968 generation added colorful variants: *cazzeggiare* is to shoot the breeze, a rough situation is *cazzi amari,* bitter penises, and a shrimpy man is *alto un cazzo e un barattolo,* as tall as a penis and a tin can. For positive metaphors Italians turn to the female equivalent, *la fica* (from *fico,* fig). A snappy suit is *fico,* a clever act is a *ficata,* and someone who's *sficato* or bereft of a *fica* is a schlemiel.

Whatever words they use, Italians have an admirable ability to talk about sex without freezing up. When I asked my mother-in-law, a home-schooled bourgeoise then in her sixties, about a mysterious journalistic expression, she explained nonchalantly that "*festini rosa*" meant orgies with children—my own liberated mother couldn't have handled the question with such aplomb. An American woman will tell me she has an itch "on the outside," wherever that is, an Italian provides graphic specifics. One came to me because of pain in her *grilletto* (trigger), a dynamite term for the clitoris. Americans excuse themselves to "go to the bathroom," Italians to "make *pipì*"—after all these years I still don't understand why they need to announce to the whole dinner table exactly what they're going to do on the toilet.

Italian has its euphemisms, of course, often with an ironic

edge: "*fare i suoi bisogni*," which means to do his needs, is a delicate way to defecate, and a man with his fly open may be said to have "*gli attributi di fuori*," his attributes hanging out. In a folk song on one of my old LPs, a woman hoists her skirt to reveal her "*come-si-chiama*," her whatchamacallit.

Sex: Walking the Walk

> Italians the Best Lovers, Poll Shows
> —Headline in *La Repubblica*

Italians are as proud of their sexual prowess as Americans of their two-car garages. They have a dozen colloquial words for the female genitalia but none for "wham bam thank you ma'am," and they don't consider fancy lovemaking to be sissy stuff. Their macho is different from our macho: even in a brief fling a guy will take pride in trying to satisfy his partner, and he's likely to make at least one symbolic follow-up phone call the next day.

For an American wolf the goal is to get a woman into bed, but for his Italian equivalent that's a relatively minor detail. Seduction is a refined pseudo-romantic game whose greatest triumph is inducing the woman to fall in love. Even the usual Italian for a sexual encounter is *un rapporto*, literally "a relationship." Italian men are themselves addicted to the heady, ephemeral intoxication of falling in love, with the downside of—beware!—often requiring serial affairs to keep getting their fix.

A ramble around the internet confirms that the gallant culture of seduction *all'italiana* is still alive and well as of this writing; we'll see a few years hence whether the tourist-primed introduction of Saturday night pub hopping wipes it out. What *has* died is the old fetish of virginity—no more bloody sheets hung out the window of the bridal chamber.

When a patient comes in with a venereal disease physicians routinely ask about sexual partners. I don't think I've ever had an Italian woman answer, "I never got his name." Italian youth are still, mercifully, stuck in a bygone age: plenty of premarital sex but usually with a steady boyfriend, often given the honorific of *fidan-zato* (fiancé) whether or not the couple actually plans to ever tie the knot. They start relatively late (at 19.4 in Italy, 18.4 in the US), they're way behind in teen sexting (twenty-six percent in Italy, sixty-nine percent in the US), and the hookup culture is light-years away.

Puritanism, and Not

"Close your eyes and think of England."

"Non lo fo per piacer' mio, ma per dare un figlio a Dio,"
"I'm not doing it for my pleasure, but to give a child to God."

—Culture-specific wifely mottos

As teenagers without online porn to help us out, my girlfriends and I had such a primitive concept of our anatomy that we learned to use Tampax by shoving the little tube around at random. I re-discover my inner prude in Italy when I involuntarily avert my eyes from the putatively artistic nudes that decorate my dentist's office, my hairdresser's wall, my janitor's apartment.

Underlying American hypersexuality is Puritan culture. The proverbial English wife hates sex but grits her teeth and submits, whereas if Italian wives once embroidered "I'm not doing it for my pleasure" around an appropriately placed hole in their nightgowns (yup), they were admitting they were horny but claiming it didn't count.

Italy has spelled sensuality since Roman times, onward to Titian, and beyond to the nineteenth-century Grand Tour that had northerners of all sexes and proclivities trooping southward to dally among the ruins with the natives. What drew Americans into postwar art-house movie theaters? The intellectual allure of Rossellini's neorealism, or the zaftig prostitutes and the house-wives hanging around in their slips? We had Doris Day, they had Sophia Loren. Two of English literature's most famously scan-dalous books, Lord Byron's *Don Juan* and D. H. Lawrence's *Lady Chatterley's Lover*, were both written in Liguria. The paganoid Mr.

Lawrence even briefly flirted with his own version of Italian Catholicism, re-imagined as a cult of marital pleasure.

Nudity and sexual imagery are casually ubiquitous in Italy. At the time of the royal marriage in 1981, a front-page cartoon in *La Repubblica* created a Union Jack out of the arms and legs of a naked Prince Charles atop a spreadeagled Diana. I once bought apricots from an old woman who had embellished her roadside stand with a long watermelon set up on its end flanked by a cantaloupe on either side, and wedding guests will bring the bride and groom a cucumber and two peaches arranged suggestively on a plate. Keep your eyes peeled on beaches for men changing out of their bathing suits, you may catch glimpses of the real thing.

Italian television stations don't have a scout sitting at the monitor ready to hit "cut" the instant an athlete's hand reaches down in the direction of his crotch. Nothing wrong with visibly scratching your balls here; a woman may even mime the gesture for good luck.

Back in the seventies when I was still living in the States, I remember TV viewers being scandalized by a deodorant ad that panned slowly 360 degrees around a marble statue before focusing in on the armpit. In Italy, advertisers were going it one better, in prime time. Image: a girl floating on her back in a pristine waterfall pool, having her feet massaged. The camera ever so slowly zooms in on the triangle of her bikini bottom and dwells there at length watching the ripples before crossfading to the photo of an intimate cleansing soap.

I once knew an American adman, in Italy to push a brand of diaper, who picked up on how Italian kiddies ran around naked on both beaches and TV screens. The sight of those bare fannies sent him into a creative rapture of freedom from the strictures of the American boob tube, where even the tiniest of buttocks must be covered. Determined to out-Italian the Italians, he pitched an ad for local TV where *mamma* removed her baby's diaper, ran her finger down his bare buttock, and took a contented sniff. Alas, this was too raunchy for Procter & Gamble, even in Italy.

Italians are blessed with physical beauty, and attractiveness is a guiding principle of their culture, entering into the choice not just of lovers but of same-sex friends. *"Stefano non mi piace"* can mean either "I don't like Steve" or "Steve doesn't turn me on." Music reviews will describe the clothing of the pianist, political commentators the cut of a politician's suit. I was amazed one slow morning to arrive on my gastroenterology ward and find the entire professional staff discussing a male colleague's *culo sceso*, droopy derrière; I doubt many male American physicians would notice the shape of a colleague's buttocks, and if they did they'd keep it to themselves.

And they've always been bling-masters. Check out those 2,000-year-old painted rooms or the Gesù Church in Rome: ancient Romans and Baroque priests alike knew how to lay on the glitz. The Italian acceptance of nakedness doesn't rule out adornment, and on certain beaches you'll see women strolling the water's edge in nothing but a necklace, their nudism being not principled but esthetic. People here are Catholic by ritual but pagan in essence, tying beauty, truth, and virtue together in a single knot. Americans, *sotto sotto*, consider not just sex but bodily beauty just a mite sinful.

A doctor's office is a privileged vantage point for seeing how comfortable people are with their bodies. When you could still buy contraceptive diaphragms in Italy I'd allow a half hour to fit one and teach the woman how to insert it. That was about right for Americans, but with an Italian it left twenty minutes to spare (some Englishwomen, true to their stereotype, couldn't learn, period).

Rigidity about sexual matters is often, I've found, skin-deep. Blair was a sophomore in boarding school, left behind in Rome while her American parents worked at a hardship post in Africa, and she was pregnant. She planned to keep the baby because "My parents and I don't approve of abortion." I persuaded her to call her mother, who instantly phoned me at home and screamed, "Have a baby at fourteen? Is she crazy? You've got to talk her into having an abortion!" I did. Then there was Francesca, engaged and pregnant at thirty-five, in tears over having to move up the date of her wedding—her Sicilian parents would never forgive her. Forgive her? They were delighted, even back in the 1980s, having practically given up hopes of a grandchild.

Cleanliness and Contamination

The Great Bidet Mystery: what's it for? Americans can live here for decades thinking Italians go to the trouble of installing bidets just so they can soak their feet. If they've read Henry Miller, they add so women can wash before and after sex. The truth is that every Italian of whatever gender uses the bidet daily—you're not clean after defecation if you haven't cleansed away every trace of feces. Except in case of dire necessity they won't move their bowels anywhere but home, next to their own bidet. I remember on a visit to Italy in the early seventies somehow innocently revealing to an Italian my assumption that he pulled up his pants after only using toilet paper. A major gaffe.

Americans say "shit" in frustration and "hot shit" in admiration but have barely a nodding acquaintance with the real thing, with the unfortunate corollary that many of them walk around emanating a faint fecal odor. Italians' acquaintance with their stool is hands on. When they grasp each other's habits of anal hygiene, each side cordially considers the other filthy ("Americans just use toilet paper?" "Italians wash WHAT with their fingers?"). Fastidiousness lying in the eye of the washer, an Italian is disgusted by the idea of having bits of feces clinging to her, but finds it normal to wash daily there and only there; an American is disgusted by the idea of getting up-close-and-personal with his anus but can't imagine a day without a shower.

Italians don't get their bidet habit from France, where the fixture is indeed ladies-only, but from their neighbors to the south: Arabs, like Asians, wash every time they move their bowels, and bequeathed this healthy custom to the Italians. "Doing the bidet" for your baby or your aged mother is a far more intimate gesture of tenderness than Jesus washing his disciples' feet.

American female hygiene used to leave much to be desired, but as a daily observer of vulvas I was happy to see around the turn of the millennium that it began improving—due to an uptick in the popularity of cunnilingus? Italian women are always washing, some of them after every *pipì*. It's part of a general acceptance of the body and its natural functions. They believe in being clean but not in being Sanitized, in bidets but not Bidettes. The same company's brand of panty liners will be perfumed in the US, scentless here.

I was once having coffee with a dozen middle-aged friends in a house so new it still lacked internal doors. One of them said to the host, "Why don't you leave the place as is? That way people can keep conversing while they're on the pot." Everybody smiled and nodded. There's long precedent—a classic subject for tourist snapshots is the twenty-four-seat marble public toilet in the ruins of Ostia Antica, just outside Rome.

Another time I was enjoying a sauna along with several Roman women, when an American came in and sat down naked on the bench. The Italians glared. Seeing that she didn't take the hint one spoke up and sent her out to find a towel to put under her butt, giving them the chance in her absence to rail against filthy foreigners who thoughtlessly contaminate public spaces. Not only won't Italians sit directly on the wood in a sauna, but they will endure painful thigh cramps to avoid putting bare skin on public toilets, which in the name of hygiene are often stripped to seatless porcelain. An Italian patient who works as a tour guide told me, "Foreigners are horrified that we don't have toilet seats in public restrooms, we're horrified that they would consider sitting down on one."

A medical corollary: Italians find the rectal route a perfectly fine way for getting drugs into the system. I once co-authored a scientific paper with Professor Prantera's ulcerative colitis research group showing that an innovative enema twice a week worked as well for warding off relapses as the standard six horse pills a day, and gave fewer side effects. The paper got turned down by an American medical journal with the puzzled comment, "Who on earth would choose an enema when they can take a pill?"

Italians are finicky about other body parts as well. They shudder when the French carry unwrapped baguettes under their arms, they ask fellow-passengers to remove their feet from the facing train seat, and they slip their shoes back on to cover the two steps from my dressing room to my exam table.

My take is this: Americans consider our whole underside to be intrinsically dirty and mentally airbrush it out. Italians think bodies are amenable to cleansing, so they're constantly aware of its potential contamination. Goes back to when the Romans, with their mania for washing, lost out to Christians, who for centuries considered bathing a sinful cult of the body.

Crimes and Misdemeanors

By age fourteen I had encountered exhibitionists, wolf whistlers, and other marginalia of womanhood, but they didn't prepare me for being physically molested. The perpetrator was a thirty-four-year-old man named Garry Winogrand, a New York photographer known for suggestive pictures of adolescent girls but not for a secret hobby of levering his fame and charm to cajole the same into being groped. I never mentioned the incident to anybody until after Senator Roy Moore was outed as a sometime violator of girls that age, by which time Winogrand was long dead, but it sure colored my attitudes.

A chance for displaced retribution came a few years into my practice, when an *au pair* I'll call Maryanne called the office and asked to speak with me. She said she had been waiting at a bus stop past midnight, when a guy palming himself off as a policeman offered her a ride home, then proceeded to drive her out of town and rape her. I encouraged her to make an appointment and, two days later, in she slouched, dressed (I was relieved to see) not fashionably hemline-at-crotch but in an ankle-length gunny sack and hiking boots. After the visit she agreed to go to the police, and found the courage to trap the rapist after the dumb cluck showed up at her home the following week to invite her back for more.

It gave me pleasure to testify at the trial. The bastard landed a four-year sentence—heavy by Italian standards—plus a divorce and, I gather, a good chance of being raped himself in prison. His lawyer mentioned halfheartedly that the victim wasn't a virgin, but seemed glad when the judge shut him up. He didn't even hint at the classic "She was asking for it" defense that, during the same period, got a suspended sentence for four men arrested at Rome's Piazza Navona, one of them atop a woman who was being held down by the other three while screaming "Stop!" and banging her head on the ground.

The 1979 documentary exposé *Processo per Stupro*, Rape Trial, seen by half of Italy on TV, blew the cover off the most blatant victim-blaming, but less overt forms are still deeply rooted. A feminist lawyer who defended both the victim in *Processo per Stupro* and my own Maryanne once claimed to me in private, woman to woman, that someone who dresses and behaves correctly—"like you or me"—would never, for instance, be felt up on a bus. I protested energetically. Her husband sighed. "Come off it, honey, you've never been on a bus in your life."

There are plenty of gropers in Italy but, I'd say, fewer exhibitionists than in the US. Does unzipping in public make Italian men feel vulnerable? Or is it that they can explain wandering hands as the natural reaction of a virile man to a female body—irresistibly attractive, thus seductive, thus asking for it—whereas flashing is for wusses? Or maybe it's that Rome is a small town and you don't want *mamma* to find out? Once I was walking alone in Trastevere, alongside the wall that shores up the Tiber River, when a pasty fortyish man with long stringy hair appeared in my path a few dozen yards ahead. There was something fishy about the way he stood planted on the sidewalk, so I wasn't entirely astonished when he opened his trench coat to reveal he was sadly bereft of other clothing. Flashers used to upset me when I was a teenager, which I think is what they're after, but now I was mature enough that with those few seconds of forewarning I managed to produce a snappy comeback as I passed by: "So small, and yet you show it in public." That's the only time I've seen anyone plying that particular trade in Rome, and I bet he didn't last long.

Dottoressa

Since about 2000, I've witnessed a modestly growing epidemic of international date rape in Rome, a toxic product of encounters between Italian men who think foreign women are nymphomaniacs and American college girls who believe in boozing it up to the point of unconsciousness. Occasionally one will stumble into my office asking me to figure out whether she had sex the night before. Never Italian girls, though; they find Anglo-Saxon party culture alien, uninviting, borderline repugnant.

Italians commit plenty of random larceny but rarely random rape. Though the *mano morta*, the dead hand of a groper, lands on even the best-dressed buttocks, actual rape is more often an extension of courtship by other means—an ex-boyfriend raping the girl who left him—or punishment for a woman who didn't "behave right"—a village girl who went to the wrong party, or a tourist who accepted a ride from someone she just met. Foreign women are prey because they don't know the rules; talking to a stranger doesn't put you at risk, but going up to his apartment or hitchhiking does. Once I was pedaling home at two a.m. when a guy with a nasty smile tried to block my way, though nothing could have been less of a come-on than my sweaty t-shirt, and I was clearly not out looking for a good time. Think in terms of incest taboo: a woman on a bicycle late at night is from a different tribe, thus fair game.

Adultery beats soccer as the national pastime, played, according to polls, by seven out of ten Italian husbands (only two out of ten own up to it in the US). They'll admit their infidelity to a pollster but deny it to their wife even if caught in the act. The Catholic Church historically turns a blind eye, in the service of keeping unhappy marriages limping along, thus creating an army of Other Women whose status is often permanent. When painter Renato Guttuso's wife died, rather than marrying his long-time lover Marta Marzotto he broke off relations with her altogether, providing the scandal sheets with juicy scenes of his abandoned paramour pounding all night on the door of the Palazzo del Grillo near the Roman Forum.

Italian physicians do their part by telling men they could have picked up their gonorrhea from a toilet seat or—I kid you not—from "a metabolic imbalance."

The flip side of adultery is jealousy, and I'd bet good money that pathological jealousy is a particularly common psychosis in Italy, where not long ago women were cloistered behind their balconies. Even inside her own home, one dying patient of mine found no peace—her husband was convinced any male doctor who entered the bedroom would try to possess her cancer-wracked body, so he would hang around during medical visits, pacing, and then rain abuse on her afterward. Moralizing about fidelity is anti-Italian—Berlusconi's babes outnumber Clinton's by orders of magnitude—and learning of a husband's fling could induce an Italian wife to throw dishes but probably not, as her American counterpart might, to pack her bags and leave.

Until the 1970s crimes of honor were licit in Italy but divorce was not; in the movie *Divorce Italian Style*, Marcello Mastroianni pushes his wife into adultery so he can kill her with impunity and marry his lover. When I moved to Italy a rapist could still clear his record by marrying his victim, and it was another two decades before the penal code reclassified rape with murder and robbery as a crime against the person, rather than against public morality.

Prostitution, another pillar of Italian family life, is legal. On occasion, a city will raise a brouhaha by briefly sending cops to photograph cruising johns or otherwise poop the party, but street hookers are ubiquitous. I was once waiting for a cab at 9:00 p.m. at Piazza Barberini, dressed in a business suit after a long day seeing patients, when I got mistakenly tapped on the shoulder. I turned around and caught a momentary glimpse of a young man's beet-red face before he skedaddled. At a prominent curve along our Friday route out of Rome a young woman in hot pants used to occupy a folding chair all afternoon, reading a book through large black-rimmed glasses. Farther outside town it's small clusters of trafficked Nigerians, and in the 1980s along the road that climbs behind the United Nations' Food and Agricultural Organization girls would flip their skirts up as you drove past at night so you'd see they were *puttane vere*, real whores, not transvestites.

Birth Control

When I arrived here in 1978 modern contraception was as foreign as kimchi, and it's made surprisingly little headway since. Thanks to Catholic mores, fewer than half of fertile-age Italian women currently use any (as of 2015 only sixteen percent used hormonal birth control, thirty percent condoms or IUDs). Italian law used to consider both vasectomy and tubal ligation "permanent maiming," as illegal as lopping off someone's hand, and though the Church lost that particular battle in the courts, they won on the ground. Sterilization is now theoretically lawful, but I've never known an Italian who'd had it done and have rarely found an Italian doctor willing to perform even the quick snip of a vasectomy. "In Italy we have the Vatican," one urologist explained to a journalist.

So how come Italy has the lowest birth rate in the world and one of the lowest abortion rates, half that of the US and falling steadily? Chiefly, everything you and I were taught about periodic abstinence ("What do you call women who use the rhythm method? Mothers") and withdrawal ("That tiny drop of pre-come is where all the sperm cells are") is wrong. Most Italian couples avoid pregnancy by combining the two—counting days and pulling out in the woman's most fertile period—and call the dual package *stare attenti*, being careful. It took me years to figure this out.

Stare attenti laudably shares responsibility between men and women, and prudently avoids relying on technology: Italian condoms tend to split (or, as a Russian woman complained in print about shoddy Soviet ones, "They break the first time they're used"). I suspect the American medical establishment party line dismisses withdrawal partly because it's free of charge and doctor-independent. Many Italians think it's "natural" and therefore acceptable to the Church, but that's an illusion—the biblical Onan's sin was not masturbation but *coitus interruptus*.

Another surefire mutual shocker for inter-cultural conversations: tell your Italian friend that most Americans never learned how to pull out, and tell your American friend it's Italians' main means of birth control.

Italian women are more likely to object to oral contraceptives for interfering with Mother Nature than from concern about side effects. Childbirth is closer to nature here too, at least linguistically: American obstetricians "deliver" babies, but Italians just *assistono* (attend), the same word they use for watching a play. But the call of the wild isn't loud enough to keep down the rate of cesarean sections, which is higher in Italy than anywhere else in Europe, beating out the United States thirty-six percent to thirty-three percent.

Italians' nature fetish can seem ultramodern when they reject processed foods and artificial fabrics (their sheets require ironing), backward when the taxi driver refuses to turn on his air conditioning. Most of those super-sophisticated, hyper-sensual women you admire on Via Veneto use sanitary napkins rather than tampons, not because they fear toxic shock but because of a sense that internal protection is, like the Pill, vaguely artificial. A country term for the female genitalia is "*la natura.*"

Diaphragms disappeared mysteriously but permanently from Italian pharmacy shelves in the 1990s—perhaps a blessing, since Italian gynecologists had never been taught how to prescribe them. I saw with my own eyes the prescription given to an American patient for "One contraceptive diaphragm." She had protested, "But I thought you had to fit me for it." The doctor, caught unprepared, waved his hand in the air and said, "Buy a medium size" (they actually come as 55, 60, 65, 70, 75, 80, or 85 mm). By the time she showed up in my office two months later, she was pregnant. When diaphragms were still around, I noticed that the gels sold to use with them were oddly irritating to delicate tissues. Turned out they were formulated with caustic ingredients that had permitted them to be sold as antiseptics in the days when birth control was illicit.

The Church wasn't happy when birth control was legalized, and I suspect its long hand behind both the vanishing diaphragm and small continuing sabotages: contraceptives are not paid for by the National Health Service like other essential medications (neither is Viagra—in the puritanical UK, you can get one a week free), and birth control pills are sold in twenty-one-pill packets without any user-friendly sugar pills, increasing the risk of error.

Hormonal contraceptives, like all powerful medications, deserve respect, but dangerous side effects are so uncommon that the Pill can be sold without a doctor's prescription in several American states. In Italy you'd think it was as toxic as cancer chemotherapy. Gynecologists promulgate that myth by demanding vast arrays of preliminary tests, often repeated every year.

Many women show up at my office asking for the morning-after pill after waiting for hours in a hospital ER and then being turned down. Sometimes the physician is a conscientious objector to abortion who oversteps his exemption by refusing to write a prescription for emergency contraception. Other times it's paramedical personnel. In 2008, an undercover Radical Party investigator surreptitiously filmed an ER nurse telling her the physicians couldn't prescribe the morning-after pill because the patient has to give "informed consent," as though she were having her appendix removed, and the ER had run out of the consent forms. (Admittedly this petty lie doesn't hold a candle to the pernicious mendacity mandated in some American states' "informed consent" forms for abortions, the ones that claim the procedure causes everything from breast cancer to drug abuse.) In 2015, the Italian Drug Agency cut back on all that theater by making Ella, a variant of Plan B, supposedly available without a doctor's prescription.

I say "supposedly" because some pharmacists play conscientious objector to all emergency contraception, though they have no right to by law. Some take their Catholic zeal even further. In 2012, an eighteen-year-old patient showed me the prescription her gynecologist had written for a birth control pill, which specified "For acne of the face and neck." Looking at her resplendent complexion I asked, "What's up?" She said the gynecologist wanted to make sure the pharmacist would fill the prescription—"Often they won't, you know."

INTERLUDE

A Baby That Wasn't

During my breather between New York and Rome, watching all those gracefully bent Kenyan women work the fields, apparently unencumbered by the infants strapped on their backs or the toddlers playing alongside, I started thinking about having a baby. In a Taita Hills village, laughing mothers tied a one-month-old to my back with a green-gold-black patterned length of cotton to show me how it was done. When I felt the squirming die down and the nestling begin, the die was cast. I trashed my diaphragm.

I was then thirty, and had always figured one bout of unprotected sex and I'd be knitting little booties. As a Neapolitan song goes, "A 'e vvote basta sulo na guardata," sometimes all it takes is a glance. My next period surprised me by arriving on schedule, and the one afterward, then all the rest, year in, year out, like ducks in a row.

There was no obvious reason. Ovulation every month, check. Tubes open, check. Plenty of happy sperm cells on Andrea's side, check. After which, in those days, there wasn't much to do except copulate and hope. We timed it with thermometers, spaced it according to now-obsolete theories, stretched out my luteal phase with progesterone, but those damned periods just kept on coming.

As a physician I got to help some women get pregnant, convey good news ("Remember my first visit? I thought I had a stomach flu but you told me it was Angela!"), and follow pregnancies for a few months here and there, but the pleasure was always bittersweet. The worst was helping to arrange abortions.

Then came a patient encounter that could have changed my life. A lost Australian waif I'll call Aileen, who was bivouacking under an ancient Roman bridge, consulted me because of abdominal swelling. The vigorous kicks of a six-month fetus met my examining hand. When given the diagnosis Aileen immediately asked, "How can I get rid of it?" I said, "I'm afraid you can't, it's too late for an abortion. You're going to have a baby." We looked at each other. I had been trying to get pregnant for four years. I can only guess at what was in her mind, but I know that through my own flitted the thought, "I could have that baby." In the end I helped her head north of the Alps, where she thought she could obtain a termination, and I never learned the outcome . . . Visions of Aileen's vague eyes and disheveled clothes have often come back to me. What would have happened if I had had the courage or the folly to leap out of my medical role, from one moment to the next, and make that unspeakable proposal?

opera buffa
ma non troppo

9

The Patient Game

> You need a good bedside manner with doctors or you
> will get nowhere.
>
> —William S. Burroughs, *Junky*

One day in the eighties a small, black-clad Italian woman sat across from me, unable to start recounting her problem. Her eyes roved over my desk in search of my left hand, which happened to be hidden on my lap. In desperation, she was finally reduced to putting the question in words: "*È Signora o Signorina?*" ("Is it Mrs. or Miss?"). For women of her generation the intactness of the hymen remained the Great Divide, to be settled before you can get to your medical history.

Most people stick to a respectful Dottoressa, the occasional backslide into Signora hastily corrected by the offender. Sometimes when a patient feels the need to demonstrate particular respect the title soars upward into Professoressa, equivalent to kissing the hem of my gown. I was jealous when my husband Alvin Curran, who as a composer already gets called Maestro, told me a concert hall usher had hailed him with the even more glorious Commendatore. But never, not even in the glad-handing city of Rome where the intimate "*tu*" can get bandied about to total strangers, would an Italian patient who had not been introduced by mutual friends call me by my first name.

In my early innocence I'd invite patients my age to call me *tu* but it only made them uncomfortable, so I decided to use the formal *Lei* with anyone over eighteen. A simple rule, except that kids grow up, and should you switch? Once a twenty-one-year-old long-time patient, forever *tu* to me, referred her same-age friend. I was just greeting the new patient using the intimate form when my eye fell on her chart and saw my secretary had typed, "Profession: Policewoman." In the space of a single phrase I wriggled over to *Lei*.

Seeing Italian patients involved a learning curve; half the time I couldn't figure out why they were in my office. I'd ask, "And what is it that brings you to me today?" Instead of "sinusitis," "my foot hurts," or "to get a Pap smear," an Italian might answer, "A whole bunch of things," or "Everything and nothing," and launch into the details of her backache, slow digestion, leg bruises, fatigue, and bladder infections, giving equal billing to eczema that's been under excellent treatment by a dermatologist for ten years and vertigo that started a week ago. In American charting terms, these patients were promoting their entire Past Medical History and Review of Systems to the more pressing status of Chief Complaint.

One thing I could be sure about what an Italian patient was coming for: it wasn't a cold. Mariateresa, who gets to transcribe my scribbled diagnoses onto patients' receipts, still can't get over how many Americans go to the doctor for the sniffles. Her compatriots know not only when that's all they've got, but also how they got it (an injudicious chill), and how to get rid of it (recipes inevitably include a stiff drink).

From an American point of view, some of my Italian patients expect too much out of a doctor, others too little. One will be after the kind of life-changing transformation you might seek from a guru, or a lover. Another just wants to add my opinion to a stack they will eventually toss in the air to see which flies. Whatever else they expect, it's not explanations. Whether from cultural habit, consumer demand, or fear of lawsuits, American doctors explain; Italians don't. I've heard a colleague complain, "With Americans

Dottoressa

you have to explain everything, they want to make all the decisions." An Italian patient put it this way: she and her countrymen are supplicants, not inquisitors. Patients expect their physicians to pontificate, so they aim to placate rather than pester.

> For us physicians it is fundamental and useful to know how to communicate . . . Not like the old days when all you needed was a sumptuous office and plenty of secretaries and assistants to instill respect and confidence in your patients.
>
> —Dr. Maurizio Zomparelli, hospital Chief of Service, 2012

Once, a young woman I'd seen several times before came in because of a rash. At a glance I diagnosed tinea versicolor, then sent her out the door in five minutes with a surefire prescription—and a scowl on her face. Since at the time I was still too afraid of my patients to ask her what had gone wrong, I called my mentor Dr. Alberto De Feo. He said the answer was obvious: when an Italian patient comes to a private doc, he or she wants a "complete visit" every time, no matter what the specific complaint, to justify paying their hard-earned money. Explanations no, putting on a show yes.

There are two kinds of people, those who love going to doctors and those who hate it. Like most health professionals, I fall into the second group, and have never really understood that large chunk of humanity whose idea of an afternoon's amusement is having their liver palpated. Some indulge their fondness for the patient role with a single doctor, while others prefer reciting their story over and over again to new audiences. Americans call this doctor-shopping, which implies an intention to eventually "buy." In Italy it often seems more like window-shopping, with each ride on a novel examining table its own reward.

Italians are comfortable in their bodies. They flaunt their figures like theatrical props, stand with the posture of women just one generation away from bearing baskets on their heads, walk with an earth-rootedness seen along North American streets chiefly among African-Americans and ballet dancers. A 5'6" Italian fills his space more than a 6'1" American.

Their innards are anatomically precise. Italians complain of pain not in their chest but in their heart or the tips of their bronchi. They suffer twinges in their ovaries, aches in their kidneys, sore livers, stitches in their spleen. The precision may be misguided—the backache is usually miles south of the kidneys—but it reflects a comfortable intimacy with their interior selves.*

A pet Italian disease is *artrosi cervicale*, neck arthritis, which they think causes not just the pain and stiffness it inflicts in other countries but also dizziness, double vision, nausea, fainting, excessive sweating, hot flashes, and gas. Since everyone over forty has abnormal spinal x-rays, *la cervicale* provides a convenient diagnostic nail to hang symptoms on. Another favorite is "low blood pressure," meaning weakness or fatigue, a concept that, like much of Italian folk medicine, dates back to the nineteenth century. Tired people have always craved medical diagnoses, and doctors have always obliged, though the specific labels spin in and out of fashion like pop stars—think hypoglycemia, yeast syndrome, food allergies, yuppie flu, multiple chemical sensitivities, and chronic Lyme disease.

Anglo-Saxons are oblivious to one vital organ, the liver, which becomes a prime source of bloating, exhaustion, itch, and general malaise for Italians if strained by overindulgence, as in "Your liver is a little swollen, eat lightly for a while." At first I took this locution seriously and would dutifully press my fingers up under the patient's ribs to check whether the organ was actually enlarged. It never was. I used to spend time tilting against such linguistic windmills, explaining over and over that migraine doesn't come from cervical arthritis or runner's stitch from the spleen but, in the end, I find it makes everybody's lives easier to let sleeping metaphors lie.

*The desire for intimacy with their *outer* selves can come into conflict with the more powerful desire to look good: many Italian full-length mirrors are rigged to narrow you down in the waist area. In the fitting rooms of fancy ladies' clothing shops some are additionally engineered to enhance your bust. This is a true fact.

Dottoressa

A serious or lethal prognosis can be hidden from the patient, but not from the family.

    —Italian Medical Code of Ethics, 1978

Information about prognoses that are serious or lethal, or could cause worry and suffering, should be provided prudently, using non-traumatizing language and without excluding elements of hope.

    —Italian Medical Code of Ethics, 2006

In 1988, when I was back in the States taking a brief epidemiology/biostatistics course at Johns Hopkins University, a conversation with my non-physician fellow-students turned to the subject of bad news. I mentioned casually that in breaking an awful diagnosis you sometimes had to listen to how much the patient wanted or could stand to hear at that moment. To a person, they jumped down my throat: "You mean you'd consider keeping the truth to yourself? Lie to patients?" Their unanimity and passion astonished me—when I had been in training just a decade earlier we rarely told a patient a diagnosis of cancer unless asked point-blank. And families had the last word; I have never forgotten one elderly black woman with advanced cervical cancer who kept begging in tears to know what she had, and on her daughters' insistence nobody would tell her. One of my chief residents preached the contrarian gospel of brutal honesty, but confessed that when he'd done a rectal examination on his own aged grandmother and felt a large cancer, he'd said, "You're fine, grandma, there's nothing there."

During my first decades in Italy everyone connived to shelter patients from bad news. I knew an Italian woman physician who for a week after an amniocentesis couldn't get her obstetrician to return her calls. Turned out the results showed Down's syndrome, so he wanted to talk not to her but to her husband. Another colleague told me that if he himself had cancer he wouldn't want to know. Doctors would go to such lengths to keep cancer patients in the dark that I couldn't trust pathology reports—the one a patient handed me could be a fake where the pathologist had penned a falsely reassuring diagnosis such as "chronic inflammation." Even the genuine version given to his family behind his back might still use deep medicalese to disguise his carcinoma as "dyskaryotic cells."

One hepatitis C patient of mine went to northern Italy to get a liver biopsy and came back carrying a reassuring report of "mild fibrosis without bridging"; bridging meant dead tissue and would have been bad. When I happened to phone the hepatologist on another subject he said, "I'm glad you called, let me tell you something about that biopsy. I didn't say so on the written report so as not to upset the patient but actually there was some bridging necrosis, she should repeat the biopsy in a year or two." A fib admirably solicitous for the patient's state of mind, but potentially disastrous for her longevity.

If in the US my position makes me a throwback to the merciful half-truths of times past, some Italians still consider me dangerous, to be kept away from their fatally-ill relative at all costs for fear he'll learn the diagnosis and throw himself out the window.

Out of pride I kept up my New York State medical license through 2015—paying $300 a year for the privilege of writing two prescriptions max. For most of those years, my prescriptions had a special box where I had to check "label," otherwise the pill bottle would only read, say, "Three times a day," without the name of the medicine. In some US states this is still the default.

In Italy that kind of secrecy is impossible, because pharmacists don't drop pills into bottles but hand them out blister-packed in labeled, factory-wrapped boxes. Their fine-print information sheets not only boost patients' sense of control but give them a chance at picking up the ball in case their doctors forget a contraindication or a drug interaction.

For most of my years here this admirable truth-in-advertising was marred by the spotty content of those informational inserts, aptly nicknamed *bugiardini* or "fib sheets." One might blandly state of a powerful medication that the only side-effect was occasional nausea and its only contraindication "allergy." Others would list different indications and side effects for the same drug marketed by two companies. Patients have shown me package inserts that say not to use Metamucil for more than a week, never leave Tampax in at night, and don't take ampicillin (the antibiotic most harmless to the growing fetus) during pregnancy. Fortunately the Agenzia Italiana del Farmaco, the Italian Drug Agency, has been gradually imposing consistency and accuracy.

Italians may be less well-googled than Americans—in 2017, fewer than a third looked for medical information online (it was sixty-seven percent in the US)—but in a practical sense they are more empowered. Patients are often handed snippets of their own intestine in a specimen jar to carry to the pathologist after a colonoscopy. And they pick up all their own results, getting to pore over the reports of ultrasounds, mammograms, and stress tests before their physician does.

Patients will tell me, "I do my blood tests twice a year," or "I had a cough so I went and got a chest x-ray." At least once a month I'll see someone who's concocted and carried out, on their lonesome, a haphazard checkup including everything from blood cortisol levels through Doppler duplex. American storefronts peddling direct-to-consumer CAT scans and 23andMe are nothing in comparison. It's the same for treatment; rather than consulting a physician for a sore throat or painful urination, an Italian will often take a course of antibiotics on her own, abetted by the free hand of her local pharmacist.

Between the ease of self-prescription and skepticism for doctors' expertise, Italians are accustomed to taking more responsibility for their own health. Recently, while instructing a longtime expat not to take Ativan more than once a day, I stopped writing to look up at her: "But of course we both know this is Italy, and you'll be able to buy, and take, as much as you want."

> Europeans think of the right to privacy as a fundamental human right.
>
> —Jennifer Granick, quoted in *The New Yorker*

Not *my* Europeans. Germans, yes; they're such fanatics that in 2015 psychiatrists who had wanted to hospitalize a Germanwings pilot for suicidal depression let him crash 150 people into a mountain rather than report his condition to his employer. Italians' only inviolable space is the confessional. They don't even have a word for privacy, and had to borrow ours (the Italian Data Protection Authority is called "*Garante per la privacy*").

In the doctor's office, an Italian is often less an individual than a member of a family, accompanied by parents, siblings, and/or offspring who crowd first into the waiting room and then into my office. I subvert the system at examination time by throwing out everyone except the protagonist, so a woman can talk about her disappointment in her son's career, or a man ask for help with premature ejaculation.

Once a very *simpatico* teacher from an American "abroad" program brought in a sullen student with a cough. I was sorry to have to stop exchanging pleasantries with the professor and usher him out. My patient looked so shrouded in storm clouds that, after excluding serious illness, I asked how things were going at school. I was rewarded by an explosion of anger against the professor's patronizing overprotectiveness: escorting him in like a baby, ignoring the moves he'd made to take responsibility for his own health, such as calling his sister in northern Italy. When I asked whether he'd like me to say something to Professor X, he nodded gratefully. Lesson learned: everybody, not just Italians, must be seen alone.

Glossary: *cura*

A handful of medications and some dietary restrictions, strictly temporary.

Aldo was eighty-five when he had his first attack of gallstone pain. He showed me what his doctor had prescribed: Actigall, which dissolves gallstones, plus five placebos—liver tonics, vitamins, amino acid pills—added like a sprinkling of holy water. Many Italian docs can't shake the habit of treating untreatable conditions with appropriately dubbed placebos: Dima Hepa for fatty liver, Vitreoxigen for vitreous detachment.

My patient Marco, a seventy-year-old banker who jet-sets between London and Rome, has a cholesterol level over 300 but won't take statins because his barber told him they're bad for your liver. Italian men really really don't like long-term medications. They do like *cure ricostituenti*, though, literally building-up treatments, a few weeks of intense vitamin preparations equally appropriate for a yearly overhaul, housewives' fatigue, lazy schoolchildren, or convalescence from pneumonia. It took years before I dared imitate my mentor Dr. De Feo and tell my vitamin-craving patients, "Tonics tonify only those who manufacture them and those who sell them."

Given the choice, Italians always go for root remedies, *cure di fondo*, billed as returning the body to its previous state of natural balance. They shrug off mere palliatives, preferring vitamin C for a cold, supposedly curative, to pills like Actifed that just dry up your nose, and with a headache or menstrual cramps they're more likely than Americans to simply grin and bear it. The Italian passion for root remedies may seem to contradict their love of tonics and *ricostituenti*, but it doesn't: those placebos are billed as the ultimate *cura di fondo*. A pet complaint, "I've been getting sick a lot lately," or "My immune defenses are low," implies that the organism as a whole is out of whack and that the specific symptoms are incidental, so the solution will be to rebalance the humors. Americans take medications to browbeat their diseases into submission; Italians hope they'll nudge the body into rediscovering its natural equilibrium.

Which may help explain why acupuncture and homeopathy are big in Italy, and why Italian docs don't view them as a threat.

Where Italian physicians love to prescribe placebos and time-limited *cure*, Americans insist to a fault on medications anointed by double-blind scientific trials, and treat the pills prescribed by a colleague with a respect bordering on the fetishistic. Once a patient of mine had a mystery disease I couldn't diagnose, whose symptoms I tried unsuccessfully to abolish with one medication after another. She happened to be on drug number seven, the calcium-blocker nifedipine, when we agreed she'd try her luck at the famed Mayo Clinic in Minnesota. After three weeks hospitalized there she came back with no diagnosis and unchanged symptoms—still taking the same futile drug. I laughed, visualizing the word "nifedipine" being copied in turn by the medical student, the intern, the resident, the attending physician, and the nurse. In the anthropology of American medicine, prescription is a cumulative process: once on a drug, forever on a drug, they stick like barnacles.

One of my few daring decisions as a resident at the Martin Luther King Clinic in the Bronx was to stop renewing one woman's unnecessary digitalis prescription. I still remember how my heart sped up as I wrote out her shortened list of medications, afraid of Aesculapius's punishing thunderbolt. Over time, I got the bit between my teeth. One American man I saw in Rome had been taking Naprosyn every day for ten years since a single bout of bursitis, a diuretic for twelve years because his blood pressure had once been elevated, and allopurinol for nine, following an attack of gout probably caused by the diuretic. I managed to convince him that, as my iconoclastic teacher Dr. Matz used to preach, "Life is not a drug-dependent state," and we both held our breaths until he had gradually tapered and stopped all his medications without any deity striking either of us dead.*

In the US, once you've written a prescription the visit is over. Not in Italy. I used to be puzzled when a patient with, say, bronchitis would linger to ask what he should eat. Dr. Anna Kohn cleared up the mystery by explaining that no *cura* is complete, whatever the diagnosis, without ordering some change in diet. Maybe no salt, maybe lots of salt. Maybe nothing but liquids, nothing but fruit, nothing but grilled meat. Maybe no meat, no alcohol, a glass of wine daily, small frequent meals, no fiber, plenty of fiber,

---

*Well into the twenty-first century this medical sacrilege acquired a name, "deprescribing," and proponents who, somewhat timidly, have begun urging American physicians to give it a try.

a hearty breakfast, a light breakfast, yogurt every morning, no fruit with meals, no vegetables, eight glasses of water, no eggs, no citrus, no fried food, no sweets, no coffee, no bubbly water, or no dairy products.

The fallback sickbed diet is called *in bianco* (white)—pasta with oil, rice with butter, boiled chicken breast, potatoes, codfish—as though the red of tomato sauce or the green of spinach would zap your immune system. Italians are infinitely solicitous of their palates when they're healthy, and for anyone with such veneration for the Great God Taste Bud eating *in bianco* seems a fate worse than death. Is it a penance, a vestige of the notion that our sins make us sick? Or is the washed-out diet a symbol of how illness has put life itself on hold?

I met Elena, an Italian psychologist, in the eighties. After a dozen lunches over several years I remember the exact moment we became friends: during a phone call when I asked how she was. She hesitated a moment, then took the plunge by giving a real answer instead of her usual "fine." Italians are curious and welcoming with passers-through, but beware of mistaking their friendliness for friendship. The American habit of pouring out your marital troubles to someone you hit it off with at a cocktail party is tantamount in Italian eyes to a one-night stand.

Glossary: *amico*

Stronger than the American "friend." Italians are quick to strike up a conversation, slow to let you get close. They're expert at both deep friendship and cultivating their coterie, and obsessively analyze and re-analyze the character and behavior of everyone they know.

In the Eternal City, even the smallest interactions are personal. A speeding car will halt to let you cross if you catch the driver's eye and stare him down. Someone who hits a pedestrian is surprisingly likely to stop, take the victim to the hospital, and weep for hours on the formica bench in the corridor waiting for the doctors to say everything's OK. Until the nineties a bank wouldn't let you open an account unless you were introduced in person by someone they knew.

Italians enhance the borders of their social encounters like kids crayoning the edges of figures in a coloring book. They wish every shopkeeper "Hello" as they enter and "Goodbye" as they exit, and never leave a party without making the rounds of the back rooms to be sure no cheek is left unkissed. They neglect introductions just as salesgirls neglect first-time customers, putting less value on making new relationships than on cultivating old ones.

This set of mores can hyperpersonalize the doctor-patient relationship, making for blurred borders that send me up the wall. Once when I was on a week's holiday in Paris, a patient's son wormed my hotel number out of my secretary, and phoned at eight in the morning to suggest that as long as I was there why didn't I stop in at the Villejuif Hospital and have a chat with his mother's oncologist? Another time it was my home phone that rang: an Italian patient of mine in tears, just a block away, could she possibly come up, she had to talk to me. I sat with her in my living room and listened to her romantic woes, offering a common-sense interjection here and there. After an hour she thanked me and left, without offering to pay: talk belongs to the realm of friendship, not medicine, and has no monetary value.

Friendship does, however, permit gifts. At holiday time I used to receive a dozen baskets from grateful patients: *torrone, panettone,* and *spumante,* surrounded by scatterings of walnuts and hard candies. A colleague appreciative of my referrals might send one too, enriched by a Gucci bag or a silver salt shaker, a genteel version of fee-splitting I never had the heart to refuse. There are fewer baskets every Christmas, as the old mentality fades, but Italy is still a gift culture where tablemates battle to pay the restaurant bill. Don't lavish excessive admiration on a friend's necklace, she'll take it off and put it around your neck.

A physician who treats himself has a fool for a patient.
—Sir William Osler

Dottoressa

Treating your friends and family is, in theory, nearly as taboo as treating yourself. In the words of the American College of Physicians, you should "usually not enter into the dual relationship of physician-family member or physician-friend." English authorities have been known to strip a doctor of his license for writing his brother a prescription.

I see it a bit differently. While I wouldn't go as far as an Italian surgeon I know who removed his own mother's gallbladder, I don't shut my friends outside the office door. After all, if I were one of those old-fashioned country docs we'd all love to be if it weren't for the 24/7 on-call, all my friends would be my patients and all my patients my friends.

In my New York days, one friend's grumbling about pudginess and lack of energy rolled off my back; I was off duty. It was only when he got diagnosed with a sluggish thyroid, which I should have suspected years before, that I guiltily recognized that you can't doctor by the timeclock.

Certainly, friendship can complicate a doctor-patient relationship. It's been shown that getting blood transfusions from friends rather than anonymous donors carries a higher risk of AIDS, because friends don't want you to know about their former life on heroin or evenings cruising for rough trade. Your friend may keep her problems to herself rather than bother you by taking an appointment, or on the contrary may bug you inappropriately at home. If your friend-patient's medical problem is trivial, you may tactlessly dismiss it as lightly as you would an illness of your own. If it's middling serious and needs a workup, you may overdo the explanations and counterproductively expose too many of your doubts. And if your friend is very sick, your judgment is really not to be trusted—I once continued treating a friend with galloping ulcerative colitis as an outpatient for weeks after she should have been in the hospital.

I set myself the rule of never initiating a social relationship with a patient. I promptly broke it by suggesting to a musician we get together for some cello-and-piano sonatas.

I've always insisted even friends pay something, partly to emphasize the professional nature of the encounter. This mix of money and friendship is extremely un-Italian. In Morocco, my ex-husband and I became friendly with a shopkeeper during the long process of bargaining over a major purchase, and were invited to eat at his house. Over tagine Mehmed began to introduce another object on which, he said, we might reach an excellent price. But for Andrea the dinner invitation had changed everything, and he cut him off abruptly: "We're friends now. Whatever you ask will be appropriate, and I will pay it," bringing the negotiations, and the possibility of a sale, to a grinding halt.

Even in the US, the separation of the Church of Medicine from the State of Friendship is less absolute in practice than in theory. In one essay in *The New England Journal of Medicine*, a woman doctor described saving her father's life by doing a rectal exam and showing his black, blood-laden stool to the hospital staff.

Glossary: *fare antecamera*

Literally to sit in the vestibule, figuratively to cool one's heels. A sign of deference.

Italians are always double-parking and blocking other people's cars, and those other people are always getting in their own cars and leaning on the horn. Watch carefully: the double-parked Italian, invested with momentary clout, emerges from the *caffè*, saunters toward the offending car, climbs in, closes the door, adjusts the mirror, turns on the radio, and drives off at a crawl. A deliberate piece of slo-mo theater.

In Italy, punctuality is a vice. Dinner guests invited for 8:30 arrive at ten, staff meetings scheduled for three p.m. start at four, concerts never begin within fifteen minutes of the scheduled time, plumbers show up a week late, a carpentry job can take years. But when it comes to a doctor's appointment, Italian patients always walk in on the button. Why? It's a power calculation: if you make someone wait you're placing yourself higher in the pecking order. Insulting your doctor that way could compromise the relationship forever. Conversely, by making patients phone back over and over, doctors underline their own superior status.

One evening in 1986 I was the last person left sitting outside a gate at JFK, hoping to board a Pan American plane home. As their doc on the ground in Rome I had the right to travel first class on a standby basis, but first was full up and the gate rep was fuming. He loved doctors, he told me, they had saved his wife from cancer. He disappeared into the gate, leaving me alone. Five minutes later he was out again and on his walkie-talkie: "In seat 3B there's a woman wearing blue jeans. Kick her out of first class and put her in the empty seat in row 29." Another five minutes to overcome protests from the sartorially incorrect traveler, and I was in row 3 taking guilty sips of champagne.

American physicians top Supreme Court judges in surveys of occupational prestige, and enjoy a nearly unchallenged monopoly on conventional medical knowledge. So depending on their attitude toward authority, American patients arrive at the doctor's either hat in hand or chip on shoulder. When I was young I was definitely a chip-on-shoulder type, awarding physicians the same impotent scorn I heaped on all authority figures, from my parents to Lyndon Johnson, geniuses or dunces. I encountered both types my first week at Radcliffe, when I got doubled over by stomach pain and found myself tête-à-tête with a young doctor and vomiting inelegantly while he tried to get me to admit I'd had sex. Deciding that if I couldn't be pregnant I must have appendicitis, he checked me into a hospital bed. The surgeon came to the rescue, trailing a coterie of students, performed the pelvic examination the nosy intern had been too prudish to do, found an ovarian cyst, and saved me from surgery.

A year later the head of the Harvard University Health Services, Dr. Curtis Prout, wrote me a prescription for the Pill, saying "I guess once you've started you're not going to stop." The way that line remains engraved in my memory is a scary warning of the power a doctor wields: a remark I toss off to a patient may be remembered, accurately or not, forever.

The authority of American medicine is collective and based on consensus, doctors channeling a Platonic reality of scientific Truth. From Oregon to Florida, there are only minor doc-to-doc or hospital-to-hospital variations in the approach to any given disease. When I was in training the dogma was handed down verbally, where now it's officialized in the form of guidelines, but there's always been a line to toe even if it boomerangs from one year to the next: for diverticulosis "avoid roughage" flipped in the seventies to "lots of roughage," for menopause "everybody take HRT" became in the early 2000s "nobody take HRT" (and now, sensibly, "take it if you need it").

The fact that the party line is practically writ on water, changing with the latest journal article, doesn't prevent the American medical profession from behaving as though it were chiseled in stone down to the smallest particulars. For a strep throat, penicillin must be prescribed for ten days, not nine, you take metronidazole three times a day for trichomonas but four times for amoebas, as though we really knew those differences mattered. Our physicians strive to present themselves as scrupulous, perfectly informed exponents of whatever is currently prevailing. One non-medical American friend confirms: "I'd be really disturbed to have two doctors tell me two different things." Another told me she'd seen two New York ophthalmologists about a cataract and was taken aback when one said she needed surgery and the other didn't.

Of course, in reality two American docs can disagree sharply, but commonly it's either because the diagnosis is elusive, they're on opposite sides of a known controversy, or one of them is behind the times.

An Italian physician typically aims instead to be seen as someone whose experience and intuition make him unique. Here, not only do doctors disagree, but everybody expects them to, just as Italians find it normal that every accountant has a different theory on whether I need to pay the "IRAP" business tax. They're not even convinced that being a doctor gives you any privileged medical knowledge, so I'm competing with homeopaths and layers on of hands and also with my patient's cousin, dry cleaner, and maid.

Physicians wield influence as much from charisma as wisdom, and are as much *stregoni* (sorcerers) as *Professori*.

When I moved to Rome the medical world was a hodge-podge of competitors, each hawking his personal ideas and remedies. That free-for-all still isn't entirely gone. As late as 2014, while international guideline committees were debating whether it's worthwhile to do any screening at all for prostate cancer, a certain Dr. Romano Rago, urologist, proposed in the Medical Society bulletin that the Italian NHS expand its cancer screening program to offer all men over fifty not just PSA blood tests and rectal exams but a yearly urologist visit, urine flow rate measurements, and abdominal and transrectal sonograms. A castle in the air that would, not incidentally, direct floods of money toward his own specialty.

Even the most straightforward remedy can be interpreted as personal magic. In 1984, I treated a patient for primary syphilis by giving him two shots of long-acting penicillin at one sitting. This had been standard therapy since the fifties, except in Italy, where they insisted on giving painful, short-acting penicillin jabs every day for six weeks. He spread the word, and I soon got a ring from Calabria asking if the caller could take an appointment with me, since he had primary syphilis and had heard that "The *Dottoressa* has a special treatment." I answered, somewhat perplexed and wanting to do him a favor, that it wasn't really necessary for him to take the night train up to Rome just to be given injections he could surely obtain (said I, naïvely) in his home town. By reducing my snake-oil to a guideline, I fear I may have driven him back to the penitence of those forty-two needles.

A common Italian approach in the face of a serious disease such as cancer is to decide what to do on the basis of weight-for-weight doctor-shopping: they'll collect five or six opinions from as many specialists, and follow the majority opinion. Americans are more likely to spend time searching out one top team, then put themselves blindly into its hands, for better or for worse.

One corollary of treating their doctors like sorcerers is that Italians are less likely to demand a guarantee of cure. American physicians offer two alternative self-images: technical whiz or

Almighty. In either case, their patients expect to be returned to perfect health, and see it as a failing of the medical profession when the fix fails to materialize, or is partial, or is temporary. I remember the exact moment I had this insight. I was listening to the tale of an angular woman who'd been diagnosed with an overactive thyroid three years earlier, in Chicago. After two treatments with radioactive iodine she still hadn't achieved hormonal balance, leaving her infuriated with her doctors. This seemed somehow off the mark. Thinking about it, I suddenly grasped why, and gently pointed out that it was actually her disease that was at fault, that she would have been better off not getting sick in the first place. If doctors play God they'll get blamed whenever their omniscience and omnipotence slip up. Italians already have a God, thank you very much, and their physicians are content with the role of priest or shaman.

Romans have a wisecrack when they're caught in a thunderstorm: *"Piove, governo ladro,"* "It's raining, thief of a government," as though corruption in high places were responsible for all the world's woes, down to and including bad weather. Similarly, Americans will tack onto "My father died of cancer" the reflex postscript, "Damned doctors didn't catch it in time." Or else they're blaming the patient, a disease-as-punishment-for-your-sins guilt trip that's undergone conceptual creep from cirrhosis (too much alcohol) and emphysema (too many cigarettes) through heart attacks (too much meat) and diabetes (too many sweets) to the distant reaches of pancreatic cancer (too much coffee), breast cancer (too little breast-feeding), and high blood pressure (too much griping). No guilt trips for Italians—after centuries of priestly absolutions, they're blessedly immune.

> When an Italian mother calls to say you must come immediately to see little Guido who is desperately ill, I give her an appointment in a week. When an English mother calls saying can you please give me an appointment for little Eric next week, I answer come right over.
>
> —Dr. Eva Lewin, legendary Rome expat pediatrician

One afternoon I got two phone calls from patients with colds, and both of them knew exactly how they'd gotten sick. The Italian had put his head out the window on a rainy night to greet a friend; the Englishman had spent an evening in a stuffy room with no fresh air.

Treating a global clientele keeps me on my toes, because according to which country a patient hails from I may err by kicking the husband out or letting him stay, explaining too much or too little, telling a cancer patient her diagnosis or hiding it, prescribing a pill or sending the person off empty-handed. It may be as offensive to offer an examining gown to a naked French woman as it is to ask an American to climb onto the examining table barebreasted.

The line between cultural sensitivity and stereotyping can be delicate, with PC Americans bristling at some casual European assumptions: "Being Finnish, he just stood staring at his shoes . . ." (watch any Kaurismaki film and you'll understand) or "You know how picky Germans are . . ." Familiarity with culture-specific expectations is most crucial when you choose to defy them. When I'd come in from the cold with my jacket open, horrifying my Italian friends, I used to joke that American babies get vaccinated against drafts, only stopping after I realized some believed it.

Italian family members get deeply involved in each other's health care, but Asians top the charts. I used to treat an elderly member of the Chinese diaspora, who was perfectly *compos mentis* and in fine health except for some prostate trouble. After a half-hour listening to his symptoms, looking at his lab tests, examining him, rebalancing his meds, and discussing my conclusions, just when I'd think I was done his daughter would march down the hall, knock on my office door, and make me repeat every word.

Another Asian lesson: you can put a patient off by smiling too much or not enough. I thought New Yorkers came from the bottom of the smile scale, until I found that nobody undersmiles a Korean. And nobody, not even a San Franciscan, outsmiles the Japanese, especially when they're embarrassed or ill at ease. The biggest smiles I've ever seen were on a Japanese diplomatic wife the week before she drowned herself.

There can be unexpected challenges. Once a new patient was scheduled to see my male Italian partner, Dr. Vincenzo Bacci, who was so overbooked he asked me to take the case. When I went into the waiting room to fetch the patient, a bearded face stared at me transfixed. Turns out he was a consular representative of the Islamic State of Iran, abruptly faced with a triple whammy in a single doctor: female, American, and Jewish. We both took a bit to reorient, especially since his complaint required a rectal exam, but in the end, between my professionalism and his intrinsic gentility honed by diplomatic training, the visit was a success.

A young Italian woman who walked bent under the weight of gold necklaces came in several times to complain about her Saudi husband, and I offered unwavering sympathy. When one day she sobbed, "Yesterday was the last straw—he hit me!" I insisted she bring him in for a talking-to. A week later my secretary Maria-teresa buzzed to warn me that the monster was being escorted down the hall, setting me to anxiously checking the length of my sleeves and the buttons on my blouse. What walked in the door was an apple-cheeked, sheepish boy child who spoke fervently about the covenant of marriage and was more distressed than she was that he'd given her that slap. He leaned forward and asked, "Doctor, do I understand from your name that you are Jewish?" I replied frostily, "Well, yes, I do happen to be of Jewish origin." Him: "Then you will understand me, we Semites have similar reactions. My wife and her Italian family are driving me crazy!"

Doctors' minds can wander during an examination, sent off unexpectedly to distant worlds by, for example, a pair of unusual feet. One afternoon in 1979 my ex-husband and I walked into the bush surrounding Juba, the South Sudanese capital, following the sound of a distant drum. An hour of hiking brought us to the source of the music: a clearing occupied by one hollow tree trunk and two young boys who sat on it pounding rhythmically. As night fell a dozen more musicians joined in, playing polyrhythm for a hundred men in loincloths whose dance consisted of jumping vertically up and down in unison. Afterward, the exhilarated dancers ran full tilt toward town through the forest, impossibly barefoot, leaving us to pick our way homeward in their wake. I understood how they did it only when a Kenyan graduate student sat gowned on my exam table twenty years later. Splayed-out shovels dangled at the end of his legs, twice the size of any foot I'd ever seen, thickly padded underneath. Clearly they had trod the earth for decades before ever getting cooped up in shoes; going barefoot just in the summer, as we all did as kids, won't flatten your bone structure. Observing those feet close up, as I never had in Africa, I now saw how those dancers had been able to run like panthers, microadjusting to any surface.

The absolute best patients are the English. They're affable, tell their story succinctly, take the medicine you prescribe, don't gripe, and show proper appreciation. A British army man once sat across my desk, his back like a plumb line, describing leg pain that had worsened over four days and culminated—he said—in a 105 degree fever. This seemed unlikely: "But sitting there now, you look perfectly fine." "Actually," he replied, "I fear I could fall over any minute." He had erysipelas, a skin infection that looks minor but packs a mean punch, and his blood pressure was dangerously close to zero.

As I am constantly reminded by patients, every country has its own alternative medicine. Frenchmen take magnesium for their nerves, Indians posted in Rome import herbs from home . . . In the age of the internet, I'm constantly if unenthusiastically doing due diligence on my clientele's preferred panaceas. Usually the best reaction is a smile, but sometimes silence won't do, as when (I've seen all these) a patient with abnormal liver enzymes turns out to be taking kava, a liver toxic supplement, for her nerves, a heart attack survivor is depending on Ayurvedic medicine instead of Lipitor, or a patient is sabotaging his blood pressure meds by chewing betel nuts.

The British National Health Service infamously allots five minutes per visit, which I thought unique until I told a Canadian colleague I allow a half hour for each appointment. He asked, "Once you've taken the history, examined the patient, made the diagnosis, and prescribed the therapy, what do you do with the other twenty-five minutes?"

Fortunately most medical talk is straightforward, and dire consequences of minor misreadings unlikely, but a single unexpected word or tilt of the head occasionally opens a crack through which I glimpse profound differences between me and my patient in how we see the world and how we experience and interpret the events we're talking about, and I intuit how much better my work could be if I *really* understood.

But just because a patient is a fellow American doesn't mean there are no cultural issues. When a new patient I've greeted as Mrs. Jones replies by calling me Susan, for example, it never fails to throw me for a loop. And the type of person who calls me by my first name also considers it good form to repeat it five times per sentence: "The way I look at it, Susan . . . And then, Susan, I got this terrible cough . . ." I checked with male colleagues about how they deal with patients using their first name; none had ever faced the issue. I worked through the syllogism and concluded that some time after 1978, when I moved here, woman-to-woman first-naming gained unprecedented ground in the USA. Sociologists take note.

10

The Doctor Game

The Aventino Medical Group used to do its banking at the Banca Nazionale del Lavoro until our local branch started randomly shuttering their door fifteen, thirty, or forty-five minutes ahead of schedule. One in four checks the Veterans Administration mails me from Texas to pay for my disability evaluations disappears en route. At least we're no longer in the quaint 1970s, when entire railroad cars full of mail would be dumped for landfill.

Glossary: *pressappochismo*

Pressappoco means approximately, so *pressappochismo* is more-or-less-ness, the dark side of flexibility. Modern-day Italians are geniuses in aesthetics, human relations, and fantasy, but attention to detail is an object of mild aristocratic disdain. Their ancestors were masters of precision—both bridges to the Tiber Island have carried traffic since the days of Caesar—and I've always wondered when the switcheroo took place.

Small-change medical *pressappochismo*: I've almost gotten used to the frequent but absurd GP prescription telling hypertensive patients to take an extra pill any day their home blood pressure machine reads high. But until I saw it in writing I couldn't believe one patient with lifelong normal blood pressure had been prescribed a diuretic for her to take "in case your pressure goes up."

Mid-range medical *pressappochismo*: When a friend's demented eighty-three-year-old father wanted to renew his driver's license, she was relieved that they called him in for a special old folks' competency test, assuming he'd never be allowed behind the wheel again. He was in and out of the examiner's office in a flash, and told her the exam had consisted in answering three questions: "Do you see well or do you wear glasses?" "I see fine." "Do you have any diseases?" "Nope." "Do you have trouble driving?" "Nope." He'd passed.

An Italian woman described her hysterectomy as, "They sewed me up." Metaphorical, I thought, until I examined her and discovered to my dismay that an older breed of Roman gynecologist didn't bother to leave behind a vagina deep enough for intercourse. To what extent their reasons were technical (it does take an extra couple of minutes), theological (why have sex if you can no longer procreate?), or ageist (women getting a hysterectomy are usually over forty) is anyone's guess.

High-stakes medical *pressappochismo*: Karen R. came to my office with a puffy neck and upper chest after being sent home from two different emergency rooms with prescriptions for tranquilizers. In actuality, a huge tumor in front of her heart was cutting off her circulation (the "superior vena cava syndrome"). I sent her to the Gemelli Hospital, where they promptly did a biopsy—but the pathologist's report revealed that their needle had missed the tumor entirely. Stuff happens. For unfathomable Italian reasons the oncologists said they wouldn't be able to repeat the procedure for two weeks, during which time she might well die. What to do? The Gemelli team powwowed and came up with a bright idea: they would give her chemotherapy aimed at the worst kind of cancer they could think of in that location, a rare tumor called a thymoma. Medically speaking, that kind of improvisation was utter madness. After asking advice from trusted cancer specialists, I got her out of their hands and into another hospital, where within forty-eight hours her lymphoma (an entirely different and much more curable disease) had been properly diagnosed and was under treatment. But the experience set off a shock in my own nervous system, one of my earliest premonitions of death, a flash of terror of what the choice to live in Italy might mean for my personal survival.

In Morrisania Hospital in the South Bronx, where I did my internship, an emergency room patient would get shipped upstairs and within an hour the ward staff would have assigned a diagnosis, devised a treatment plan, hooked up the tubing, and moved on to the next case. We would be drawn and quartered if we didn't have at least a tentative diagnosis by morning. Diagnosis was easy, cure difficult. When I set up shop in my lonely Roman office the equation reversed: the process of committing to a diagnosis paralyzed me. I felt unsure pronouncing on the simplest urinary tract infection, and worried that every runny nose might really be lethal midline granuloma (to steal from George Thomas and Lee Schreiner's book *That's Incurable!*). Responsibility looms scarier when you don't have a hospital full of colleagues to back you up.

I've found some Italian physicians oddly indifferent to pinning down exactly what the patient has. My friend Ruggiero died in Naples without a diagnosis, after languishing in hospital for weeks. A pulmonary disease specialist treated one of my patients for tuberculosis without ever sending a sample to the lab, because he saw what "looked like a tubercle" through the bronchoscope. When I suspected an infection in a recent knee replacement, a potentially disastrous complication, I rushed the patient back to her orthopedist to draw off a sample for culture and antibiotic sensitivities, only to have him prescribe a guesswork antibiotic instead.

But other times it may be better *not* to chase after a specific diagnosis. The introductory chapter of my medical bible, *Harrison's Textbook of Internal Medicine*, warned the young physician that we don't know how to explain everything and don't have to. A little list of inexplicable but benign symptoms followed, starting (I remember) with that odd stab of pain people get sometimes in the side of the skull, to encourage trainees to admit our ignorance and leave our prescription forms untouched. Italian docs are more likely to just hand out treatment. I saw one healthy twenty-two-year-old woman with nondescript abdominal pain, sent by her general practitioner for a sonogram that was interpreted as showing four vague diagnoses, all unlikely in her case, "chronic cholecystitis, liver disease, ovarian inflammation, and renal sand." The GP dutifully prescribed four placebos, one per organ.

> Italy lacks a culture in science-based policies.
>
> —Dr. Ilaria Capua, prominent virologist about to emigrate to Florida, 2016

In 1980, visiting Rome's *Ordine dei Medici* (Medical Association) as part of my vain crusade to have my Internal Medicine specialty recognized, I got to chatting with the director about alternative medicine. He startled me by saying he thought the whole lot, from homeopathy to iridology, was probably as good as anything we regular docs have to offer. Thirty years later a vascular surgeon of my acquaintance, when I asked for the scientific evidence behind one of his prescriptions, answered, "I don't go by research, I go by my experience." One of Rome's top radiologists put it to me even more bluntly in 2013: "Research is shit." On learning that a respected colleague used homeopathy as part of his repertoire, I spent hours combing through the extensive (negative) research literature. When I proposed we meet and look it over, with the goal of mutual edification, he was totally uninterested.

Once I asked an Italian doc just back from a year working in a British hospital about her impressions, expecting awe at the level of scientific medicine. Instead she vented her disgust at the doctors' slavish respect of guidelines, finding the very concept anathema. Italians prefer rough edges and a dash of randomness, much as traditional musicians in Asia prefer imperfect tunings and quasi- rather than perfect unisons.

Italians have a point in insisting there may be more than one way to skin a cat. Maybe changeable weather does cause headaches as everyone here believes, including me, and maybe vitamins can cure chronic hepatitis after all. The crucial point is that all medical assertions, whether about distance healing or Prilosec, could, and in theory should, be tested using the scientific method and then accepted or discarded depending on research results.

In their heart of hearts, it sometimes seems to me, neither Italians nor their physicians fully believe in scientific evidence. Italy's largest political party in 2018 is officially anti-vaccination, and Italian medicine is full of odd remnants of what may have been up to date when docs now pushing ninety were kids. An overworked liver triggers conjunctivitis, a dental abscess causes maladies from arthritis to cancer, and most everything else can be explained by the malefic power of drafts. A woman whose heavy periods have left her exhausted with anemia should wait until summer is over to take iron pills. By law, dead bodies must wait twenty-four hours before being autopsied or embalmed, in case the patient wakes up. If you visit a private hospital after sundown you find vases of flowers all along the hallways, removed from patients' rooms for the night because of the rather charming concern that the flowers will steal oxygen from the sick.

When I lived in the States my fellow citizens universally believed that getting their lungs listened to and their blood drawn every twelve months would ward off the evil spirits of disease, no matter how many Big Macs, Camels, and boilermakers they consumed, and the passage of time hasn't fully eradicated the conviction that year-to-year survival hangs on a physician's benediction.

Checkups in Italy include mammograms and Pap smears, but mostly feature *le analisi*, routine testing showered on healthy people as though they were refreshing their permanents. A gynecologist may routinely order five blood cancer markers plus a pelvic ultrasound, spawning interminable chains of further testing, cancer scares, and unnecessary surgery. And when the profit motive comes in, there's shameless self-referral. I've seen reports of privately done normal bone density (DEXA) tests which brightly conclude, "Repeat in twelve months" (guidelines say three to ten years), and normal breast sonograms that say "Repeat in six months."

Though only physicians will really get the joke, I can't resist listing some of what I've seen ordered in one or another doc's yearly routine: alpha-fetoprotein, anti-thyroglobulin antibodies, beta-HCG, CA-125, CA-19-9, CEA, cyfra 21-1, factor II, factor V Leiden, ferritin, fibrinogen, free thyroid hormones, homocysteine, lactic dehydrogenase isoenzymes, partial thromboplastin time, progesterone, prolactin, protein C, protein S, activated protein C resistance, prothrombin time, resistance to antithrombin III, thyroid stimulating hormone, and tissue plasminogen activator; carotid artery duplex studies, echocardiograms, panabdominal sonograms, stress tests, thyroid sonograms, and transrectal prostate sonograms; examinations by cardiologists, gastroenterologists, and urologists.

I consider it a personal mission to try to break both American and Italian patients of the habit of excessive testing. When a patient protests, I'll quote my wise teacher Dr. Matz: the less the reason for doing a test, the more difficult it will be to interpret the result.

> The specialist or consultant who examines a patient without the primary care physician being present must produce a detailed report of the diagnosis and the suggested therapeutic plan.
> —Italian Medical Code of Ethics, 2006

Outside the Code of Ethics fantasy world, there's no such thing in Italy as a proper consultation note, where the specialist commits to grandiloquent writing for benefit of the referring physician his exhaustive history, meticulous examination, tour-de-force diagnosis, and scrupulous therapeutic plan. Here in Rome, at least, I rarely receive even a terse scribble. But then, Italy rarely encourages written prolixity; within living memory, if you wrote over five words on a postcard the stamp cost more.

So I was impressed by the report given to one patient of mine by an orthopedist, ex-Chief of Service at a major Rome hospital, who had seen her a few days earlier in relation to a disability claim. He conscientiously described her limping gait, tenderness and limited motion of the lumbar spine, weakness of the left leg, absence of sensation along her calves, severe pain on straight leg elevation, and knees that were swollen, tender, and fixed in a bent position. There was only one problem: when I examined her I discovered that all those abnormalities were pure fabrications. He had been hired, after all, not to treat her but to get her a pension.

Long ago, a patient told me she didn't believe the surgeon she had paid was the one who had actually operated on her. I dismissed that as paranoia, but colleagues in the know have since disabused me: once a private patient has been put under in the operating room, the big-name surgeon who commands the hefty fee may secretly play second fiddle to someone who's billed as his assistant but is better at handling a laparoscope or just better, period. An Italian surgeon who told me he's often invited to operate in place of klutzier colleagues added, "It's the same all over the world"; seeing me unconvinced, he shook his head at my New World naiveté.

It may reveal an excess of faith in American medical training, but I stick with the notion that my colleagues back home have it easy, that they can assume the locum tenens, specialists, emergency room docs, and hospitalists who share their patients are more or less competent. Rushed or insensitive perhaps, making a mistake here and stealing a patient there, choosing an antibiotic you wouldn't, irritatingly following a guideline you find inappropriate, but basically knowing what they are doing. In Rome I can't take that bottom-line know-how for granted, having seen, for example, a gynecologist creatively attribute vaginitis to lactose intolerance and an ophthalmologist give a patient with a small painless eyelid cyst written instructions to permanently stop eating fried foods, nuts, and strawberries. So at times I'll find myself venturing beyond my comfort zone to treat complex patients I'd have preferred to refer elsewhere.

> The relationship between physicians should be inspired by principles of solidarity, mutual respect, and consideration for the other's professional activity.
> —Italian Medical Code of Ethics, 2006

All the other doctors kept telling me my doctor was nuts.

—A patient after surgery for intestinal obstruction

It wasn't easy to control Arnold C.'s high blood pressure, but I had finally succeeded using a combination of enalapril, hydrochlorthiazide, and atenolol. The Italian cardiologist he consulted for a second opinion looked at my prescription, raised his eyebrows, and wrote a new one: ramipril, chlorthalidone, and metoprolol. The names were different but the three drug classes were the same, so all he'd done was disparage my advice without actually changing anything.

I was taught to abstain from criticizing colleagues to patients, and to attempt to avoid even the appearance of a difference of opinion. There are excellent reasons: a patient's report of what happened elsewhere can be unreliable, a patient presented with two different opinions may well discard both of them, and by circling the wagons we protect the dignity of the medical caste as a whole. US physicians have further managed to avoid dog-eat-dog behavior by scheming to keep their number down, so there are plenty of patients to go around and consequently less need for cutthroat competition.

For years after starting to work in Italy I would hear hair-raising tales of incompetence without breathing a word to the patient, though I'd concede a tactful second opinion if asked. My training in collegiality was reinforced by a sense of gratitude to an adoptive country that I adored and that I felt had been maligned for sloppiness and incompetence even more than it deserved. I can't remember what incident made me first stray from that line, but after the initial crack appeared it wasn't long before the whole dam came crashing down. Once you've let your eyebrows arch during a patient's story it's a slippery slope to gently suggesting aloud that there might be issues with the other doc's treatment to snorting at his prescriptions to saying he was an ignorant fool to— in fits of frustration—dissing the entire lot of 'em.

Lengthy immersion in the Italian sea has also bleached away my respect for the inviolability of another doc's professional relationships. More than I'd care to admit, I've gone native. I have been shocked to hear phrases spill from my lips ranging from, "Seeing the number of unnecessary expensive lab tests, it looks like the doc's brother-in-law owns the laboratory," to "That cardiologist doesn't seem familiar with two decades of guidelines on lowering cholesterol after a heart attack," and "You shouldn't believe any physician at that clinic—they kicked out all their experienced staff three years ago and only have docs fresh out of training." At times I've even muttered *"paese di merda,"* shit country, to Mariateresa. Other long-time expats who have awakened from their honeymoon with Italy will commiserate.

American medical solidarity seems as firm as ever. A 2012 Medscape survey asked physicians what they would do if their patient was scheduled to undergo a procedure with a colleague "whose skill you knew to be substandard." Fewer than half said they would warn the patient off.

Reporting dangerous incompetence to a supervisor or a medical board, as you might in the US, does not seem to be an option here, as I learned after discovering that a colleague often examined patients while falling-down drunk. I could find no trace of hospital peer-review committees or formal regulatory authorities, and the Medical Association apparently limited its policing to bureaucratic slip-ups.

In 2010, an Italian medical daily described a *Journal of the American Medical Association* article reporting that seventeen percent of US physicians had had direct knowledge within the past three years of impaired or incompetent colleagues. The American researchers noted with shock that only two-thirds of those seventeen percent had turned the culprit in "to the relevant authority," as demanded by the AMA Code of Ethics and many state laws. The commentator wrote, "With Italian eyes, we can't see what all the fuss is about."

11

Filthy Lucre

He Went Around in a Lamborghini but According to the Tax
Authorities He's a Total Evader
—*Il Messaggero* headline, August 5, 2014

$\mathbb{M}$y friend Annabella was showing me proudly around her country house, but when I admired the stone-crafted fireplace she
sighed. It had been hard, she said, to get the mason to accept payment in cash. "Why in cash?" "Yes, you know, my husband doesn't
pay taxes so everything has to be under the table."

That was the first I heard of the Italian tax dodger supreme,
the *evasore totale* or "total evader" who's found the final solution to
the tax problem: never file a return. Akin to living off the grid, but
without the primitivism. The idea is you're less likely to get caught
if you're flying entirely under the radar than if you simply under-
report your earnings.

Most doctors can't achieve total evader status, because of their
on-the-books day jobs in public hospitals or NHS offices, but in
their private practices they gleefully play cat and mouse with the
tax man. A doctor's receipts or *fatture* are numbered legal documents, and taxes get paid on exactly the sum of your *fatture*, no
more, no less. The fear of alienating one's physician by request-
ing a receipt used to enable whopping tax evasion. I remember

one patient many years back, a bureau chief at the United Nations' Food and Agricultural Organization, who had relentless, undiagnosed leg pain. After dozens of fruitless consultations and failed therapies I referred him to Professor T., an anesthesiology whiz. One nerve block stopped the pain—temporarily—and the giant fee didn't faze my grateful and well-insured patient. But he was never reimbursed, because Professor T. simply would not give him a receipt. I phoned to beg him personally and was told, "I'm sorry, dear colleague, but my accountant tells me I've earned too much money already this year." I proposed he scribble something on his letterhead instead of giving an official *fattura*, since my patient's international insurance company wouldn't care; no go.

Back then, in the early eighties, no physician would spontaneously offer a *fattura*, and they concocted elaborate techniques for sidestepping the occasional request. Often the secretary who took the patient's money wouldn't be authorized to give receipts, so if you wanted one you had to wait humbly until the Great Man himself had finished his office hours and then be readmitted into the doctor's scowling presence and blurt out your plea face-to-face. Many abandoned their quest rather than risk hearing "*Piùttosto non mi paghi*—if that's the way you feel about it, don't bother to pay me at all," with the implied corollary ". . . and don't bother to come back." When a Rome labor union briefly ran a tax evasion hotline for citizens to anonymously report abuses, the three most egregious offenders were bars, grocery stores, and doctors.

Insist on a receipt and the fee went up. Italians are used to this, and in their logic it's not unreasonable. They have a Value Added Tax that gets paid only if there's a receipt, so the savings get passed on to customers who pay under the table; your auto mechanic will add on the twenty-two percent VAT only if you insist on that little piece of paper. A form of petty collusion against the powers that be, like the 1960s New York cabbies who used to leave the meter off and charge less (their employers foiled them by installing pressure-sensitive seats). There's no VAT on medical visits, though, so hiking the price for someone who wants a *fattura* is pure extortion.

Glossary: *nero*

Black as in black market, i.e. off the books, unseen by the tax collector. Economists complain that they can't quantify the Italian economy since so many exchanges of goods and services never figure. Despite Herculean attempts to bring the black economy to the surface, many landlords, for instance, still write contracts for only a fraction of the real rent, taking the rest under the table in cash.

Private medicine seemed destined to stay forever in the underground economy. The *Fisco* (the Italian IRS) didn't nab doctors, since almost anyone in private practice has a good enough salary from the public system to be able to declare a plausible total income. Patients didn't care—if you weren't among the few with private insurance, why would you want a receipt? Then, in 1986, along came Bruno Visentini, a reformist economy minister who had the brilliant idea of letting citizens deduct 100 percent of their medical expenses from their taxable income. Now *that* was a trick that worked. Overnight patients began demanding receipts, secretaries received permission to disburse them, and the shadowy medical marketplace was dragged into the light of day.

Over the years the deduction has become less generous, but the culture changed to the point that nowadays I don't think any physician will outright refuse to give a patient a *fattura*. Few offer them routinely, though—and when asked the doctor's fee a secretary may politely query: "With a receipt or without?"

Many of the aspects of Italian medicine foreign patients find puzzling derive from the intricate systems used to avoid paying taxes. For a while the government was making headlines with spectacular raids on physicians' offices, padlocking filing cabinets full of medical records and then rifling through them at their leisure. Having understood that charts proved how many patients they'd seen, docs fought back. Your pediatrician has rag-tag medical equipment but a late-model computer? That's so she can carry her patient records home every night on a flash drive. Your dermatologist gives you your own chart to bring in next time? It's not to foster patient autonomy, he just hasn't upgraded yet to a computerized system (notice that his name appears nowhere on your records). The radiologist's signature is an illegible scrawl and his name isn't typed on the report? As far as the tax collector is concerned, your x-ray was never taken. The sonogram was done by one doctor but signed by another? The tax burden is being redistributed. The doctor writes nothing down at all? That way nobody can figure out how many patients he sees, even if it means starting over at every visit from your name on up.

My father was a militant atheist, who allowed a Bible in the house only if it had been lifted from a hotel room, but he was the high priest of a personal cult of Jewish ethics that treated lying and cheating as harshly as murder. (An exception proved the rule: when he urged five-year-old Susie to duck under a subway turnstile without a token I was so bewildered that I refused.) He would have turned over in his grave to know that during my first years in Italy I ran with the pack, giving receipts to only half my patients. My *fattura* rate crept up in stages until around the turn of the millennium I took the plunge and went totally legit. Whereupon, like the two-pack-a-day smoker who climbs on an abstinence high horse after he quits, I started being outraged at colleagues who kept walking on the wild side.

Most Italian patients still don't go out of their way to ask for a receipt—sometimes a true gentleman will try to block my secretary from writing one—so how many a doctor dispenses, thus how much tax he pays, is in direct proportion to his fear of being audited. That's where your *commercialista* comes in.

Glossary: *commercialista*

Accountant, accountable only to you. None of those prissy legalities that may induce a Stateside professional to squeal on you if he suspects you're cheating—an American friend once got turned in to the IRS and fined after asking her accountant a theoretical question about tax havens. The *commercialista*'s sole mission is to keep you from getting caught.

The risk of a formal audit in Italy is supposedly around one percent per year, but I've only known one person who's had the pleasure: an orthopedist colleague, who encountered in the process a rare if unwelcome demonstration of competence and zeal. A pair of *Fisco* officials combed through his desks, his computer, his *fatture*, his appointment books, his charts, his hospital's operating room schedules, his bank accounts, his receipts for everything from phone bills to syringes, and combined all the data to come up with an estimate—remarkably accurate, apparently—of what he had actually earned the last four years, the amount of taxes he had underpaid, and the fines he owed. Then they huddled with him and agreed on ten percent of the total as the amount he would give them under the table in exchange for wiping the entire investigation off the records.

Power trumps money in Italy, so it's no surprise if power relations are the deep grammar of microeconomics. Rome companies notoriously keep afloat by not settling a bill until they get sued or their tires get slashed—one office where I used to see patients put in a new AC system and a year later hadn't yet paid a penny. But Italians always, always pay their doctor, because an unpaid doctor has had his power questioned and will not forgive. The single exception I have encountered was a tubby fellow with late-blooming acne and bad breath who came into my office with a peculiar story of chest pain. He acted so oddly that Mariateresa smelled a rat when he left without paying, tried to track him down, and discovered that his name, address, phone number, and workplace were all invented. In this country only a real weirdo like him, driven by either a generalized grudge against the medical profession or a bizarre taste in sexual turn-ons, would skip out on a medical bill.

Glossary: *pezzente*

Literally, ragged person or beggar. Figuratively, cheapskate. Italians consider fussing over small change or talking about money slightly embarrassing, like children's masturbation. They find it vulgar to use monetary success as a measure of value, and baffling when Americans pass up a job that's desirable in terms of power, prestige, and enjoyment merely because it would entail a drop in salary. When a colleague attempted to lure away one of my half-time secretaries, Maura, swearing he'd hire her full time at higher pay, she answered nobly, "Dr. X, money is not the only thing in life." An Italian may not turn over the restaurant check at all, just tossing a large bill on top and pushing the lot to the far edge of the table.

Italians ask for discounts in stores, but in a doctor's office they'll hand over whatever sum is named, no questions asked—it can be difficult, in fact, to find a face-saving way to get the impoverished to accept a break. When a colleague's secretary once mistakenly asked a working-class patient for $2,000 instead of $200 he paid without a word and made it out to the sidewalk before she realized the mistake and ran after him.

> I swear by Apollo . . . to hold him who has taught me this
> art as equal to my parents and to live my life in partnership
> with him, and if he is in need of money to give him a share of
> mine.
> —The Hippocratic Oath

One day in the nineties a young surgeon, pudgy and bespectacled, insisted on coming into my office to introduce himself. I never see visitors with something to sell, but made an exception for this guy out of respect for his father, an upstanding lab director. He brought glossy handouts describing his setup at a major private hospital and an unremarkable list of the operations he performed. He boasted of a peculiar pricing policy: "We always let the referring physician set our fees, since you're the ones who know the patients best." I had heard enough, and tried to hustle him out the door. He cried petulantly, "But you haven't let me get to the most important part! The referring physician gets forty percent of my fee!"

Fee-splitting was standard procedure during my first couple of decades in Italy. Laboratories and radiologists would slip twenty or twenty-five percent of their take to the referring physician, opticians a whopping forty percent to the ophthalmologist (glasses cost a fortune in Rome). Like that first kill that initiates you into the Mafia, kickbacks bond the profession into a conspiratorial caste. Following Dr. De Feo's advice, I politely refused all offers but kept track of who made them, so if I had a down-and-out patient I could cash in my chips and ask for a discount.

Not all mutual handwashing involves money. Take the appendix. Even the best surgeon sometimes gets it wrong and takes out a healthy one—it's better to do an occasional unnecessary operation than to risk killing a patient by *not* operating on someone who needs it. In Italy, though, no appendix is innocent. Not because surgeons are better at making the diagnosis, but because they're in cahoots with their pathologists. If an organ is completely normal, the path report will read "chronic appendicitis"—a dubious disease at best—so as not to imply the surgeon operated unnecessarily.

But then, it never rains in Italian beach towns on summer weekends either, if you go by the forecasts in the papers. A Rimini city employee admitted to me that part of her job, in the interest of the tourist industry, was to doctor weather predictions in favor of sunshine.

> The surgeon's visit cost 500 euros, no receipt. It looks bad to ask a doctor who's going to lay his hands on your mother's brain for a receipt.
>
> —Letter to the glossy newsweekly *Oggi*, 2012

Mink-clad lady overheard in stationery store: "I went to Doctor X last week and was *very* satisfied. My dear, he charges 150,000 lire [a week's wages for a teacher at the time] for a consultation!" Sable-coated friend: "Well, I saw Professor Y and he made me pay 200,000 lire. He's a Chief of Medicine!" Disappointed, but with due admiration: "Ah, yes." One Italian patient refused to go back to my dentist because his prices were too low.

Not that everybody's rapacious, quite the contrary. A dermatologist friend is so squeamish about being paid that, in the days before email, he'd tell patients to phone and describe the state of their rash, instead of taking a second look in person. Some invent their fees every time, like my dry cleaner who calls back to her husband, "Remind me, how much do we charge this lady for a sweater?"

When one international civil servant brought me his colonoscopy report, I was irritated to see that a small polyp had been detected but hadn't been removed on the spot. Instead, a second colonoscopy had been scheduled to cut it out. Another unpleasant prep, another anesthesia, another risk of perforation. I figured the reason was incompetence, that the colonoscopist didn't know how to remove a polyp and wanted to bring in someone who did. A colleague in the know enlightened me: it was just a simple way to double the colonoscopist's income. The UN insurance company paid relatively little for colonoscopy, so greedy gastroenterologists would routinely do a second "operative" procedure if they had the good fortune to sight a polyp the first time around.

Doctors here may use such petty stratagems to pad their fees, but at least if you stay in a Rome private hospital you won't get outright fleeced. They will even tell you over the phone ahead of time exactly how much your stay will cost—try that one in the States. My patient Jerry, owner of the worst knee around, did. His knee was deformed when he was born, deteriorated over six decades, and received its death blow from a botched joint replacement. Several Italian orthopedists understandably turned his case down as hopeless. A little sleuthing told me that New York's Hospital for Special Surgery was the world's best for knees, and in 2012 their top surgeon agreed to take on the challenge. The next step was to get a ballpark estimate of the cost so he and his Italian insurance company could decide whether they could handle it . . . and there we ran up against a brick wall. Emails, faxes, and phone messages dropped into a black hole, as though the question were somehow indecent. I only realized a year later, from a *Time* magazine article ("Bitter Pill: Why Medical Bills Are Killing Us"), that these shenanigans were the American Way for hospitals: they conceal their charges ahead of time, sock you with outrageous sticker prices after the fact, then haggle. Only a sucker pays in full. Worse than a Moroccan souk, where in addition to all those amicable glasses of tea you get to hear an asking price and do your bargaining *before* rather than *after* agreeing to buy.

For all I know it was no different in the seventies when I was working in New York hospitals, but we trainees lived in blessed ignorance. The only billing issue to penetrate my consciousness during those years pitted Mount Sinai Hospital against an uninsured Portuguese fisherman who had cut his palm on a fin in mid-ocean and arrived in New York with a septic hand the size of a baseball glove. We medical students were spellbound watching the surgeon clean infected material from the tendons in a series of painstaking operations, thrilled to see the hand gradually shrink to normal size, and appalled that the hospital administrators came by the ward every day, pressuring Dr. Oh to discharge him. They had allowed the sailor to be admitted as a fascinating case, but charity only goes so far. This was my one glimpse of the financial wheels that were grinding away underneath while we scuttled about with the illusion of professional independence and doing good for humanity.

12

Playing Doctor

Pharmacists Play Doctor

My longtime patient Carlo, whom I've seen through everything from athlete's foot to stroke, decided to haul his paunch in for a checkup. In the two years since I last saw him, he reported having had only one medical encounter, an emergency room visit for a sprained ankle. I ask, "But what about your atrial fibrillation, your diabetes, your hypertension, your cholesterol, the plaques in your carotid arteries?" "Oh, I take care of all that myself." I raise an eyebrow. "I check my prothrombin time every few months to make sure my anticoagulant dose is OK, I check my blood sugar and blood pressure at home once a week and adjust my insulin dose and my Vasotec. The pharmacist knows me, so he never asks for a prescription."

Italian patients can play this kind of Russian roulette only because their pharmacists wield real clout, rather than being mere complements to physicians. Petitioned meekly as *"Dottore"* or *"Dottoressa,"* they will dispense advice and provide guidance to the purchase of pill boxes laughingly labeled, "Not to be sold without a doctor's prescription."

My very first prescription: I had just gotten my license and my husband strained his wrist, so I laboriously followed the instructions I'd been given and wrote a script for indomethacin, the ibuprofen of its time. The pharmacist took the prescription and brought back a box of prednisone pills (a steroid). I had a moment of disorientation, then said, "Excuse me, ma'am, you've brought me the wrong drug by mistake." She: "I know, Signorina, it's not what the doctor ordered, but the one I'm giving you is much more powerful, it will work better."

OK, that episode was a long time ago. So here are a few recent ones:

- In 2011 my patient told a pharmacist he'd be traveling to Tanzania and walked out with a box of chloroquine, a malaria preventive (prescription-only, of course) that hasn't worked in East Africa since the 1970s.
- On May 1st, 2013, I heard a pharmacist greet a well-dressed elderly man: "Here you are, on a holiday! What do you need today?" Man: "Clexane or Calciparina" (two different injectable blood-thinners, which require not just prescriptions but precise dosing). Pharmacist: "Which one?" Man: "Either one, whichever you have." Pharmacist: "I have Clexane. What dose do you want?" Man: "Oh, I don't know, one and a half, maybe two . . ." Pharmacist: "It comes as four, or six . . ." Man: "Four then." Pharmacist, "OK." Sells man Clexane.
- In 2015 I listened to a pharmacist peddling sumatriptan (Imitrex), a migraine medication that often gives nausea or dizziness and can occasionally cause heart attacks, convulsions, and strokes. "But of course there aren't any side effects. Would I give you something that had side effects?"

Some of the potentially deadly drugs I've known pharmacists to dole out for *years* without the patient ever seeing a doctor or doing any testing include methotrexate (a cancer chemotherapy and anti-arthritis drug that can zero out your blood cells and your liver function), Coumadin (an anticoagulant that can easily revert to its original calling as rat poison), interferon (an immune suppressant that can cause lupus, liver failure, and suicide), insulin (low blood sugar can kill you), and prednisone (its myriad complications can include diabetes, tuberculosis, and insanity).

In northern Italy they're more likely to insist on a prescription, and progress has been made even down here in Rome, but patients still regularly tell me their pharmacist keeps giving them meds for depression or high blood pressure or diabetes because he "knows my face," "trusts me," "is nice," or "is my friend." With friends like that . . .

Laboratories Play Doctor

> The lady doctor who did the blood test told me I should have an ultrasound examination.
>
> —A perplexed patient

In the US your doctor draws your blood, sends off the specimen, and gets the report without your having any idea who or where the laboratory is. In Italy medical labs are yet another player wielding power beyond the reach of the medical profession. By law physicians can't draw blood in their offices, and you can always walk into a lab without a prescription and choose your own tests. When the results come back a white-coated individual introduced as Doctor so-and-so, whose degree is in biology, not medicine, may warn you to watch out for your kidneys, or tell you to get a CAT scan.

Medical laboratories offer the usual Italian mixture of kindness, ingenuity, professionalism, and sloppiness. I've seen urine cultures done on samples brought from home, generating false-positive results, or discarded after only twenty-four hours, generating false-negative ones. When asked to do a glucose tolerance test, some labs have the patient consume table sugar instead of glucose, saying the glucose solution "tastes terrible"—true, but with table sugar the test is uninterpretable. A cynical endocrinologist colleague said most likely they just don't bother to stock the glucose.

Doctors Play Doctor

Where the rest of the world has technicians, Italy has physicians. It's a neurologist who clips the EEG electrodes onto your scalp, a pulmonary specialist who urges you to blow harder into the spirometer, a cardiologist who straps you up to the ECG machine;

in the US they'd just be sitting in the back room writing interpretations. This can give the patient a special sense of being cared for. But whereas the back-room cardiologist would never dream of giving the patient advice, one who attaches the leads to your arms with his own hands and forks over his report personally from across the desk may be sorely tempted to offer clinical counsel along with his findings.

And that's exactly what happens. Italians are accustomed to having a test report conclude with prescriptions for therapy, and generally take them in the spirit in which they were written: half-hearted and half-informed suggestions that rarely prompt an actual trip to the pharmacy.

This quirk, which to Italians seems entirely normal, divides Italy from the rest of the world by a yawning gulf and leaves foreigners bewildered. As one told me, after having Prilosec prescribed by an endoscopist, "I don't understand. In Australia, after you do a test you go back to your own doctor to get the treatment."

In its most benign form, inappropriate advice is part of the official test report: "Surgical consultation advised" for a tiny sonographic thyroid nodule, "Venoruton and arnica gel suggested" for a Doppler exam showing varicose veins.

One step worse are the friendly extras, diagnostic findings that the examiner tells the patient verbally but doesn't put into the report—a fatty liver, say, or an aortic aneurysm, as though the patient were more capable than his or her physician of handling an unexpected abnormality.

Still more nefarious is unwritten practical medical advice. A radiologist asked to do a pelvic sonogram slides the probe northward and tells the patient, without writing anything down, that she has stones in her gallbladder and really should go see a surgeon.

Worst of all is the Magical Materializing Prescription, pulled from the hat of a doctor who's asked to perform a diagnostic test but instead blithely dispenses treatment. I've had patients with abnormal chest x-rays walk out of the radiology department with scripts for antibiotics. "Angiologists," veins-and-arteries specialists, are other major offenders. One of my patients emerged from an examination of her leg veins with a report saying, "Normal and unchanged from previous study" and a prescription for "Ten sessions of lymphatic drainage and four sessions of acoustic muscular modulator therapy"—acoustic muscular modulator machines being this guy's personal invention.

Such pranks not only undermine the patient's relationship with the referring physician, especially when opinions clash, but can escalate into assault and battery. One radiologist interpreted the mammogram of a Swedish patient of mine as showing a suspicious calcification, performed a needle biopsy on the spot, gave her a report a week later saying it was cancer, and referred her to the surgeon down the hall to plan a definitive operation. At which point it occurred to the terrified patient that something might possibly be fishy, and she phoned me to get directed to a surgeon I trusted. He proceeded to remove what turned out to be . . . normal breast tissue. I encouraged her to try to get her hands on the slide that had been misreported as cancerous—honest error or fraud?—but she was so shaken that she preferred to put the whole episode behind her.

Professionalism

To err is human. From my training years in New York I remember a kidney biopsy that got interpreted, over the signature of Mount Sinai's distinguished head pathologist Dr. Hans Popper, as "Chronic glomerulonephritis and chronic active hepatitis," i.e. the biopsy needle had been pushed in too far and had picked up a sample of liver. I remember the man who walked into the Morrisania Hospital Emergency Room, told the clerk he'd been shot in the heart, and was sent to wait his turn on a bench, where he toppled over dead. I remember a wrong leg being amputated, a heart fatally punctured by a chest tube, and a cardiac surgeon who earned the wicked nickname of "Butterfingers" by dissecting out a piece of leg vein and dropping it on the floor.

What knocks the ground out from under my feet here in Rome

are not the mistakes, but the lapses in medical professionalism. Proudly labeled *deontologia*, it seems honored as much in the breach as in the observance. It's friendliness that moves the sonographer to tell the patient a finding that she doesn't write down, kindness that makes the liver pathologist write a falsely optimistic finding on the report, collegiality that drives the pathologist to write "chronic appendicitis" to cover for a surgeon who's removed a normal organ—laudable motivations all, but outside the *bel paese* these expressions of them are, as far as I know, not found in medicine.

A young American woman who'd come to Rome for a vacation, then muddled on for ten years giving English lessons, told me about the one time she'd needed a doctor. She was broke, had no insurance, and didn't know that Italian emergency rooms see you gratis, but being resourceful tracked down a "clinic for foreigners" in the National Health System. When she got to the front of the line the nice lady at the desk told her she was sorry, but the clinic doctors couldn't see Americans, every other kind of foreigner but not Americans, because the United States refused to see impoverished foreigners for free and Italy returned the favor. My young woman burst into tears and said, "What can I do? I have this terrible burning when I pee and I have to see a doctor and get some medicine." Whereupon the nice lady at the desk, the secretary, wrote down the name of an antibiotic on a leaf of clinic stationery, scrawled an illegible signature, and said here, bring this to the pharmacy and take the pills, you'll get better. And she did.

It took me decades to put my finger on what's wrong with that cute story, which is the same thing that's wrong with many ugly stories: it reveals that the physician's professional role has gone so moth-eaten here that not even the secretary of a medical clinic respects it. In the US, or elsewhere, the receptionist might possibly have slipped off to plead with the doctor for special dispensation from the rules, but would never in her wildest dreams have considered writing a prescription herself.

Neither of the universal cornerstones of professionalism—uniform training and standardized performance—are strong suits in

Rome. Each of my hairdresser's assistants has her own method of doing a perm, and each rep at a call center will give you a different answer. Medical professionalism includes an additional cornerstone: a doctor-patient contract that's as indissoluble as a Catholic marriage. When we take someone on as a client, we're implicitly shouldering responsibility until death or retirement do us part. Which is why, as I see it, the lines need to be sharply drawn. Practitioners who have not signed up for a formal relationship shouldn't be tossing out advice to patients, and docs who have accepted that responsibility shouldn't be taking off on vacation without arranging backup. Or am I just a hopeless stick-in-the-mud, too rigid to carry off the brilliant balancing act of pure Italian improvisation?

13

Sex in My Office

On first hearing the facts of life I imagined my parents had performed exactly two acts of coitus, in the bathroom somewhere among the hygienic fixtures, once to make me and once to make my little brother. As a medical student I bought into a similarly sanitized narrative: the doctor's office as hallowed ground where the patient's body is stripped of sexual connotations along with its clothes, and where sex reverts to the "the penis is inserted into the vagina" neutrality that it had for me at age five.

This myth was shattered the first time I performed a pelvic exam. Nowadays American medical students are usually taught on paid models, but my own initiation involved a slender sixteen-year-old with a demure Afro who had come to the emergency room for abdominal pain. Luckily for both of us, the resident instructing me that day showed unusual respect for her youth and her lack of gynecological experience—he drew the curtain, spoke gently, and handled her with delicacy. (A more typical and more brutal gyn resident once told me pelvics were useless, since women always tensed up their muscles when he examined them.) But the very humanity of the encounter left me undefended for my reaction when my turn came. The patient trustingly reopened her legs on the examining table and I was so bowled over by her magnetic, earthy odor that I took a small involuntary step backward before getting hold of myself and going on with my lesson. The objectification had failed: I was in a room with a beautiful woman, being admitted to her most intimate being, and however heterosexual I was, my training had left me utterly unprepared for the intensity, the sexuality of the encounter.

If normal genitals can throw the medical student for a loop, imagine the impact of abnormal ones. I'll never forget my first sighting of a clit ring or my first encounter with genital mutilation, an Eritrean woman all smoothed out between the legs. Equally shocking to observe that a woman's sexual parts could be beautiful—not everyone's, just as not everybody's face is beautiful. Sometimes it will happen that a woman who I know thinks of herself as unattractive happens to have a pretty vulva, and I regret there's no way of letting her know without sending her screaming out the door. I once told this over dinner to a friend who was also a patient. She responded not with amusement but with horror: "Good god, I'll never let you do a pelvic exam on me again."

Many Anglophone women, as they place their feet in the stirrups and renounce their self-protective instinct, will make a ritual declaration: "I hate pelvic examinations." An Italian is more likely to think of my reactions: "I'm sorry to put you through this, it must be so unpleasant." Then there was one fiftyish Englishwoman, years ago, who announced—smack in the middle of my examination—that the gynecological speculum turned her on. I worked to keep the shock off my face while I extracted the damned thing and withdrew to a safe distance. She went on to say with visible pride that she knew this was extremely unusual. Somehow I felt more assaulted by her sexual arousal than by the occasional man with an erection. Thinking back now, older than she was then, I'd say she was throwing down a gauntlet in the face of impending menopause.

When I was in training most of the all-male group of gynecologists who taught us seemed to have chosen the field to exorcise their hatred for women. Far from targets for seduction their clients were, as one doc told me, "all pus pots." Mount Sinai's gyn clinic patients awaited examination in a row of booths whose partitions weren't quite long enough for their whole bodies, so that what you saw as you came in the door was an array of two dozen stirruped legs and thighs and dark mandalas of pubic hair, getting smaller and smaller toward the far end of the cavernous room. It still chills me to remember another instructor's quip, in that same clinic, about the difference between a good gynecologist (gesture in the air with two fingers pointed out and thumb cocked up like a gun, which is how you do a pelvic examination) and a popular gynecologist (same gesture but rotating the thumb, as if to massage the clitoris).

The classic American pelvic examination is encased in border rituals designed to blot out any trace of intimacy by setting it off from ordinary interactions: dressing room, gown, paper-covered table, tucked sheets, a white-clad nurse who takes care of preparing the patient. The gynecologist enters to see only a vulva surmounted by an impenetrable wall of drapes, while the woman lies flat on her back staring at the ceiling. Decades ago I read someone's proposal to elevate the head of the examining table, and once I'd tried it I never looked back. The shift from supine to half-seated and eye-to-eye transforms the woman from a slab of meat into a person (with the side benefit of facilitating examination by relaxing her muscles).

Anne was almost out my office door when she stopped, turned, and asked, "By the way, can it damage you to masturbate with a carrot?" A patient with a sexual issue will often rattle on for a half-hour about his cholesterol and his stiff neck, screwing up the courage to get to his real agenda. That's why medical students are taught about the doorknob phenomenon: when the patient is already on his way and stops to say something, hear him out even if five other patients are fidgeting in your waiting room, because he's telling you why he really came.

Some talk about sex with nonchalance. I remember one college kid coolly reciting everything he and his girlfriend did in bed, their sexual fantasies, and how often each of them masturbated, with the punchline: neither gave a hoot whether they got it on or not. Sex *should* be a loaded topic. If it's not, there's something wrong.

Most doctors are nearly as ignorant about sex as anybody else, just as prudish, and just as wary of discussions on charged subjects. If you manage to project comfort and acceptance, patients can discuss even the most delicate concerns. One of my tricks is to toss a casual question into my routine with new patients, "Do you have any sexual issues you'd like to discuss?" Even if they say no, they've received permission to come back another time to talk.

Physician embarrassment can lead to major mistakes. Daniel, one of my early patients, had pain just in front of his scrotum, and I sent him off to a urologist after a quick glance. Only after prostate surgery failed to relieve his symptoms did I put Daniel into the "gynecological" position, feet up in stirrups, so I could really examine the area—and discover the obvious cancer growing at the base of his penis. That experience cured me of examination shyness . . . The only thing that can be said in my defense is that the urologist missed it too.

Only once have I been asked for a certificate of virginity.

Venereal disease used to be rampant among my world-wandering clientele, and I got so good at making the diagnosis patients would think I had a crystal ball hidden behind my desk. It's easy: if a man sits down, looks from one corner to another, and doesn't open his mouth, it's time for a politer version of "So which is it, hemorrhoids or the clap?" One guy who returned from a business trip with an itch and proved to be crawling with critters drew himself up in outrage at the diagnosis: "Impossible, I only had sex with one woman over there and she couldn't have had crabs, she was staying at the Hilton."

We're in the safe sex era now, so I see fewer sexually transmitted infections. The bogeymen of herpes and AIDS have scared my American college kids into (mostly) using condoms and my international civil servants into (mostly) skirting Third-World bordellos. But disease phobia persists. I had a patient named Marcello, an Italian physician, who once had chlamydia and couldn't be convinced he had shaken it, no matter how many tests came out negative. After a year of his haunting my waiting room I finally caught on: this guy wasn't cautious, he was nuts.

A proper sexual history can sometimes solve a puzzling diagnostic problem. Young American woman with strange red spots on the roof of her mouth. I ask, "Any idea where they could have come from?" She shakes her head. I think a second, then ask, "Did you happen to have oral sex with a man the night before they appeared?" She nods. "Would you say it was particularly vigorous?" She nods. Guess she didn't want to seem too forward, the way a teenager won't take the Pill because that would seem like she was planning on getting laid. Another time a man asked me about a pale, thickened patch under his tongue. I'd have never figured out the diagnosis was repeated trauma if he hadn't volunteered that he regularly used that particular area to perform cunnilingus.

One man came in with soreness at the base of the penis. He denied everything: no heavy session with his wife, no other women, no trauma. Normal examination. Me: "Well, I don't know what to make of it, since you are sure you didn't do anything out of the ordinary . . ." Him: "Well I did actually buy a kind of sex toy and was trying it out a little yesterday by myself." When I raised my eyebrows, he laid on the desk an orange rubber whatsit whose name I understood later to be cock ring.

But my gold medal game of medical Twenty Questions involved a British businessman with the world's worst case of urethritis. Screams of pain came from inside the bathroom as he worked on producing a urine specimen, and the one drop he managed was pure pus. The picture was classic for venereal disease, but he was fresh from four weeks on a Greek island, cloistered twenty-four hours a day with his wife. I grilled him about local girls, local boys, sex toys, exposure to chemical products, but all he could suggest was maybe the Ionian Sea was polluted. He pleaded not to be catheterized, so I sent a sample to the lab, sent him home with painkillers and antibiotics to cover every known infection, and phoned all the specialists I could think of. When my patient called as instructed a few hours later I admitted, "Not many new ideas. One dermatologist did tell me about a case he'd read about, a man who had gotten urethritis from masturbating in a bubble bath . . ." He broke in: "That's it!" Turned out the symptoms had begun two hours after he had masturbated using body shampoo as a lubricant, straight from the tube. If I hadn't more or less spelled it out, he'd have never confessed. Later that day, when I reported back to two of the Italian male colleagues I had consulted by phone, each of them separately asked, "What BRAND of shampoo?"

Once it was the other way around—the general medical history was the key to a puzzling gynecological problem. A thirty-five-year-old woman began to have migraines after every orgasm, so severe that she needed testing to be sure it wasn't something dangerous. A year later she came in complaining of aching in the pelvic area. A gynecologist who didn't know her history would never have thought to ask, as I did, "You're holding back your orgasm, aren't you?"

> A father and son are in a car accident. The father dies, and the son is taken to the hospital. The surgeon, on entering the operating theater and seeing the patient, turns white and says, "I cannot operate on this boy. He is my son." How is this possible?
>
> Answer: The surgeon is his mother.
>
> —Brain-teaser, *so* twentieth-century

In my time, the instruments they used to keep women out of medicine were breathtakingly blunt. The MCAT asked guy stuff, like whether flashlight batteries were AA, A, B, C, or D. Med school interviews featured easy quizzes on female candidates' procreative ambitions ("Planning on having children while you're in medical training?").

If you did get into medical school, you found yourself in a boys' club. For us trepidatious trail-blazers in the early seventies, our instructors' crude sexism was both infuriating and distressing. Our lecturer on the anatomy of the breast peppered his slides with images of overendowed Playmates; when one of my female classmates complained about it to a psychiatrist, he asked, "And how large are YOUR breasts?" We heard from our endocrinology teacher that hairs around a woman's nipples meant a hormonal disorder (guess his girlfriends plucked theirs) and from our gynecology teacher that menstrual cramps were a sign of neurosis. Our urology lecturer told us women were anatomically inferior because we have to bear down to start the flow of urine whereas men can just unzip, point it, and gush.

As graduation drew near, we found that our well-meaning teachers were trying to keep weaker students from doing too much damage by steering them into the "harmless" fields of pathology, psychiatry, and . . . gynecology.

Occasionally the locker-room atmosphere could be amusing. No one could forget the twelve cranial nerves—olfactory, optic, oculomotor, trochlear, trigeminal, abducens, facial, auditory, glossopharyngeal, vagus, accessory, and hypoglossal—after memorizing them using the time-honored mnemonic: "Oh oh oh to touch and feel a girl's vagina approaches heaven."

I'm sure all this falderal disappeared once the percentage of female medical students passed a critical level . . .

Contrary to some people's dire predictions, my gender hasn't held back my career, maybe not despite but *because* of moving to Italy—in the 1980s the speaker of the house was Nilde Iotti, the best known astrophysicist was Margherita Hack, and the latest Nobel laureate in medicine was Rita Levi-Montalcini. Other aspects of Italians' notorious machismo can be more apparent than real as well; in a country where calling someone a *frocio*, a faggot, was an invitation to a knifing, the post of prime minister had, when I arrived here, recently been held by Emilio Colombo, widely considered a closeted gay man.

As a foreign female internist in private practice I was an exotic anomaly, which helped. By now more than half of Italian doctors under forty-five are women, a higher percentage than in the States, but a disproportionate number of them aren't working, and many of the rest push pencils—one friend screens disability applications—or eke out a living as overqualified technicians. Women physicians who do treat patients mostly stick to the beaten paths of psychiatry, pediatrics, or dermatology, while sidestepping surgery, orthopedics, and God forbid urology. Many female clinicians assist their Chiefs in private practice, but few strike out on their own, and most of the numerous female gynecologists don't perform surgery. One colleague told me when she became a university hospital *aiuto* or associate professor, "For a woman, *aiuto* is the top—you'll never be made *primario*."

Back in the 1980s I had a lemon of a washing machine. The drop-dead gorgeous mechanic who came whenever it broke down always acted stiff and wary in my presence, like a beast fearing a trap. One time, though, a girlfriend was visiting, and he instantly became easy-going and teasing. When a plumber invades a housewife's space to fix her sink, the kitchen air tingles, so universal, undiscriminating, and impelling is the sex drive assumed to be. The two circle around each other at a distance, avoiding the jokey flirtatiousness usual for interactions between Italian men and women but taboo in a situation where all really could be possible.

An Italian man won't follow a woman into an otherwise empty elevator without asking her permission first (*"Posso?"*), just one step short of Turkey, where apparently a man and a woman who have been together alone are presumed to have had intercourse.

Traditional Italy was two worlds, one male and one female, intersecting chiefly under the influence of the sex drive. Passing through a village you would see men, nothing but men, sitting on benches or standing on the corner according to their age, watching life go by. The women would be indoors with their sisters-in-law, female cousins, and neighbors' wives, rolling out the pasta and chewing the fat.

Though being left unattended with a woman may leave a man ill at ease for lack of his usual courtship dance, he's still ordinarily the one holding the reins. In a female physician's office the tables are turned, and the woman is in charge—enough to make a fellow lose his mojo. When I set up shop, a Roman colleague warned that no Italian man would ever darken my office door. He was wrong: about twenty-five percent of my patients are men, about par for the course in a practice that includes office gynecology. But in my early years the Italian men were mostly dragged in by foreign wives, and it could be exhausting to deal with guys there under duress who brought their lifelong habit of lording it over women.

I think even some of my fellow-countrymen consult me only because they feel duty-bound to consult the only genuwine Amurrican doc in town. They may recite their symptoms through clenched teeth, but at least they've chosen their own fate, and stick out the visit. Back when I was working at the Martin Luther King Clinic in the South Bronx, one guy assigned to me walked into the room, took a look, and walked right back out, calling, "Ain't no lady doctor laying a hand on me!"

In the 1980s, a New York colleague told me the story of a man who came to her hospital's emergency room with fainting spells and was admitted. Per protocol, when he hit the ward the first person to take his history and do a physical examination was a medical student, who happened to be a woman. Then came the intern; her history and physical were more focused but just as thorough. He patiently fielded the few pointed questions and brief examination of the female second-year resident who came next. When my friend, who as chief resident was the head of the medical team, poked her head in to check that things were going smoothly, he said, "Yes, ma'am, everything is just fine. *Now* do I get to see the doctor?"

During my training years in the Bronx, I remember a junkie who passed out drunk while waiting on line for his methadone, got stripped stark naked by the Morrisania ER staff for his workup, was diagnosed as needing to sleep it off, had a sheet tossed over him to preserve his modesty, woke up a half-hour later, looked around, saw he was surrounded by female personnel including yours truly, grinned, and . . . tore off the sheet to expose his limp penis.

One day a fellow resident received a call inviting her to moonlight by performing urological examinations for an insurance company. Never spit on a few extra bucks. In order to ascertain her competence, a representative of the company had her meet him at Montefiore hospital where, wearing her whites, she duly palmed his testicles and palpated his prostate. He explained that the complete urological examination involved confirmation of the organs' functional capacities, and proceeded to manipulate his member. After ejaculating under her attentive gaze, he handed her an appropriate fee in cash and promised numerous clients would be forthcoming. It was only after another couple of months passed without word from him that she realized she had been had.

The men who have the hardest time with a woman physician are probably Latin Americans, but I've examined so few that I'm a poor judge. One was tricked by a co-worker into thinking I was a man (she had fiendishly talked me up in French, since "le médecin" covers both sexes); when he was ushered in he froze in the doorway, incapable of stepping forward or backward. Arabs behave with greater aplomb, at least the ones who choose to see me. The easiest male patients are the English, who don't seem to notice.

At first I was afraid I would be constantly assailed by passes I couldn't handle. Back then, if you went to the movies alone in Rome some guy was sure to sit down next to you and let his hands wander. Once when my husband was away I tried anyway, barricading the seats on either side. Halfway through the film an arm dropped from the row *behind* me, landing ever so casually on my breast.

As far as my office practice was concerned, it was wasted anxiety. It turns out that female doctors are not sex objects for their patients, much less archetypal ones like nurses. An occasional disturbed man may act flirtatious, but that's easy to ignore. The single exception I've encountered was when a well-known Rome intellectual reached up from the exam table while I was listening to his heart, and squeezed my butt. Grotesque, from a man stretched out helpless and nearly naked on my chopping block. I later found out this particular individual habitually felt women up on crowded buses—the famous *mano morta* or dead hand—and I was pleased to learn eventually from his wife that his real sex life was pathetic.

The last act of one diplomat at his final visit before heading to his next posting was to come around my desk and plant a kiss on my lips, saying, "I've been wanting to do that for three years." I'd never felt any erotic tension during our professional relationship, but in the event, to be perfectly honest, I didn't mind.

Once male patients are in, they keep coming back. "Physician" trumps "female," men are used to confiding in women, and, besides, the slimmer the finger the easier the prostate exam. How about women, do they prefer female doctors? Many do, but one shouldn't generalize—the only woman gynecologist I ever personally consulted had Chinese-red, lacquered, needle-sharp fingernails.

It sometimes seems that Catholic monks and priests consult me disproportionately for maladies located between the waist and the knees. One will seek help in suppressing erections or infatuations, another express the fear that a rash might mean years-old indiscretions come back to haunt him; the challenges presented by their celibacy can be interesting and even moving. A monk about to leave as a missionary to Africa came in to discuss his terror of the imagined temptations ahead—bare-breasted women, boys asking advice about sex. While all medical encounters carry a tinge of intimacy, a celibate man with few chances for legitimate tenderness may be particularly grateful for the chance to receive the nonjudgmental attention and professional touch of a woman.

It can be risky. An elderly and dignified religious brother once sat on my examination table in tense expectation with a blue cotton patient gown knotted around his neck. On feeling the first tap of my fingers on the back of his lungs, he ejaculated. For ten seconds, as the stain spread on his gown, I stood paralyzed in a jumble of shock, embarrassment, pity, guilt, and amusement, before mumbling something and taking flight. Some kind of sexual misconduct seemed to have taken place, but who was the abused and who the abuser?

Pelvic congestion, the nagging ache in and behind the scrotum that teenagers call blue balls, is unsurprisingly common among monks and priests. I prescribe the key component in the treatment protocol, frequent ejaculation, as professionally as possible. Though I usually refrain from checking up on their compliance, I had to break that rule with my worst case, a priest who came back stolidly week after week for prostatic massage but never improved. He was taking his medications and doing his hot baths but—I had to ask—could not betray his vows by masturbating. The visit where I suggested he discuss the issue with his confessor was the last time I saw him.

Some Catholic religious observe celibacy lite, as I discovered in the early years of AIDS. At the time I would beat around the bush in inquiring about risk factors, simply asking whether the patient was "sexually active." One Massachusetts monk answered no. Three months later, after a trip home, he came in with secondary syphilis he had gotten from the man he shacked up with on weekends. I asked, surprised, "Didn't you say you weren't sexually active?" Reply: "Well, honey, I don't hang out in the bathhouses any more." From that day my standard question about risk factors for AIDS became brutally explicit.

I was perplexed to learn that the foreskin often gets snipped off young priests and monks in hopes of curbing their sexual desire. Coming from a country where newborn circumcision was common I could guarantee the hopes were vain, but on the other hand I lacked expertise in penises *au naturel*. A young monk once asked me whether it was normal if his foreskin didn't retract fully when his penis was erect. I reassured him that it was—then ran off to the hospital to check with my male colleagues. They all roared with laughter and informed me the foreskin always started out that way, that to get it to retract you had to put in a lot of work . . .

Nuns, too, sometimes get cut. Until recently many orders had all their novices surgically deflowered, then subjected to yearly Pap smears, an exercise not just humiliating, but useless. Even in the Dark Ages when I was studying medicine we had caught on that cervical cancer was a sexually transmitted disease, though we didn't yet know to blame human papillomavirus. Telling a celibate woman she can stop having gynecological exams is a guaranteed gift of joy.

One day during my training in the Martin Luther King clinic, a fellow resident came over from his office to ask, "Hey, Susan, what do you prescribe to men who come in for impotence?" I was floored. "Men who come in for impotence? Never saw any." When it came to male sexual issues, I must have radiated discomfort.

In my early Rome years some did dare complain of erectile dysfunction, but the visit was inevitably awkward. I vividly remember trying to measure the blood pressure in the penis of one victim, sure he could see I was red from the neck up as I bent over his body in a parody of sexual intimacy, sweating so hard I couldn't fasten the tiny cuff.

One day a young military man, in a whisper just this side of inaudible, sat staring into the corner, confessing his relationship with a rubber doll. All of a sudden he leapt up, cried, "There you are in your miniskirt and those sexy boots and I can't stand it!" and rushed out of the office never to return. I never wore *that* outfit to work again.

Then I hit The Hill. Living in Italy, I had learned to field calls of "Hey, gorgeous" on the street, slip my buttocks out of range of wandering hands on the bus, and ignore the guy touching himself under the next tree while I picnicked with a girlfriend in Villa Borghese. Until age forty-three, when I abruptly found myself wrapped, practically from one day to the next, in a cloak of invisibility. No more catcalls, no more gropers, no more flirtatious looks or even once-overs—I had stopped being an object of interest to the Italian male gaze.

I reacted, like most, with relief tempered by outrage. The mirror told me, aided perhaps by the aging of my visual acuity, that I looked better than ever, and women in their forties have been proven scientifically to be at the height of their sexual functioning. Science does not, however, impress the aspiring Casanova.

Professionally, there was a silver lining. Once considered beyond the flirtation game, neither a babe to conquer nor a Circe to fear, a woman is the ideal ear for men's sexual problems. My psychologist mother added "sex therapist" to her card when she reached middle age, long before Dr. Ruth Westheimer founded her famous call-in radio show. When I reached that first stage of cronehood I was rewarded by male patients starting to ask me about everything from whether it was okay to masturbate through their pants to how to stuff it in following a prostatectomy.

When I passed fifty it was the women who noticed. Women coping with menopause will tell any old doctor about their hot flashes, but when it comes to sex being, as one patient said, "just not what it used to be," they sense that only a woman their age will get it. Members of my own American second-wave-feminist cohort were particularly thrown if their libido took a dive, as happens to half of menopausal women—nobody mentioned *that* in our consciousness-raising groups. My brochure "Sexual Issues in the Menopause" now has pride of place in my desk display, alongside "Tip Sheet for Future Ex Smokers" and "Taking It Off and Keeping It Off." I have the impression that Italian women are more accepting about losing their sex drive along with their periods—perhaps because the Catholic church binds sex so firmly with procreation?—but more embarrassed talking about it.

Evolution may have known what she was doing in engineering women to lose interest in sex after menopause: frustrated males who turn us in for a younger model can continue to make babies. This may be great for propagating humankind, but it sure wreaks havoc on relationships. I've considered it my sisterly duty to become an expert at fighting Mother Nature's species boosterism by helping women keep their sex life going if they so desire—using lubricants from spit to Astroglide, vaginal hormones from Vagifem to Estring, individualized recipes of pills and patches, libido-building hormones and pseudo-hormones, pornography, bedroom tips, and a healthy dose of good humor.

American and English women patients often have the impression they're getting propositioned, or at least ogled, by Italian doctors. I've heard complaints about virtually all my consultants, even the least likely offenders, because the national *modus operandi* leaves room for misunderstanding.

Italian medicine builds few of those bulwarks against positive-to-negative electricity that set off American physician encounters from everyday intimacy. No chaperones, no drapes, no gowns, rarely even a separate exam space. Some Italian docs consider it normal to tell a woman, "Strip!" and settle back to watch the show. Or chivalrous to comment (I'm quoting my patients here), "You have a body like a statue," or "I *love* the breasts of a nursing woman, so *big!*" Leaving the clothes on can be nearly as bad. A cardiologist may undo a button on a woman's blouse and slide in his stethoscope hand like a boy in a dark movie theater. Gynecologists commonly have their patient take off her underpants and hike up her skirt, lovers' lane style; I was personally examined by one who additionally turned the lights down low and piped in mood music.

(Prurience and puritanism are two sides of the same coin. In my time at Mount Sinai there was a chief of surgery who observed that the bosoms of women in the intensive care unit were always being publicly bared for purposes of examinations, ECGs, or cardiopulmonary resuscitation. Solicitous for his patients' modesty, he devised and enforced a novel solution: Band-Aids over the nipples.)

I find the ritual trappings helpful. I'll have a patient climb onto the examining table even if it's just to look at his hand, and I'll always offer a gown. After thirty years of ordering examination gowns from the States, I was delighted to sight a stack in an Italian medical supplies store, and grabbed up a half-dozen. They turned out to be designed for a dwarf orangutan: cut plenty wide but so short the crucial organs risked hanging out, with sleeves as small around as a child's arms. Someone without sartorial skills must have been trying to reinvent the patient gown from scratch after watching *Grey's Anatomy*—as my husband says every time a bold and ill-conceived project falls through, "Italians are dreamers."

To keep sex out of the office, appropriateness of body contact is as crucial as the professional setting. Medical touch is a learned skill: firm, aseptic, but tinged with humanity, walking a tightrope between brutality and Eros to make our space safe for patients.

The only time I heard it mentioned in medical school was when my classmates and I were learning to look at each other's retinas through an ophthalmoscope and I had trouble holding the instrument steady. The instructor said wisely: "Remember, Susan, you're a doctor now. This patient may eventually need to trust you with his nakedness. It's OK for you to put your hand on his shoulder—it may even be reassuring."

One of my nonmedical sidelines is watsu, a form of body work performed in warm water, and I know how different the healing touch I use in watsu is from what I use with my patients. The physician's reassurance is negative—"Your body does not disgust me, I accept it," the watsuer's positive—"Your body is a treasure, feel good in it."

I first dabbled in body work during the eighties, in a survey course that covered massage, meditation, Feldenkreis, Jacobson's progressive relaxation, and bioenergetics. As a young and naïve practicing physician I enthusiastically put what I learned into use by trying to treat the anxieties of a Polish businessman using the bioenergetic approach. My own boundaries were clear, but I didn't yet realize how powerful body-based techniques could be. At one point when my hand was resting gently on his abdomen, following the rise and fall of his breath, the patient opened his eyes and said, "Susan, I love you." End of my stint as sorcerer's apprentice.

14

Madness and Misery

The madmen of Rome are well fed and well dressed, *mamma* makes sure of that. One of them used to preside over Piazza Barberini when I had an office nearby. He wore a set of floppy toy antennae on his head, shouted insults at strollers, pulled his pants down to moon passing cars, and took the 56 bus to and from "work" every day. I sometimes rode home on the bus with him: never a word or a gesture out of place. Once Sandro Pertini, who was then President of Italy, walked through the *piazza* on his way from a Via Veneto restaurant to the presidential palace atop the Quirinal hill. When he had antennae and a bare backside wiggled at him, Pertini was incensed and ordered the man arrested. His police escort demurred, explaining that the culprit was the soul of the neighborhood and better left untouched. No arrest.

Though an occasional lunatic may be hidden away by his family, more are out there mingling with the crowds. Plus, it's perfectly respectable for an Italian to have an *esaurimento nervoso*, literally nervous exhaustion, a term that covers the gamut from momentary ennui to a full-fledged nervous breakdown. The term suggests something that might land you into a rest home in the mountains rather than a mental hospital, and is a convenient way of getting off work. A bank teller once told me without embarrassment, from behind his window, that he'd just gotten back on the job after six months off for an *esaurimento*.

On a bus passing through Piazza Venezia one winter day, I overheard two women agreeing, "How cold the poor dears must be." Turning to look, I was amused to realize the delicate souls they were talking about were the soldiers standing at attention to guard the eternal flame of the tomb of the Unknown Soldier. Newspaper articles will lament how the traffic police "have to work without a moment's rest, in barely tolerable psycho-physical conditions," or say of a cop who pulled out his gun or discovered a dead body how upset he was by the experience. For someone who comes from Ramboland it seems odd when armed men in uniform are permitted, even presumed, to have on-the-job anxieties and insecurities.

Soft hearts, too. In the certificate-collecting days that led up to my Italian medical license, I once reached an end-of-the-bus-line office at 12:10 and found an armed cop guarding the locked door while the last clients shuffled their papers at the windows inside; this particular office, the only place in Rome to get a Certificate of Existence in Life, for reasons known only to itself, closed not at the usual 12:30 but at noon. I burst into tears, and the policeman immediately unlocked the door for me. Try that one in New York.

My mother was a clinical psychologist, my father a psychiatric social worker, and dinner table conversations often featured their more interesting patients. But being raised by psychotherapists didn't mean I was on speaking terms with insanity, quite the opposite: nothing was more taboo at home. The faintest odor of irrationality hanging around a person disqualified anything he had to say, like a taint of pinkness for a McCarthyite or a touch of the tar brush for a Klansman. Being slightly mad would have been like being slightly pregnant.

During my early months working in a state mental hospital, fresh out of college, I had nightmares where the line between sanity and madness blurred over, or patients and staff took each other's places. Even awake, I managed to see a bit of myself in every patient on the ward, from the Irishman who preached to an unseen congregation in the kind of utterly unhinged language psychiatrists call word salad, to the bird-faced boy who paced the halls all day masturbating. Eventually the boundary markers got cemented back into place and the job became tolerable.

Then one day I woke up with bad menstrual cramps and my boss, the late psychiatrist Gideon Seaman, brought along a sample pill of Talwin, a brand-new, slightly altered opiate, for me to swallow while he was driving us to work. By the time we arrived at Creedmoor, I was loopy. I opened the great iron-barred door with my massive key and heard it clank behind me, locked myself in with a hint of foreboding, and proceeded to walk the corridor feeling like an automaton with zombie eyes, through the TV room full of psych patient reek, becoming more and more terrified they'd never let me out. I was about to run up to a staff member and cry, "I'm not a patient! I'm one of you!" when a thought penetrated my rewired brain: that little pink pill! I shut myself up in an office until it wore off. (Talwin eventually became notorious for triggering paranoid reactions.)

Gideon was on a modernizing mission to train the professional staff in the proper use of antipsychotic medications and the ancillary staff in running community meetings. My job was to document the clinical effect of both interventions by conducting before and after interviews with a sampling of inmates, all—it seemed—irretrievably insane. They had inhabited locked wards for an average of twelve years. Only once, outside my nightmares, did I encounter the interface where reality's grip was still in the process of being loosened. A polite, tidy new arrival in a paisley print dress answered my questions reasonably but would hesitate every few minutes and interrupt with, "Excuse me, but did you just call me a whore? No? That's all right, I didn't really think so." Three days later she had bare feet and torn buttons and looked just like all the other patients. It seemed my parents had been right: either you're crazy or you ain't, there's no straddling the edge.

After Gideon got the medical staff to start prescribing adequate doses of Stelazine and Thorazine we had the privilege of watching many patients return across the border of madness and rejoin the world, miraculously cured like the first meningitis victims saved from certain death by an injection of penicillin. The Irish preacher went from word salad to talking sense—but was very, very sad when he realized he had lost twenty years of his life to a curse from the fiend Schizophrenia.

Not all madmen are incapacitated by their demons. Some, instead, book flights to Rome. There they are surrounded by strangers who act funny and speak an incomprehensible language—great for transforming latent madness into the real thing.

A young graphic designer from Chicago arranged a job here to get away from the FBI; when she started saying the agents had caught up with her, her worried roommate called me. It was August 15th, Ferragosto, the holiest of holidays because it celebrates the Great Spirit of Vacation, when nothing, whether restaurant or psychiatrist, is open for business. So I felt no choice but to send her to a public hospital's psychiatric emergency room. She was discharged a week later, no longer raving aloud but on such low doses of medication that her voices were still telling her to kill herself.

A Kenyan lawyer, in Rome for a conference, seemed to fit the pattern. In the fancy hotel room where I was evaluating her sore throat, she told me her first impression of Europe was that it was crawling with vermin. While I contemplated whether to send her to a psychiatric ward or ship her home to her family, a mouse ran across the floor a yard from my toes.

Between my original calling as a psychotherapist, Gideon's training in interviewing and medication, and enough experience in mental hospitals to lose my fear of psychiatric patients, my practice has attracted quite a few. I thought I already knew the varieties of insanity, from Creedmoor to the characters who haunted New York emergency rooms—Aida who got ambulanced in once a week cataleptic after fighting with her husband, Texas Mary who'd haul off and swing her shopping bag at the staff. But in the shelter of my Rome office I encountered a different bunch: the near mad, the formerly mad, the closet mad, the just-one-corner-of-their-mind mad. Psychosis is probably more common than you think—it's certainly more common than I thought—and isn't my parents' all-or-nothing. A young dancer would hear voices for months after a toke of hashish but was otherwise fine, a successful professional has reached age sixty-five without his delusions being blessed with diagnoses or treatment and I'm not going to be the one to rock the boat, a hairdresser spends every winter and spring warding off fellow-workers trying to poison her but is cured for six months a year by summer vacation . . .

Many are Italians. One of the first patients to descend into my office on Via Scialoja was an impeccably-groomed matron who explained that she had chosen me to consult about her nerves because I was new in town and unlikely to know her husband, whom she named, an important figure on the Rome medical scene. I was anxious to please, but her story smelled fishy. She had just gotten off the train from France, had escaped the night before from a mental hospital, the police were after her . . . Only years later, when I met the real, life-long wife of the physician in question did I realize it had all been a fabrication.

A patient I will call Rocco originally came to me for a stomach-ache, and I fell into being his *de facto* psychiatrist. For years, with a specialist's coaching, I enjoyed the challenge of prescribing medications, exploring his bizarre take on the world, helping him negotiate its traps. Rocco went to work in a ministry every morning, lunched sociably in the cafeteria, and ate dinners cooked by a wife of twenty years who didn't know that his every move was ordered by the CIA. He was so used to hiding his psychosis that when I got him to apply for a disability pension he told the commission about his headaches but not about the voices emanating from a radio transmitter planted in his tooth. What threw him off after a decade of doing fine under my treatment was the abrupt end of the cold war, when his delusional system collapsed along with the Berlin Wall. As soon as Rocco no longer needed the CIA to protect him from the KGB, threatening voices that only he could hear returned with a vengeance, and he wound up knifing his butcher (not lethally, I'm glad to say).

Munchausen's syndrome—named for an eighteenth-century baron who embroidered fantastic adventure stories—means factitious illness, faked with the purpose of torturing doctors. Usually its practitioners choose easy conditions such as fever (thermometer under the hot water faucet) or low blood sugar (judicious self-injection of insulin). Signora L., instead, had neck pain, which she whined on about so interminably and aggressively, never letting me say a word, that to keep myself from running out the door under the assault of her diatribe I kept scribbling notes to self on her chart: "unbearable," "the worst patient ever," "I'm going nuts," "help." Five years later she showed up in my office totally transformed: polite, smiling, and succinct. It was part of a victory tour, to let me know she had finally found a doctor who had taken her seriously, and operated on the slipped disc in her neck that had been the cause of all her misery. Unfortunately now, six months later, she admitted on questioning, the pain was coming back . . . I felt such distress and guilt on seeing the neat scar on the back of her neck that I called up the neurosurgeon for some details. He screamed so loud I had to hold the phone away from my ear: "That crackpot! I curse the day I laid eyes on her! How could I have been such a fool as to let her talk me into operating on her non-existent disc disease!!!" But the deed had been done, and for the rest of her life Signora L. had a scar to wield any time she felt like tormenting a new victim.

Other mental cases were foreigners. I remember the American tourist, nicely dressed in an old-fashioned way, who showed me a dozen red pimple-sized spots on the front of her chest. After examination with a magnifying glass I pronounced them mosquito bites. She asked politely to please put that in writing for her to show her hotel manager, to aid in their ongoing discussion of whether, as she had previously suggested to him, the bumps might be the sites of hypodermic injections administered by an intruder to drug her in her sleep. She added, "They've done it to me before." Beneath the Chanel No. 5 and the pearls, she was mad as a hatter. But what could I or should I do? This was many years ago. Today, older and cursed with hubris, I might have tried some real treatment. Instead I sent her back to the hotel manager with the requested note.

Then there was the accountant who had left New York after, according to her unlikely tale, being thrown out of the Bellevue Hospital Emergency Room. She had chronic sinusitis due to a jinx by upstairs neighbors who galumphed around in wooden shoes at 4:00 a.m. just to harass her (all apartment dwellers will empathize). I prescribed antibiotics and psychiatric follow-up and considered the visit over. Nobody moved. I said kindly that it was time for her to leave. She refused to get up, or to quit talking. After another ten minutes of her unstoppable monologue I had to have her forcibly escorted to the door. Stupid me, not to have believed her story about Bellevue.

One long-time Rome resident, originally from Australia, would telephone choked by tears, sobbing that she was going to obey the voices that told her variously to stick her fingers into the electrical socket or strangle her children. Then all of a sudden she would break into a matter-of-fact voice and say, "Oh, my husband's come in, gotta run. Talk to you later!" Concerned for her children's safety, I hunted down her counselor at a suicide hot line. It turned out he had been talking with my patient several times a week for years, and begged me to believe that she'd never do any harm. I count her as my one case of Ganser's syndrome, a variant of Munchausen's where the chosen make-believe illness is psychosis.

My most difficult deranged foreigner was an ex-sailor, his brain pickled in alcohol, who had to be accompanied over to a nursing home in Denver after thirty years in Rome. Problem: how to get away with a plane trip including two stopovers, when the man's favorite activities were yelling dirty jokes and pinching all female bottoms within reach. Solution: transport him lying on a curtained-off stretcher and shoot him up with a tranquilizer every two hours. It worked fine, and since TWA puts their stretchers in First Class he made his last voyage nibbling, between catnaps, on caviar. I was so relieved when we survived our final layover in Detroit without getting bounced that the minute we hit cruising altitude I broke a prime rule of duty and toasted him in champagne.

If I want to consult a medical book from behind my desk, I reach over my shoulder. In the age of the internet the books get less attention than the bookcase itself: "MisuraEmme Tensolibreria," a narrow seven-foot tower of rust-colored steel, bent sideways into a bow shape, with a sturdy-looking metal cable strung between the top and the bottom of the decorous curve to give the illusion that the cable is pulling the ends of the bookcase together. It turns out to provide a kind of Rorschach test, inspiring reactions from scared ("That thing is not going to fall down, right?") through solicitous ("Did you know your bookcase is leaning over?") and practical ("I know a metalworker who could straighten it out") to hip ("Cool bookcase"). In a class of his own was the American writer who once sat across from me, as booze-drenched as a Baba au rhum. He squinted for a while at the structure behind me, then shook his head: "You can't fool me, doc. That thing's crooked!"

More office time than any of us imagined in medical school is spent handling emotional problems. Not just the worried well and the stress-triggered ulcers and the depressions hiding under physical symptoms, but also the purely psychological, people who could have consulted a therapist or a priest but chose you instead. I used to feel uneasy when patients came in just to talk about their misfortunes without a physical complaint as the ostensible reason for the visit—afraid, despite all my training, of being inadequate, of not knowing how to help.

One incident helped me get over that: a junior year abroad student managed to hunt down my home address and knocked on the door instead of phoning my office. She found my surprised husband Andrea alone in the apartment, who seeing her in tears courteously invited her to wait until the doctor came home and offered her a coffee as Italians do. Since he was so friendly, she began to pour out the story of a jilted love affair. After a half-hour, her tears dry, she jumped up and announced perkily that she was going. Andrea said, "But the doctor's due back any minute now." She replied, "Oh, I don't need the doctor any more, I'm all better."

During my New York residency, Andrea and I had attended a few workshops in Re-evaluation Co-Counseling, a kind of mutual aid movement whose cardinal principle is "Listening is always enough." That has probably served me better in my day-to-day work with emotional distress than anything I learned in my medical training.

One young woman from Ghana, for instance, was brought in because of depression. It was difficult to get her husband out of the room, but once that was accomplished I wormed out of her that she was depressed because her in-laws had put a spell on her. Just confiding in me and coming back a couple of times to talk lifted the depression—and maybe the spell?

I have had the fortune of receiving considerable supervision in the psychiatric side of general medicine, first (along with my colleague Vincenzo Bacci) from the German psychoanalyst Alice Ricciardi, then, less formally, over many years with English psychiatrist Harold Bourne, who in addition to case-by-case advice wisely hammered home invaluable general lessons, such as that I myself am as important a drug as any I can prescribe, my patients may feel rejected if I refer them to a psychiatrist or a therapist, I can dare to ask patients real questions, and if they ask me questions I can dare to give them real answers.

I gradually became comfortable with one-on-one counseling, but family dynamics remained beyond my skill set. When a couple would march in asking me to fix their marriage (usually one marches, the other is dragged), I'd feel ganged up on. I figured out that a pinch of common sense could sometimes treat both their marital problems and my performance anxiety. One Afghan man was planning to take his Italian wife home to Kabul, and demanded she start following his country's customs right away. I negotiated a compromise: she'd wear a hijab on the street, he'd let her smoke. They left wearing smiles, though one might predict more storms ahead.

Monks, priests, and nuns present special challenges. At first it seemed odd that they'd choose to come tell their problems to a Jewish woman, but going outside the Church hierarchy may be part of the point. I've gotten to know the dynamics and dialectics of collective religious life, where self-esteem can be crushed by a difficult relationship, or what one could call convent mobbing, and I've become pretty good at deciding whether to refer a depressed priest to an ordained psychologist, a lay therapist, or his confessor. Or to suggest one of the approaches used by a surprising number of Catholic religious to soothe their jangled nerves: yoga, quigong, Tai Chi.

An outwardly perfect Italian woman may complain of depression, or a dashing man of paralyzing anxiety, but they rarely want pills. With so many Americans demanding antidepressants and tranquilizers, I find it refreshingly difficult to talk Italians into taking either. Americans like to blame their symptoms on their genes or a "chemical imbalance," while for once it's Italians who play the moralist, the ones with the stiff upper lip, who insist they should be able to shake themselves out of it. Yes, the medicalization of misery is making inroads here as elsewhere, but still only about three percent of Italian adults are taking antidepressants, versus fourteen percent in the US (though I have known several Italian psychiatrists to advise the wife of a depressed man to slip him medication in his food).

On September 10th, 2001, I saw a patient with an unobtrusive coin-sized patch on her scalp where the hair had fallen out: alopecia areata, an unpredictable condition that, as I explained to her, might get worse, stay the same, or go away. My patient was devastated, less out of fear the condition might spread than because she saw it as a stigmatizing imperfection, a mark of Cain that would draw the attention of everyone she encountered. I spoke with her for a half-hour, trying to explore the mental habits and past experience that might be making her overreact, then sent her home with prescriptions for a medicated cream and a tranquilizer. Two weeks later she returned as I had requested. She hadn't bought the cream or the pills, and the spot was still there, but it had stopped bothering her. "Partly it was talking to you," she said. "But mostly it was the attack on the Twin Towers the next day. Compared to that, who cares about a little bald spot?"

Almost all teenagers have some melancholy . . . But that's not a reason to give them medications.

—Gustavo Pietropolli Charmet, Italian psychologist

Melancholy, yes. Sturm, Drang, and raging rebellion? In Italy, from what I see, not so much. A 2010 survey said nearly eighty percent of fifteen-year-olds found at least one of their parents "easy or very easy to talk to." I might be wrong, but that doesn't match my memories or impressions of attitude-ridden American adolescence.

At least one in every three American college students I see is on some psychiatric medication. I remember one girl with infinite lashes around wide eyes and a beauty so extreme as to be distracting, who came in complaining of anxiety, nausea, fatigue, and weight loss. Turned out her physician had prescribed the amphetamine Adderall five months earlier to help her concentrate on her studies, then added the antidepressant Zoloft and the tranquilizer Ativan when she became jumpy. When I told her all her symptoms were side effects and she cured herself by going cold turkey, that was one happy young woman.

Italians that age take lots of drugs too, but their pushers are their friends, not their doctors. Local regulations make it particularly hard for them to get their hands on stimulants, because Ritalin and its cousins have always been legally prescribed only to children and only in strictly controlled public settings. Which has made it easier for me to deal with the American college kids who come in asking for Adderall: I just say, "They don't sell it here," and help them learn to live without. But in 2015 a single Rome private psychiatrist somehow finagled permission to prescribe stimulants to adults, rendering that line sadly obsolete.

Reliable comparison statistics are hard to come by, but here's the best I've found: in 2013, 6.3% of US adolescents had taken a prescribed psychotropic drug *during the previous month*; 1.5% of Italian fifteen-year-olds had *ever* received such a prescription. Considering the difference in time scale, I'd guesstimate that American physicians prescribe psychiatric drugs to fifteen times more adolescents than Italians do. How much is that difference due to a drug-heavy medical culture? How much to an American lifestyle that drives teenagers to despair?

Two countries, two styles. In the technocratic United States, psychotherapy is increasingly dominated by cognitive behavioral therapy, while in relationship-gifted Italy, psychoanalysis still holds sway. Analysts are on a world-class level here, their ranks disproportionately heavy on Jungians, non-physicians, and aristocrats.

Otherwise, therapy in Italy is a bit catch-as-catch-can. There are licensed psychologists and psychotherapists, with degrees and practical supervision, but also plenty of unlicensed counselors—not entirely unlike the American plethora of self-styled life coaches, professional listeners, life consultants, and hypnotherapists. Italy being Italy, I'm unsurprised to hear of therapists personalizing their professional relationships by talking about their own life problems in the therapy session or hanging out afterwards over drinks. Role-bending may be particularly common with foreigners, who are fair game in Rome (where they get sold the Trevi Fountain) as in New York (where they get sold the Brooklyn Bridge). I once helped a docile schizophrenic woman, a former nurse, escape from the clutches of an Italian psychiatrist who as part of his treatment had her living in his house and sharing his bed. The Italians call that *plagio*, plagiarism, which can mean stealing either a person's words or his soul. A colleague and I escorted her personally to a Boston-bound plane.

In my years here various top Italian therapists' reputations have been clouded by charges of *plagio*. Psychiatrist Massimo Fagioli, a psychoanalytic heretic who gathered a flock of worshipful followers known punningly as *fagiolini* (green beans). Training analyst Carlo Traversa, whose habit of sleeping with his patients led the Freudian Italian Psychoanalytic Society to split in two. Aldo Carotenuto, founder of the Jungian society, expelled for the same peccadillo . . .

When an Italian is feeling stressed out he can always bypass the mental health professions altogether and just take a week or two off from work, with blessings and funding from the National Health System, to soak in hot sulfur baths in Viterbo or Saturnia. The persistence of that tradition, and of herbal sedatives such as valerian and chamomile, may be yet another reason Italian doctors are so open to non-mainstream approaches.

During the 1990s, in fact, it was an open secret that one of Rome's biggest public hospitals had on staff a psychiatrist who specialized in detecting demonic possession. Once the diagnosis was made, he'd call in a priest to perform an in-hospital exorcism. They may still be at it—in April 2016, Father Pedro Barrajon, presiding over a course in exorcism at the Pontifical University of Regina Apostolorum, told *Il Fatto Quotidiano*, "We will continue our close dialogue with the psychiatric profession."

I've witnessed one in-hospital exorcism myself, not in Italy but the Bronx. The patient's family and friends held hands in a ring around his Montefiore bed, intoning incantations against the Devil. His medical diagnosis was herpes encephalitis, 100 percent fatal at the time, so we figured why not let the family feel they'd left no stone unturned.

When it comes to psychiatric care, the United States has little to brag about. Working at Creedmoor during the great deinstitutionalization reform of the late 1960s, I was infected by the fever of enthusiasm for the marvels of antipsychotic drugs, the capacities of nursing aides transformed into group therapists, the future of long-term mental patients released into the community. The old snake-pit hospitals would close, the "out of sight, out of mind" lifetime banishment of the mentally ill would end.

They did close, and it did end, but as a denizen of the Upper West Side of Manhattan I soon had a front-row seat at the disaster that followed: masses of ex-mental patients dumped on the streets, the promised halfway homes and outpatient facilities having evaporated not long after the locked wards were emptied. Psychiatric patients, often powerless, uninsured, and low-profit, have been appallingly neglected ever since; if Obamacare's coverage parity between mental and physical illness survives, things may improve.

In 1978 came Italy's turn, with Dr. Franco Basaglia's "180 law" zeroing out long-term inpatient psychiatric care. Again the baby was thrown out with the bathwater, leaving even fewer beds than in the US, all on psychiatric wards of general hospitals, with even the briefest involuntary confinement near-impossible. The newspapers regularly describe the tragic odysseys of families seeking urgent hospitalization for their loved ones, making their pleas in one ER after another, culminating in suicide or homicide.

Deinstitutionalized mental patients have fared better here than in the US, with fewer in prison or sleeping under bridges, thanks to universal health care (Community Mental Health Centers) and, as ever, the solicitous Italian family. For a while there was even a psychiatric branch of the Guardia Medica, NHS specialists on call to calm the agitated in their own homes or escort them to the hospital, twenty-four hours a day, but, alas, it succumbed to cutbacks.

There are several for-profit psychiatric hospitals in Rome, all expensive and idiosyncratic. While your garden-variety private hospital maintains a lengthy roster of affiliated docs, encouraged to admit and treat as many of their own patients as possible, the psychiatric ones are often the private fiefdom of a single *primario* who takes over everybody's care, and can be a one-product shop: at *clinica* X patients all get old-fashioned sleep therapy, at *clinica* Y it's electroshock.

As so often in Italy, a touch of humanity can take the edge off. I once sent a manic patient with several episodes under her belt to an Italian public hospital during a phase of flagrant psychosis. She later told me she far preferred the ramshackle lice-ridden pavilion, whose staff was a bit shaky on the expertise but treated her like a person instead of a case, to the cold-blooded efficiency of an American psychiatric ward.

Colic in the Coliseum, Cystitis in the Sistine Chapel

In a practice heavy on passers-through, I've seen plenty of exotica—Dengue fever, intestinal tuberculosis—but more often it's the context rather than the disease that's out of the ordinary. Twisted ankles from navigating the cobblestones, depleted pill supplies from a purse snatching, herpes from Latin lovers, kidney stones from touring the Forum under the summer sun, and allergies that shift into high gear between mildewed apartment walls, shedding plane trees, and the parietaria plants that poke out from between Rome's ancient stones. Plus, my medical training didn't prepare me for those truly vital everyday questions such as what's the malaria situation in Bhutan, can you obtain the Pill in Japan, and is it permissible for a Muslim to let a gastroscope enter his stomach during Ramadan.

There was the traveler who stumbled out of the train station and into my office after being drugged and robbed in his couchette. The Pan Am pilot whose first face-to-face sentence, pronounced from his hotel bed, was a slurred "Sit down and have a drink." The tanked-up college student who demonstrated his perfect balance by heel-toeing along the parapet of the Garibaldi bridge but misjudged when hopping down to join his buddies and jumped off on the wrong side—luckily crash landing on the Tiber Island, a few steps from the Fatebenefratelli Emergency Room.

Even the most mundane medical condition can be complicated if the patient arrived yesterday and is leaving tomorrow. How bad a case of asthma can you fly with? Where can a woman with gonorrhea get follow-up in Vietnam? If the patient's been having diarrhea but is off on mission to Africa should I do testing now or wait until he gets back?

I have to pay special attention to vaccine histories, think parasite when something looks like irritable bowel syndrome, try to keep follow-up from slipping between the cracks—ambassadors' wives tend to fall behind on their mammograms. For elective surgery or a complicated pregnancy I'll often send patients back to their home country, not because the treatment will necessarily be any better, but so that they won't blame Italy if something goes wrong.

With newbie expatriates I've learned to tailor my routine intake questions to their national origin. For Brits: "How is your new life going?" ("I love it, of course.") For Americans: "How are you managing to adjust?" ("It was awful at first, of course, but I'm past the worst now.") Transplanted Americans suffering from Mall Withdrawal Syndrome often take advantage of their visit to ask where they can find peanut butter or extra-narrow shoes.

Then there's the bewildering medical system. Americans new in town balk at going to a laboratory to have their blood drawn, and feel a smidge naughty picking up their own results. Pharmacists dispense nearly any drug for the asking, and if you do have a prescription they may suggest scrapping it in favor of their own favorite nostrum. The only safeguard for my scripts is the conviction of a fast-shrinking minority of Americans that the doctor's word is Holy Writ. I remember once arguing with a sniffling patient: he came in asking for an antibiotic, I said he didn't need one, we squared off. I thought I'd end the discussion by remarking that if he felt that strongly about it he could go into any pharmacy and just buy whichever antibiotic he pleased. But no, it wasn't just the pills he wanted, it was my imprimatur.

opera seria
ma non troppo

15

Doctor Susan

After a freshman year of excessive studying, partying, and French fries, I went to my rotund hometown doctor complaining of exhaustion. Tweedledum tilted his hinged leather chair perilously backward, then mortified and incensed me by saying, "Of course you're tired, it's all that extra weight you're carrying around." True, I'd gone from a size ten to a size twelve, but compared to him I was positively anorectic.

My first medical encounter that wasn't one-off, hostile, or both, was one day when I was twenty-two and it hurt to pee. I knew the drill, so I headed for the UC Berkeley student health service. The luck of the draw was a thin woman doctor with dark straggly hair who instead of playing her part in the drill—doing a urine test and prescribing antibiotics—asked whether I had ever had these symptoms before. When I said five times in the past year, she wrote out instructions to take an antibiotic every night for three months, and if that didn't work to come back to get further testing. My story had gained a history! A doctor had taken the trouble to think about what might lurk beneath today's problem! And her treatment worked!

Eventually I took her as a model, aiming to always look one step deeper, but when I first opened my practice I was barely capable of handling even a case of laryngitis. After so long away from medicine and thrown completely onto my own resources, I felt like a child dressed up in a white coat. I'd try to ingratiate my patients, Zelig-like, by mirroring their behavior: shy with the shy, rigid with the rigid, chummy with teenagers. I remember asking one young patient who was being hostile what I was doing to tick her off. She considered a moment then answered, "Nothing actually. I'm just used to acting that way with doctors." Exactly like me at her age.

An office visit gone wrong with an American Embassy employee eventually pointed me in a new direction. The encounter had seemed perfectly cordial: first we quickly planned a workup for an abnormal urine test and then moved on to a few words about her obesity. I only later learned from the Embassy nurse that she had left furious with me for being so offhanded about the terrifying blood that had been found in her urine and for going on to humiliate her by bringing up her weight for no good reason. I was left feeling guilty, but perplexed as to exactly what I should have done differently.

Soon afterward I saw a United Nations staffer, a massive black woman with knee arthritis. I recited the standard advice: weight loss and an anti-inflammatory drug. She accepted the prescription but looked sour, at which point, without thinking, I blurted out, "How does my plan sound to you?" I don't recall her specific objections, but I remember the life-changing freedom I felt at being open to hearing them. Expressing uncertainty had always come easy to me, partly as a boast turned upside down: "I'm so strong and knowledgeable that I don't have to pretend to understand everything." But asking patients what they were thinking felt different, courageous, really putting myself up for grabs.

I began regularly asking patients how they felt about what I was saying, inviting them to correct me if I had gotten things wrong, pausing to take their answers into consideration, and discovered that there was an infinite peace of reassurance all around if I slid into a space of trust and mutual respect instead of living with the fear that any negativity on their part would destroy me. Now I often end examinations with a touch of show-biz, summing up what the patient has said, what I've found, and how I see the state of their health, pulling everything together if I can, listing problems and possible solutions if I can't, ending with punch lines like "So does what I've said make sense to you?" and "If my advice doesn't work, let me know." I'll bet lots of docs do the same thing.

> To err is human, but to really mess things up requires a computer.
>
> —Dr. Robert Matz, "Principles of Medicine"

While at last call my US colleagues are spending fully half their office time fiddling with Electronic Medical Records, I stick with paper. I'd rather look at my patient than my computer, I worry about privacy ("Hack of Community Health Systems Affects 4.5 Million Patients"—*New York Times* headline), I like to keep hopelessly discursive notes, and you know what they say about old dogs. Plus, every American physician I know detests them.

For years, I toyed off and on with the idea of moving to California and getting a job in a clinic. I even checked out how complicated it would be to get licensed (an outfit named Medical License Direct said give 'em $1,400 and four months and I'd be in business). What wrecked that fantasy was EMRs and their thirty-two clicks per flu shot, which are apparently driving half of US docs to contemplate throwing in the sponge. One doctor complained in the *LA Times* that after the EMR came in he saw only the back of his own internist's head. Another claimed he had seen a computer-bound ICU nurse, her back to the patient, interrupt her typing when a respiratory alarm went off only long enough to shout, "Breathe!"

Even without the distraction of an EMR, the doctor's mind may stray to her shopping list while a patient is describing a sore throat instead of listening for what might distinguish this case from the last thousand. Menopausal symptoms used to be guaranteed to shut down my attention mechanism, perhaps as an unpleasant premonition of my own future. One afternoon in 1983 a new middle-aged Australian patient who'd taken the train up from Naples, I'll call her Mary, was droning on about her irritability and facial hair, provoking daydreams of ducking out the window, until her voice broke into my consciousness with, "I'll have to start at the beginning. When I was a boy . . ." Whoah. Recalculating. As Mary continued without any prompts, looking intensely into my eyes, my mind cycled rapidly from boredom to fascination to morbid curiosity to awe for the secret she was about to place in my hands. Trying to hold her gaze, and to radiate calm and acceptance despite inward turmoil, I sat in silence as she described a carefree boyhood shattered when puberty took a bizarrely wrong path toward female curves . . .

So how did she wind up in my office telling me this astounding tale? Medical tomfoolery. She had been feeling tired, so an Italian doctor prescribed anabolic steroids—stuff weight lifters dope with. A mustache sprouted, her hairline receded, and her voice deepened, conjuring up, to her horror, the ghost of a gender she had fought forty years to forget. Learning that the symptoms were side effects, not manhood revenant, sent her out of the office filled with gratitude but also, I suspect, some regret at having revealed so much.

Neuroticism, like Barolo wine, softens with age. After thirty, people find the sharp edges of their youthful misery rounding off, their anxieties less overwhelming, their loneliness not quite so unbearable. And, for me at least, doctoring bolsters those benefits of the ticking clock. Having a front-row seat at the spectacle of life, a fly-on-the-wall view of how other people eat, defecate, make love, worry, and screw up their marriages, drives home that you aren't the center of the universe and drains the urgency from your own woes. The very act of helping others can be curative—one of my pet prescriptions for overcoming depression is to work a suicide hotline.

Practicing medicine cured me of a lifelong habit of procrastination—I have to plow through that stack of things to do *now*, or my patients will suffer. I also lost the illusion that nobody listens to me the first time a patient recited from across the desk, as revealed truth, an opinion I knew had originally come from an article of mine.

Of course doctoring is, as the Italians say, not all roses and flowers. Burnout can drive us to drink or suicide, three out of four medical trainees are said to be on uppers or downers or both, and the "impaired physician"—lush, junkie, or madman—has generated a slew of publications and even a few laws. But overwork only burnishes the image of Superdoc. I have one friend who invariably says, with maddening solicitousness and even if I'm fresh as a daisy, "You look so exhausted, Susan. I understand, poor dear, you're always working too hard."

> In the middle of the journey of our life I found myself within a dark woods where the straight way was lost.
>
> —Dante Alighieri, *The Divine Comedy: Inferno*

By our twentieth reunion, most of the Harvard-Radcliffe class of '68 said they had experienced a midlife crisis. Mine started insidiously, with a creeping sense that my practice consisted of endless repetition. Next I found myself reallocating mental energy from medicine to music, then fantasizing about moving to a hut on Bali, finally arriving at utter dissolution of the internal drive that had carried me through fifteen years of professional life. I felt demoralized, confused, indifferent.

In a psychologically-oriented practice like my own, a little demotivation goes a long way towards bringing down the whole shebang. It requires a special kind of concentration to catch the fleeting clue, the word a patient wishes you would pick up or the unconscious gesture that inadvertently reveals what's really going on. The moment you pinpoint the key piece of history, or put an angry or anxious patient at his ease, the easing of the tension in the room is as palpable as the tug of a fish on the hook. When the spark from my own unconscious faded during my midlife crisis, doctoring became flat and meaningless, reduced to the brain-death of prescribing Actifed for colds and Flagyl for vaginitis.

I went off on a slow-paced country vacation. One day I was sitting and reading, with Tom Waits in my ears, and, suddenly, saw myself from the outside paralyzed forever in that chair. Something cracked, my motivation mysteriously rebooted, and the next morning I felt ready to start anew.

One of my first patients back in Rome was a girl who planted herself in the waiting room without an appointment and refused to leave. I squeezed her in using a colleague's examining room. It turned out she had lost her virginity a week earlier, and the guy had given her gonorrhea. There was something about her plight that touched me, and for the first time I felt my heart open to a patient without covertly seeking admiration or gratitude. The devotion of the country doc, which as a modern technocrat I had dismissed long ago as paternalism, crept in through a back door; I started caring about my patients.

I remember an elegant dark-skinned housewife. Turning down her gown I discovered a mosaic of color, an entire body decorated with the pink-and-brown of vitiligo. Hopkins's poem "Pied Beauty" came to mind as I admired her dappled body and saw the beauty of her differentness. For her, of course, it was a defect to be hidden. Likewise the adorable little extra breast that appeared under one young girl's armpit when she raised her arm, the velvety black mole that covered half of a boy's forearm. You couldn't blame them for wanting to have their special marks obliterated, to join the common herd, but I started seeing those stigmata as I would the scars and freckles on a lover's body. It was always hard to know how to respond, though: silence might fuel their shame, estheticizing might violate our intimacy, commiseration might verge on betrayal.

I rarely dislike a patient, even one I'd take a distinct aversion to if we were introduced at a cocktail party. Listening empathically to someone's problems, the fears and weaknesses beneath his or her social mask, the vulnerable underbelly, makes even the hardest-boiled sympathetic. With some patients there is a deeper connection, and for a few I would use the word love. I love Mrs. R., whom I have communicated with at least once a month since 1981, in person or on the phone or by email, about everything from vomiting blood to how to raise her children. I love Amy L., whose career and romantic oscillations I have followed for thirty years along with her asthma. I love Father M., whose hormones I have been balancing for fifteen years since his surgery for a brain tumor. I love Signor P., Ativan addiction and all. I loved Mrs. B., who had lost two breasts to cancer years before, as she courageously fought her last doomed campaign.

I feel special affection for the widows and old maids who come in every few months to recite a litany of cramps and stomachaches and dizzy spells that varies only slightly at every visit. They used to leave me frustrated. Now, as the decades pass and more of my patients enter that phase of their lives, their social circles shrinking with age, and as I see old age threatening on the horizon of my own life, I understand why they come: less for a cure than for a listen.

Actions that save lives are part of our routine, but most of them don't count. A guy has pneumonia, you prescribe an antibiotic, he survives, ho hum, any medical student could do just as well, probably the barista at your local Starbucks too. I can count on my fingers the people who stayed alive because I *really* went the extra mile to get them diagnosed and treated, and I can list their diseases from memory: meningitis, leukemia, Hodgkin's disease, non-Hodgkin's lymphoma, encephalitis, carcinoid tumor, myeloma, cerebral arterio-venous malformation. (I've asked a few colleagues my age, and each came up with a similar number.) Between me and each of those patients persists another kind of special bond and, I suspect, an unspoken assumption that I will always be there for them above and beyond the call of duty.

No therapeutic success, however, can cancel the blow to self-esteem that comes from failures. For physicians, the survivor's guilt that follows all deaths is magnified by the injury to our professional omnipotence—and that same injury gets repeated, writ small, in daily practice. A patient gets worse instead of better, a medication gives awful side effects, a family turns its frustration against you . . . If you learn to absorb it all without wilting, are you becoming mature or just thick-skinned?

My medical training in New York didn't just neglect empathy, it positively discouraged it. We despised our patients' self-destructive behavior and, when we already had twenty others to take care of on the ward, resented them for coming to the emergency room.

Emotional distance was easy. We were young and they were old, we were almost all white and they were almost all black, we were fit and sharp and they were frail, senile, or both. Occasionally a patient's humanity would break through: a spry, wizened Southerner who had been kicked by a horse in the pre-antibiotic era, gotten tetanus, and miraculously survived; a nice lady who came in with a simple heart attack and the next morning woke up paralyzed and mute having had a stroke during the night. After I left the US, the AIDS epidemic shifted the mean age on the wards downward and medical schools became marginally more diverse, so my younger colleagues may be less impervious to their patients' suffering.

There's an arc of caring in medicine. As a beginning student, you're a layperson with normal human reactions, sympathizing with every patient. Medical training burns it out of you until you reach the separation necessary to start being a professional. Eventually, with any luck, compassion takes over again.

Compassion and annoyance are potentially two sides of the same coin of engagement, and having intimate encounters with a dozen people a day could be a challenge for a quick-tempered person like myself. In fact, oddly enough, those interchanges rarely ignite my short fuse. I might feel anxious when faced with a sarcastic patient, inadequate with an excessively well-informed one, helpless with one who shows up every month to report that my latest treatment has only made her worse . . . but never angry.

(What, never? Well, hardly ever! There is one patient I have never forgiven. Three days after my mother died he insisted on maintaining his appointment for a routine checkup, shrugging to my secretary who called trying to cancel it, "We all have our problems.")

Only one class of patient regularly ticked me off: my Social

Security Administration examinees. I would be irked by their transparent prevarications, their innocent exaggerations, their unlikely limps, their winces at a hand laid on their shoulder. Much as I hate to admit it, I believe the reason I felt irritated with these poor supplicants, as I never was in the face of frank hostility or arrogance from regular patients, was that with the disability applicants I was fully in charge and didn't have to answer to them in any way. Lord Acton said absolute power corrupts absolutely, and this was as close as I would ever come to the power of, say, the Italian *padre padrone* who lords it over his wife and kids. With my paying customers it was different—I was in the driver's seat, but only as their chauffeur.

I'll confess to having sometimes seen my reactions corrupted by countertransference, a psychoanalytic way of saying distorted by my own personal history. For instance, there was one father who had read too many of the wrong articles and was starving his diabetic teenage son. The boy was short, skinny, and resentful, and I did the right thing by campaigning successfully for a more liberal diet. But this was many years ago. I was psychologically hardly more than a child myself—a rebellious one who was still battling parental authority in her head—and I knew deep down that the professional satisfaction I felt whenever the boy gained a centimeter was tainted by triumphant Oedipal revenge.

My father had a heart attack when I was away at college, and I was enraged with my mother for waiting until he was off the critical list before she called to let me know he was in the hospital. Whenever I hesitate to break bad news, I remind myself how excluded I felt at not having gotten to worry about him, or sit by his side, during those three days.

We physicians get mileage out of our personal experience of illness, like the novelist who finds material in his divorce or the painter who documents her own wrinkles. Our practice is indelibly molded and enriched by our own medical history; everything looks different from the other side of the desk. I've always had a go-easy approach to managing cardiovascular disease risk factors, with a relatively high threshold for prescribing statins or high blood pressure pills: a sober, well-documented, scientifically-supported position. But the day I learned my own calcium scoring test showed a deposit in a coronary artery, I panicked like any other anxious patient, expecting to drop dead the next day. Now I could understand the impulse to reach for a magic pill.

Many great historic descriptions of diseases are owed to physicians writing the inside story, from Dr. Thomas Sydenham's classic description of his own gout to Oliver Sacks's *Migraine*. Fortunately, I haven't had to learn about cancer or AIDS on my own body, but my collection of ailments, like everybody's, swells with the years, from the acne, sunburn, and cystitis of my youth through ear wax, leg cramps, mourning, thoracic outlet syndrome, migraine, sprained ankles, bursitis, vestibular neuronitis, aging eyes, and bad knees, and for every condition I've experienced myself I'm a terrific, subtle doctor. With a hidden pitfall: the temptation to assume that my patient's experience and reactions will be just like mine.

The consulting room is a privileged space for physicians as well as patients. Once the door is shut, you leave your worries outside and draw consolation from soothing the physical and psychological wounds of others. In rare moments, though, your own miseries can blow in through the keyhole and rattle the door. I've had to do abortion counseling when I was trying to conceive, help peevish headache patients while nursing a migraine, certify two weeks' sick leave for the flu after dragging myself back to work the day my own fever broke.

When the disintegration of my first marriage was still raw, a woman my age came in distraught because her husband had walked out. Between bouts of tears she raged, disparaged, sneered he'd never get anywhere on his own, swore she missed nothing about him except his handiness with hammer and nails. As my eyes sent her in and out of focus, I hated her for her ugliness, her aging, her complacency, for myself mirrored in those crow's feet and haystack hair. The words, "You deserved it" flashed across my mind. My training held, though, I forced my reactions into the service of empathy, and I'm sure she perceived nothing but kindly attention.

In 1982, after I witnessed the Saturday attack on Rome's Synagogue, the barrier between my profession and my personal world collapsed altogether. On Monday at the start of office hours I was still pretty shaky, and when a new patient walked in wearing a huge Star of David across her sweater I broke down and cried. In a weird twist, she turned out not to be Jewish at all, but an earnest German Protestant wearing the star in expiation for her Nazi parents' sins.

I've wept other times in my office, usually during or after talks with cancer patients but also one day when an older Catholic monk with whom I had a particularly warm and respectful relationship told me he would be leaving Rome forever. I was busy shuffling papers as he walked out the door, then to my amazement found myself with my head on my desk, in tears.

Knowing the habits of Italian GPs, I'm accustomed to surprise from Italian patients examined head to toe for the first time in their lives. But since the turn of the millennium I've been hearing unexpected comments from Americans after I listen to their heart and lungs: "Oh, you're a doctor who examines! I didn't know anybody did any more!" One told me she had asked her Chicago GP to check her breasts and was told, "Oh, we don't do that now, we just do mammograms." It seems American doctoring is becoming as hands-off as Italian medical school.

Seeing colleagues in one American medical forum debunk every element in the routine physical beyond measuring blood pressure, I was inspired to contribute a post tallying the significant, curable conditions I'd detected by doing the occasional once-over: thyroid cancer, aortic aneurysm, rectal cancer, prostate cancer, non-Hodgkin's lymphoma, aortic insufficiency, aortic stenosis, asymmetric cardiomyopathy, countless basal cell carcinomas, and a good dozen breast cancers, some within months of a normal mammogram. And I'm not a physical examination genius like Abraham Verghese.

Personally, I love the ritual of examining patients. Not just in order to make diagnoses, but to deepen our connection and give myself a few moments of meditative retreat into underused senses. One of my teachers used to close his eyes and bow his head while listening to the heart; I thought that was an affectation. Now I often catch myself doing the same thing during a cardiac exam, a pelvic, or a breast check, distilling my focus into my ears or my hands, taking a break from the visible world to enter a universe of sound or touch.

If you declare physical examination a useless skill, your prophecy will self-fulfill as soon as you've produced a generation of doctors who don't know how. A recent American study claimed that one out of four hospitalized patients have important diagnoses missed for lack of proper examination. In the doctors-only website *Medscape*, Dr. Fabrizia Faustinella, an Italian working in Houston, recently snitched on hospital colleagues who had no idea their newly-admitted patient's fever came from a leg infection, because they never examined her.

Even more than Americans, Italians and their doctors adore the kind of pop psychosomatics that blames stress for everything from eczema to cancer. Those dedicated, as I am, to the rigorous study of mind-body interactions can sometimes forget how much people's belief in them is based not on twenty-first-century science but on magical thinking left over from the nineteenth.

I've always been intrigued by the influence of the mind on the body, from the way a patient's blood pressure can drop from 180/90 to 130/80 after sitting calmly for five minutes on up to the brilliant insights of psychoneuroimmunology. But however fascinating it is to, say, graph the activation of natural killer lymphocytes following the stress of a laboratory exercise in public speaking, the importance of psychosomatic influences is usually more theoretical than practical. After three decades studying the impact of psychological factors on peptic ulcer I always ask ulcer patients about life stress, but Prilosec and *Helicobacter pylori* treatment usually work fine whatever the psychological context.

Arguably more important are more prosaic kinds of mind-body interactions. If someone with a cold comes to your office instead of waiting it out, maybe it's a sign he's depressed. A woman's pain during intercourse may stem from fear that her husband's having an affair. A spell of migraines may signal binge drinking.

I'm a devil's advocate, adept at straddling the psychosomatic fence. With people who reduce everything to chemical imbalances, I highlight the role of psychological and social factors. With patients who've been told their problem is all in their head, I'll emphasize the biological.

Medical students are taught that the doctor's jobs are diagnosis, treatment, and prognosis. Early on you channel all your energies into the first two, but later you understand the centrality of the third: predicting the future. It is often less vital to get diagnosis or therapy right than to be able to tell patients whether and when they'll get well. After all, ninety percent of problems will either go away or kill you, whatever the medical intervention. Tendinitis may hurt less if you take ibuprofen, but the tiny rips in the tendon have to heal themselves in their own sweet time. Experience teaches physicians to see through the pretense that every disease requires action—the cure can be worse than the disease; medications for labyrinthitis are so sedative that many patients prefer their vertigo. And if a painless quarter-inch spot on your arm isn't going to turn to cancer, who cares whether its proper name is cherry angioma, sebaceous hyperplasia, or dermatosis papulosa nigra?

Patients often leave our prescriptions unfilled, and their "noncompliance" may make sense. When I was in training there was only one condition we were told might not be worth the trouble to treat: fungal infection of the great toenail. Nuts to the damn nail, save your energy for battles easier to win. Every year that goes by I extend that concept further.

Even those treatments we think are essential may not be. I remember a Mount Sinai Hospital patient in a jalabia and patriarchal beard who refused antibiotics for his badly infected foot, asking to be allowed to try treating it himself. He wasn't on my service, but the news of his outlandish request spread fast, so my classmates and I made little detours to sneak glances at him assiduously cleaning his wound and applying his native salves. After a week, to everyone's astonishment, his fever was gone, the swelling and redness had decreased, and pus was no longer oozing.

> After I had my first baby, Alice, [in England,] a National Health nurse came to my house regularly . . . The baby seemed to have mild eczema, but the nurse was relaxed about it. When I took Alice, at 3 months, to New York and we went to a Park Avenue pediatrician for a minor, unrelated complaint, the doctor seemed unaccountably exercised. "This baby has ECZEMA!" he said accusingly, pointing to a few reddish spots. "What are you doing about it?"
> —Sarah Lyall in the *New York Times*
> *Week in Review*, 2009

I lean toward therapeutic nihilism in the British mode, preferring non-drug treatment and the healing effects of what my favorite teachers called "tincture of time." *Primum non nocere*, first do no harm, trust Nature to heal, respect what your body is telling you—stay off that sprained ankle instead of just popping Aleve. Prescribing effective folk remedies gives me a special kick: giving an American olive oil as a moisturizer or chamomile tea for sleep, telling Italians to plunge a burned hand into cold water or soothe a sore throat by gargling with salt water.

Nonetheless, discussions of alternative medicine can get my back up. A friend starts in on her recent cure by homeopathy or the virtues of oil of evening primrose, and I get a sinking feeling as though I were walking into an ambush. I never understood exactly why I took these things as a personal attack, reverting to a defense-of-the-guild mentality, when I otherwise pride myself on being open to everything from herbs to acupuncture.

One evening at a dinner party a guest with arthritis asked what I thought of green-lipped mussels, which he said had saved the use of his hands. I felt lucky to be able to punt to a fellow-physician at the table, curious how he would deal with the question. When he said, "Actually I don't know anything about it. It might be interesting," I was impressed by his nice job of defusing a difficult situation, taking it as a variation on one hoary method for handling a foolish person who says something particularly dumb: say "You're perfectly right," and walk away. Only much later did it occur to me that a doctor might have genuine curiosity about new ideas introduced by a lay person, without losing power or prestige. If I felt like a trapped animal when somebody brought up what I considered quackery, maybe it was because of a hidden agenda to be loved by my patients for my "knowledge" and my "concern." With the years I feel less skittish about the unfamiliar, and freer to explain, for example, that the reason I particularly dislike homeopathy is because it promulgates the myth that the answer to all ills lies in a little pink pill.

Some years back I had a stomach upset that went on and on no matter what treatment I tried. After a year I decided I'd send my principles to hell, give in to my then-boyfriend-now-husband Alvin, and let a well-known Roman alternative medicine guru try his stuff on me. But my life was busy, I never quite got around to arranging the visit, and two weeks later the symptoms went away forever. What would have happened if I'd managed an earlier appointment and improved while following his prescription? Would I have converted to homeopathy despite knowing that it had been thoroughly debunked by science? I shudder to think.

Thousands of priests, monks, and nuns have passed through my office, so you might imagine endless debates over the healing power of prayer. Nope. Though a few do make a surreptitious hop to Lourdes, most of my Catholic religious seem to sequester their piety far from their health beliefs. The impact of their spirituality, as I have observed it, consists more in acceptance of disease, a dignified lack of attachment to life, an admirable willingness to look death in the face. As a researcher into mind-body interactions, I'm the one who thinks of medical benefits from spiritual practices. I once asked a monk who suffered from migraine, "How much do you pray, Brother X?" He reassured me: "Oh, we don't do much of that any more, doc." Feeling faintly ridiculous, I said, "Well, you might try increasing your prayer time. It could do wonders for your headaches."

16

Endings

I'm not afraid of death; I just don't want to be there when
it happens.
—Woody Allen

Elliott was one of the AIDS epidemic's early victims. Already
blinded by cytomegalovirus, with no flesh left on his bones, when
he was hit by a Pneumocystis pneumoniae infection in 1984, he
decided it was time to die. He gave away his belongings, said farewell to his friends, stopped taking any medications, and signed out
of the hospital to await the end at home. I went to his apartment
and wept with him, held his hand, accepted his gift of a silver bowl
with lion legs. Whereupon his battered immune system pulled out
from some prankster hat the ability to fight off the infection, leaving him to survive another fifteen months suspended between
this world and the next. Whenever my eyes fall on that small bowl
in my hall I remember his dignity and courage in facing his disease and the last terrible joke it played on him.

Physicians can stand death, they just can't stand the transi-
tion. Out of hundreds of deaths I witnessed during my training in
the 1970s only three were a simple halting of the breath, and the
doctor who allowed two of them was, in everybody's eyes, near-

criminal. All the rest were thumped and pumped and shot full of enough drugs to make it as far as the intensive care unit as a way-station to heaven, usually dying on a respirator without regaining consciousness, their prolonged helplessness and dependency lessening their physicians' sense of impotence. Lately docs are more likely to wash their hands, Pilate-like, ducking responsibility by pressuring afflicted relatives to make the call to turn off the machines.

The ancient Egyptians buried food with their dead to help them reach the afterworld, and in Jamaica the recently departed hang around as "duppy" before they find peace. Modern medicine has invented its own no-man's-land between the two kingdoms: brain death. It's less like real death than they'd have you believe. Brain-dead mothers can be kept on life support for months to carry their fetus to term. Organ transplants begin when a warm pink brain-dead patient is rolled into the operating room—unconscious but breathing through a tube like any intensive care unit inhabitant—and a sterile team scrambles in high surgical mode to remove his kidney, liver, and/or heart. After which the doctors strip off their masks and gowns, shut off the respirator, and abandon a corpse that a moment ago, to the untutored eye, was a living person.

One night during my residency I had a patient shipped down to my ward from the intensive care unit because he was brain dead and they needed the bed. In the morning he woke up and asked for breakfast.

I remember the first time I was awakened on call to pronounce a death. The body was still warm, and, alone under the half-illumination of a bed lamp, I listened to the heart and secretly gave him a shake, panicked at having to declare the end of a life, terrified he would awaken in the morgue, or in the coffin. The second time I was more confident, newly armed with a trick passed down through generations of scared interns: I assembled my ophthalmoscope and peered into a pupil to check that the arteries of the retina were reassuringly fragmented into a chain of elongated rectangles, what we called the "boxcar sign." The nurses, who knew death when they saw it, found us ridiculous.

Those lonely deaths of men and women found lifeless in their hospital beds were the decent ones. George Washington—his real name—signed out of Morissania Hospital against medical advice as soon as he stopped vomiting blood from the fragile varices in his esophagus. He had end-stage alcoholic liver disease, had endured ten such hospitalizations in one year, and now wanted to go home to die. He made it as far as his front stoop, where he collapsed, blood again spurting from his mouth. Carried back to the hospital, he refused treatment. For half an hour he survived, gushing red out of both ends, as we all stood helpless around his ICU bed watching him bleed to death. The moment he lost consciousness the hovering medical team intubated him and plugged a transfusion into each arm—ethically questionable maneuvers that would never pass muster nowadays—but it was as useless as trying to stop the tide with a colander. Horrifying and awe-inspiring: unique among the patients I saw in my training, Mr. Washington was dying the death he had chosen.

When I was an intern in the Morrisania Emergency Room, an ambulance with red lights and blaring siren once brought in an emaciated old woman who wasn't breathing. We did cardiac massage and within ten minutes had brought her heartbeat back, hung an intravenous line, intubated her, and sent her to the ICU on a respirator, when in walked her physician son, who'd called the ambulance. He said, "What a blessing for my mother to finally die after so many months of suffering from cancer." Everybody started yelling at once: why hadn't he ridden with her, why hadn't he telephoned, why hadn't he sent a note along, why had he called the damned ambulance in the first place? I walked out of the ER in a fugue state, my mind not knowing what my body was doing, took the elevator up to the ICU, turned off the respirator, waited until there were no more blips on the cardiac monitor, came back down and told the crowd they could stop arguing because she had died. I didn't weigh the pros and cons of performing this act any more than I could have debated whether to run out of a burning building.

Fast forward to one night in the late 1990s, sitting in a private hospital's intensive care unit in Rome with the body of my patient Doris. Just a month earlier she had been a hale fifty, but then her liver began to crumble, perhaps under the assault of some hitherto unknown virus. Her demise was an utter failure—not the endpoint of an inexorable disease, the lightning strike of a heart attack, or the trailing off of old age, but a reminder that death always triumphs in the end and can drag off the strongest of us. All lights were dimmed in the ICU except a yellow sconce intensifying the color of her jaundiced face, and the curtains were drawn around three sides of her bed. I was tormented by the thought that if I had somehow managed to transfer her to the UK she could have been saved by a transplant.

Not many patients have died under my care, since major illness drives Italians into the arms of the public system and induces foreigners to pull up their stakes and head home. In my minutes alone with Doris, waiting for her husband, I meditated on others I had lost. Especially Arnold, screaming through the night with inconsolable terror unleashed by the metastases in his brain, screaming as my sweaty fingers injected crescendo doses of tranquilizers into his arms. He would doze off for a few minutes, then pop bolt upright and begin screaming again, into the walls of what I remember as a huge, comfortable living room, his wife desperate in her way and I in mine. Two days later he mercifully stopped screaming, and breathing.

Several times I have been taken over by a shudder when death's minions have caught me unprepared. During a rectal examination on a sixty-year-old army major with abdominal pain, my exploring finger touched the rock-hard spiny tip of a cancer deep inside; when I pulled out the finger I no longer saw a patient but a dead man walking. The frozen pelvis I found examining a tourist with vague abdominal pain, all her internal organs trapped inside an encasement of tumor. The variegated hills and valleys of an advanced melanoma casually unveiled when a monk took off his shirt. A patient who stuck out his tongue for my neurologist officemate, and we both saw that fasciculating bag of worms which transformed him from a living person into one whose horrible end from Lou Gehrig's disease was just a matter of time.

The worst may be when you turn a familiar corner on a routine exam and there in front of you is the guy with the scythe. While reaching across to start a routine examination with a patient's left breast, the edge of my hand knocked accidentally against the sharp edge of a two-inch cancer in the right one. Having forced my usual quick full-body exam on a new patient who came in to have his earwax removed, I felt an obscenely enlarged, plainly malignant spleen. I clutched the examination table with my other hand, afraid I would faint, and I remember my voice somehow remaining calm.

But then death is always at our side. In my second year of medical school I was at Beth Israel Hospital, taking ECGs to earn a few bucks, when a boy with a mop of curly red hair looked down at our feet in an elevator and said, "Hey, we're both wearing Wallabees." Kevin Moore was a nineteen-year-old high school dropout who pushed wheelchairs for a living; I was twenty-five and on my way to being a doctor; for some reason our love affair was transformative. My slate of previous dalliances was wiped clean, and I was just making the dazzling discovery of what it was to be part of a couple who supported each other in public and were entranced by each other's every thought in private, when heading home across the Brooklyn Bridge his bicycle was hit by a truck and he was smashed on the street below. I think the arduous hospital clerkships I was slogging through were the only reason I survived the first months. They occupied my mind during gaps between guzzling whiskey and staring at the pill bottles on my shelves to gauge their suicidal potential.

As I sat by Doris's body in that Rome ICU, I thought of my father, whose lifeless body I never saw. Of how every time I came near Kevin's coffin over the three days of the wake I mussed up his hair so it would be the way he wore it, how the funeral parlor people kept combing it back down, and how he smelled of greasepaint. Of watching a flock of vultures eating a dead zebra at Masai Mara game park in Kenya and a mile further on watching a zebra mare lick the amniotic sac off her newborn colt. Of the Clarissan nuns on Ischia who used to pray every day before the sisters who preceded them, whose clothed corpses were propped up on stone seats with hollow bottoms to rot slowly into clay bowls placed underneath; they prayed knowing they themselves were destined to sit, eventually, on those same chairs.

In May 2005, my mother died in my arms. At eighty-eight she had no diseases, but every system was faltering, every step teetered, she was only pretending she could still see St. Peter's out my window or follow the dialogue on TV. Her mind was all there, though she found its pace exasperatingly slow as she toiled day and night on the second edition of her book, *Messages from Home*, about the Parent-Child Home Program she had founded. She had arrived in Rome from New York elated by a celebration of fifty years of her program but exhausted by the flight; we weren't surprised that she couldn't handle more than guest-room to kitchen and back. The fourth night we heard moaning through the wall, and I found her tossing and hot in her bed, breathing once per second, and radiating fear. I called an ambulance, slid her arms into a sweater, held her and promised she would be all right and watched her fight, terror-stricken, to breathe and then she stopped breathing and the light went out of her eyes. I frantically, competently, uselessly blew my breath into her mouth and pumped her heart all the way to the hospital.

For years she had thought of her own death every day and thought she was ready, until the moment it actually came. In my dreams, for weeks afterward, she found more peaceful ways to die. Deaths I'd seen in the hospital were nothing like this unbearable moment of transformation, as holy in a contorted way as a baby's first cry.

I once had a patient who escaped unhurt from a bad car crash but remained haunted for a year by a paralyzing awareness of the possibility of death. Any cornice he walked under might fall and crush him, any bridge collapse under his feet. Automobiles, which hurtle headlong down skinny strips of asphalt steered by inattentive humans, were out of the question. Our everyday living depends on maintaining a fiction of invulnerability, which when breached leaves us crippled by fear.

After my mother presumed to disappear while I held her, I was crippled like that. An invisibly hovering Death could appear at any moment; my husband would go into the kitchen and I imagined him dropping lifeless to the floor. Several times every afternoon in my office, while I measured someone's blood pressure or palpated their liver, I would be assaulted without warning by a split-second vision of the life suddenly fading from their gaze.

For months after my mother's death I found it hard to tolerate touching patients. Though I forced myself to go through the motions, I felt impotent, bereft of the essential professional delusions of knowledge and power. Medicine seemed a card trick, an exercise in futility, its successes insignificant. I had felt like a charlatan when I first opened my Rome office, after twenty months away from medicine. The difference this time was that I didn't so much doubt my expertise as feel it was useless.

I felt uncertain about every diagnosis and ambivalent about every prescription. I'd always had the professional vice of creating complications—asking too much, explaining too much, offering too many alternatives—but now it went over the top. I lost my grip on the usual orderly process of information gathering, diagnosis, and treatment, distracted by everything that could go wrong, fussing over the microdifferences among cases, overindividualizing my prescriptions. My charts consisted more and more of patients' own thoughts and descriptions of their symptoms instead of my translations into medicalese.

One theory of schizophrenia says patients can't distinguish figure from background, so their senses and emotions overwhelm their ability to cope. My professional block was a little like that.

I already knew plenty about mourning, after losing my young love Kevin and my father within a year of each other. Now, though, in the wake of my mother's departure, I was forced to learn about post-traumatic stress disorder, since any reference to death—they happen, in my job—triggered flashbacks, adding the insult of distracting psychological symptoms to the injury of loss. For years, when reading medical articles I had to skip over paragraphs mentioning cardiopulmonary resuscitation.

My mother chose "my100self" as her AOL password; she really wanted to hit the century mark. When very elderly patients came in I resented them for surviving when she hadn't.

But for once I was on the receiving end of my patients' support. One woman I cared for unearthed a comment I had tossed off about my mother years earlier, several recalled their own parents' deaths, many sacrificed precious minutes from their allotted time to ask how my mother had died, who she had been and, chiefly, how I was coping. Their concern left me grateful, confused—who was supposed to be helping whom?—and surprised by how many of my relationships with my patients were revealed as genuine, even deep. Those unexpected gestures transformed my interactions not just with the people who made them, but with all my patients. Our relationships felt more equal, reciprocal, authentic. An outside observer might have seen little—no lapses in professionalism, no new flurries of self-revelation—but to me, the change was palpable: we were that much closer to being present to each other not just as doctor and patient, but as human beings.

17

Native Misinformant

Informant: one who supplies cultural or linguistic data in response to interrogation by an investigator. Example of informant in a sentence: We learned the language with the help of a native *informant*.

—Merriam-Webster.com

I grew up with *The New Yorker*, and one of my first acts as a Radcliffe freshman was to sign up for my very own subscription. When I moved to Rome at age thirty, the issues that trickled into my mailbox were a lifeline to hometown culture.

The first chip in my bicontinental identity arrived two years later, when for the first time I looked at a cartoon and didn't get the joke.

The poignancy of expatriation: your native land keeps moving forward without you. American culture, the only one I profoundly *know*, evolves mercilessly elsewhere as my center of gravity drifts Romewards. It's easy to keep up with the latest antihypertensive drugs, but not with the flavor and byways of medical practice, or of daily life, back in the United States—I gain perspective on my own culture at the cost of losing my validity as an insider.

Italy's evolved too, of course. When I moved to Rome the rare brown-skinned person walking down the street attracted stares;

now they occupy half the seats in any bus or classroom. The old artisan workshops have become wine bars and jeans stores, the extracts of placenta are gone from the pharmacy shelves, and workmen no longer wear newspaper hats or sing on the job. None of these shifts have startled me, because I've watched them proceed molecule by molecule.

But dipping into American life only at intervals, I find the oddities have piled up until now my knowledge base is so far off that I sometimes wish I could fake a foreign accent. I'm not sure whether speed limits are capped at fifty-five, or whether there's a national drinking age—and would it be eighteen or twenty-one? When I lived in the States you were served at the gas station, and self-service pumps in Italy have always accepted bills, so when I needed to pump my own gas in 1990s California I couldn't figure out how to pay until a kindly passer-by pointed out the clerk behind her glass door.

If you hear my New Yawk accent you may take me for a native, but don't be fooled.

My first hint that American English was evolving elsewhere was on holiday, four years after my move to Italy, when someone yelled "Yo" in my direction across Harvard Square. I figured he was speaking Spanish, and kept walking. No, it was an old friend, who had to run over and tap me on the shoulder—it never crossed his mind that his greeting surpassed my understanding.

"Cougars" chasing younger men may date back to Catherine the Great, but when I lived in the US there wasn't a word for them. "Homogeneous" hadn't started losing its second e and "nuclear" wasn't garbling into "nucular." Rooms were free of elephants, guests didn't dine out on anecdotes, and when people networked they called it socializing. Rocket science was a job, not a metaphor, robocalls didn't exist, nobody had skin in the game or went postal, and, of course, nothing could go viral.

Many brand-new terms fit in so snugly that even a native misinformant hardly noticed, such as when I first heard "same old same old" at a party, "I've got your back" on NCIS, "shout-out" in an email, "whatever" in a Berkeley kitchen, "my bad" at an American Psychosomatic Society committee meeting. I caught on fast to well duh, been there done that, get a life, wannabe, soccer mom, air guitar, baby bump, stoner, sticker shock, and senior moment. Perp walk, high five, bootylicious, helicopter parent, hottie, ghetto blaster, gangbanger, hookup, and "the N word" took some context, and I needed serious help with bimbo (in Italian, it means male child). I'm still not sure I really get Eurotrash or LOL.

There were always several other Susans in my school class, plus various Marys, Lindas, Elizabeths, and Barbaras. In the nineties an introduction to an Alyssa was my first exposure to a torrent of novel monikers, often color coded (McKenna versus LaKeisha). In Italy parents have some leeway, but they usually choose a saint's name to be safe—while Mommy is still in the hospital, Daddy goes to the Registry office, and if he says they want to call the baby "Tiffany" or "Green" the man behind the desk has the power to turn thumbs down.

In my day nobody pooped. Or rather, boring guests pooped parties, but patients moved their bowels. The first time a patient told me her poop was hard I didn't know which end of the boat she was referring to.

I've had to quit referring to my officemate Dr. Vincenzo Bacci as my partner because patients started assuming we were a thing. I've had to stop asking about hay fever because young patients don't know it means allergies, and I stopped asking patients to take off their trousers after one giggled, thinking the word obscene. For a long time I thought anyone described in the American press as "struggling with addiction" must be in rehab, before catching on that it was a new euphemism for junkie.

At least I'm not as clueless as some of my pseudo-American patients, who learned mother-tongue English at their expat parents' knees but have never lived outside Italy.

Back when the *Times* cost a quarter, an Italian friend once went to a paper stand in my native New York and handed the salesman a dollar. The guy said, "What do you think I am, a fucking bank?"

This was normal behavior. New Yorkers are preternaturally nice nowadays, which I attribute to a population shift away from my own grouchy tribe of Eastern European Jews in favor of Latinos and Asians.

A Nigerian college boyfriend told me that while traveling alone through the South in 1963 he'd had a winning strategy to avoid lynching: always wear African clothes. In one small town he'd put on his suit to go to church on Sunday and was turned away at the door. Next day, in a dashiki, he ran into the pastor on the street and received an apology: "So sorry we didn't let you in. We didn't know you were an African, we thought you were a Nigra."

From such intimate familiarity with my home culture, I assured Europeans during the 2008 primary campaigns that the United States couldn't possibly elect a black president. Classic native misinformation, reflecting my ignorance of a vast sea change in black-white relations in America, of which Obama's triumph was only an epiphenomenon. When I lived in the States it was inconceivable that an Oprah Winfrey could be molding the literary tastes of the middle class, an Idris Elba could be a universal heartthrob, or the offspring of mixed couples might choose to put checkmarks for race next to both white and black.

Learning that lily-white Minneapolis now houses thriving Somali and Vietnamese communities was a mild surprise, but when I found out that heroin and crack cocaine had supplanted Budweiser in Nowhere, USA, I was, frankly, floored. Even more so when I had a runny nose in California in 2014 and discovered they'd removed Sudafed from the shelves for fear somebody would cook it into methamphetamine.

In my America, parents let first graders walk to school alone. Adolescents talked on the phone instead of working on their Facebook personas. Waiting on tables wasn't assumed to be a day job. I remember once in the nineties my mother being so impressed by a Roman waiter's professionalism that she asked what he hoped to be ten years hence. Puzzled, he replied, "A waiter, of course."

When Italy discovered satellite dishes, one of the first original language TV shows it offered was *CSI*. I was appalled by those bullets plowing through flesh, charred legless trunks, maggots crawling in eyeholes. But I should have caught on to Americans' growing appetite for graphic violence years earlier, when my friends heaped praise on movies I found unwatchable, like *Fargo* and *Pulp Fiction*. When I lived in the States the National Rifle Association helped pass gun control laws, and nobody dreamed of interpreting the Second Amendment as a universal right to own firearms; President Ronald Reagan said there was "no reason why on the street today a citizen should be carrying loaded weapons."

My husband and I recently watched a season of *Seinfeld*. How quaintly decent it looks after, say, *Breaking Bad*, like the benevolent *West Wing* now displaced by its evil twin *House of Cards*.

Practicing office gynecology has kept me up on styles in pubic waxing, but a California street sign offering "eyebrow threading" left me mystified. Lady Gaga has performed in Rome's Circus Maximus, and someone once pointed out an as yet untainted Lance Armstrong as he pedaled past in Verona, but Justin Bieber? Who he? My familiarity with celebrities dwindled so low so fast that I wasn't aware until after the 2017 inauguration that Donald Trump was nationally famous as a reality TV star—in my Manhattanite days he was just an outer-borough real estate sleazeball.

Gourmet used to mean New York, San Francisco, maybe New Orleans. When I was at Harvard, eating out meant hamburgers or chop suey, and in 1977 my then-husband and I ate at one of the few restaurants in Santa Fe. It's still hard to fathom, from afar, the cultural cohabitation between foodies who have blanketed the country with Whole Foods markets and television with cooking channels, and fast foodies who subsist on pizza and candy bars.

My Rome-trained palate scorned Starbucks espresso as undrinkable on first sip, and I was flummoxed to later learn that the chain and its perversely un-Italian "lattes" had become the embodiment of privileged yuppiedom.

Sex has changed too. I left the States in the raunchy seventies, before free love gave way first to the commercialized swingers scene of Plato's Retreat and then to the new Puritanism of the herpes- and AIDS-crazed eighties and nineties. Even a member of my flower-child generation can be taken aback by the current disconnect between copulation and not just love but, apparently, passion. Urban Dictionary: "Twitter Bang. Hooking up with someone who you've spoken less than 140 words to."

Gay marriage? You gotta be kidding! New Yorkers could be prescient, though. When I married my Italian first husband in 1977 the typographers, asked to print invitations to the wedding of Susan and Andrea, inquired discreetly whether this was "Some kind of . . . *alternative* ceremony."

My America survives unchanged in a parallel universe, like the spaghetti sauce of those Italian-Americans who parboil and peel their tomatoes as their Sicilian forebears did 150 years ago, or the seventeenth-century English that supposedly hangs on in deepest Appalachia. I'm always stumbling over unlikely examples of the new normal—only after the US economy tanked in 2008 did I learn, from friends' tales of woe, that your Average Joe American was juggling tens of thousands in credit card debt and had taken out a second mortgage on his house.

> Physician satisfaction across the country has declined to its
> lowest levels ever.
> —Dr. Robert Pearl, *Forbes*, 2015

In the last forty years the American health scene has been steadily evolving away from physician autonomy and toward ever more expensive medications, ever more pressure to prescribe them, and ever more outsourcing of direct patient care to nurses and physician assistants. I count myself lucky to have escaped. I've steered clear of obligatory electronic medical records, the swelling ranks of the uninsured, call centers that tell docs whom they can hospitalize and what x-rays they can order, and drug companies so omnipotent, omnipresent, and sneaky that you can no longer trust the bona fides of either journal articles or "grassroots" patient organizations. Knowing that the medical history is the key to diagnosis and is where the physician's skill really shows, I've been dismayed to hear from patients that in the States their symptoms often get recorded by the same underling who logs their weight and temperature.

An American college administrator sent me an email in 2017 asking whether she could send undergraduates to watch me treat patients in my office. Wow, inviting adolescents with no professionalism training whatsoever to snoop on the most intimate of conversations. Obviously unethical, and probably illegal! I replied with a shocked "no." But then, poking around the internet, I discovered that such shadowing has become practically a must-do for pre-meds, and that most practicing physicians—thankfully not all—think it's fine and dandy to have a teenager in the room when they're with their patients. Maybe they never get into talking about the heavy stuff.

Newspeak In Medicine Department. Driving around an American city on vacation I noticed sparkling new "Rehabilitation Hospitals" everywhere and figured that to need so many physical therapy facilities the locals must be smashing their limbs at an alarming rate. That's what rehabilitation meant in my time, either that or kicking a drug habit. Later the omniscient Mr. Google informed me that so-called rehab hospitals are actually halfway houses for patients who've been thrown out of the regular hospital when they're still too sick to go home.

In the medical culture of my US, complaints of pain elicited stony indifference. Later I was glad to read that hearts had softened and pain had begun to be treated with compassion, but for years those medical articles didn't let me in on the dirty little secret that the flip side of untreated pain had become drug abuse. In 2012, an American veterinarian admitted to me he had recently kicked an Oxycontin habit; even that recently, I took his case for a fluke rather than part of an epidemic. It was hard for a physician like myself, trained to avoid prescribing anything with abuse potential, to catch on that my colleagues in the US were handing out opiates like candy, spawning pop-up clinics that rip off Medicaid in cahoots with drug dealers, heroin addicts who have swamped flinty New Hampshire, opiate overdoses so frequent they've dragged the curve of American longevity downward for the first time ever.

I recently asked an American psychiatrist colleague for advice about a particularly annoying patient and he said, "Why don't you fire her?" I laughed at his wit until I realized he wasn't joking— some docs nowadays sever their ties with patients who fail to pay, yell at the office staff, refuse to vaccinate their children, or won't quit smoking. The concept didn't exist in my America, a foundation of medicine being, I was taught, to keep offering help no matter how many times you're rebuffed.

After college I spent eighteen months working in a mental hospital, eight wandering around Europe, twelve doing premedical science courses. I was the only member of my training cohort to have taken any time off from my schooling. Nowadays more than half of entering first-year US medical students have had at least one gap year, and it's not unusual for them to be in their thirties or even their forties. One reason they can start older is that training is less physically draining than it used to be. Even my own relatively undemanding internship meant a thirty-six-hour haul every time you were on call, and a 110-hour workweek. Nowadays, a shift generally maxes out at sixteen hours and a week at eighty, though as of 2017 those limits may be lengthening a bit; on-call residents have a night float colleague as backup, then the whole next day off. I worry those short hours could be bad for continuity of care and adequacy of training, but maybe I've become as much of an alter kocker as the senior physicians of my day who thought interns should still be working, as they themselves had, thirty-six hours out of every forty-eight.

American medical training has always inculcated a reverence for research. In my day that meant picking up on valuable innovations and avoiding what had been proven useless. Now it's gone further, with overzealous Evidence-Based Medicine poo-pooing any treatment that hasn't been confirmed in a placebo-controlled double-blind clinical trial—are we *really* sure that eating is effective in relieving hunger?—and treating all such trial results like words from the mouth of God. Which leaves us at the mercy of who's doing the research, the study design they choose, the journals' publishing policies, and the drug companies' thumbs on the scale. On the one hand, the medical establishment is so hostile to dietary supplements that melatonin was pronounced useless against jet lag on the basis of one atrociously-designed study. On the other, when pharmaceutical executives are unveiling their latest concoction they use every gimmick in the books to justify marketing it at exorbitant prices when older medications would do fine. Skepticism is imperative.

Do I count as an up-to-date American internist? I'm no longer sure. I keep up with my reading, and three-quarters of the medications I prescribe were invented after I expatriated, but the changing culture of medicine can't always be grasped by following the journals. This was brought home to me sharply ten years ago when I found abnormalities on an American diplomat's routine ECG. Further tests confirmed coronary artery disease, but he had no symptoms so I started him on intensive medical therapy as all the guidelines dictated. On vacation in the US he went for a second opinion to a cardiologist, who proceeded to send him for . . . an angiogram and two stents. I was dumbfounded. It took a while to puzzle out that in the years since I had left the country a vast, profitable industry had been built around doing potentially dangerous invasive procedures on everybody with a blocked artery, even though research had irrefutably shown stenting to prolong life only when performed in the middle of a heart attack.

I remember the moment when the words, "What's her insurance?" first entered my ear. It was during the nineties, I was on the phone with a gynecologist friend in NYC to refer a patient for a hysterectomy, and I couldn't understand why she asked.

Years later, an American patient had a series of strange infections and low levels of gammaglobulin (antibodies) in his blood. Wanting him to get a proper diagnosis and a plan of action, I tracked down a top specialist in New York and wrote asking how to get an appointment. She wrote back that the case didn't seem severe enough to warrant one.

I put two and two together: American doctors won't let you in the door if you don't have the right kind of insurance. One of those ground rules that look crazy from over here but my US-based colleagues must consider normal—like that an ECG can cost $130 in one place and $1,300 in another, a hospital won't tell you its prices ahead of time, the uninsured poor pay top dollar, and patients are expected to bargain over hospital bills.

For decades American medical culture was wildly, notoriously, to-the-max spendthrift. When I worked as a resident in the Martin Luther King Clinic in the South Bronx we were proud overscreeners, bringing in all our healthy adults every year, young or old, not just for a physical examination but a long set of blood tests, urine tests, an ECG, and a chest x-ray. Patients with any symptoms got what doctors' slang calls "million-dollar workups," and handfuls of medications were thrown at any and all diagnoses, without physicians having any idea what any of this cost or what its value was. Docs were afraid of being sued if they missed anything, and insurance companies were picking up the bill, so why scrimp?

In the last few years, common sense in the form of the American Board of Internal Medicine's "Choosing Wisely" campaign and other voices of reason has begun pushing doctors to use their little gray cells instead of all that diagnostic machinery, and to recognize that not every backache calls for an MRI. The worm is turning away from overdiagnosis and overtreatment.

Maybe it's turning too far. My first hint came with a patient I suspected of having intestinal malabsorption. No laboratory in all of Rome could perform the crucial test, a measurement of how much fat was in her stool. Fortunately she was heading home to Nevada on vacation, so I wrote a letter for her to bring to a gastroenterologist at her Health Maintenance Organization. When she got back from the States having had no diagnostic evaluation at all, much less the usual overkill, I was nonplussed. Not long thereafter I read that many HMOs were docking physicians' pay if they ordered too many tests. Some added gag clauses forbidding the docs to tell patients what was going on. Cost-cutting was trumping scientific medicine, and my patient had been caught in the middle.

That particular form of profiteering was eventually exposed, decried, and banned, but the penny-pinching revolution has proceeded in other forms—guidelines cutting down mammograms from yearly to every two years, for example, which predictably hikes the number of cancers that are found at an advanced stage. US physicians are being tossed between two pillars of profit, the Scylla of the drug and testing industries and the Charybdis of the insurance industry.

I often wonder how satisfied I'd have been with my medical life if I had stayed in the US instead of escaping a week after my Board Certification exam. When I was a clerk on the pediatrics ward at Mount Sinai, long before the current scourges of prior authorization and diagnostic coding, I remember a practicing doc bewildering a bunch of us students by telling us that *this*, our stretch of playing doctor without real responsibility, would be the best time of our professional lives. We just stared at him, all chafing to escape from med school purgatory, none willing to believe there could be downsides to the professional paradise we would soon enter.

In the end, I wouldn't exchange my Roman career for any other. Every time I read new ways the American medical system is shaped by greed, or the Italian National Health Service hobbled by penury and *pressappochismo*, I can't believe my luck: perched atop the Aventine Hill, far from every fray, happily doing my doctoring whatever way I think best.

A Moral, or Three

> European heaven is where the policemen are English, the
> cooks French, the bankers Swiss, the post office German,
> and the lovers Italian. European hell is where the policemen
> are German, the cooks English, the bankers French, the post
> office Italian, and the lovers Swiss.
>
> —Venerable joke

Health heaven: the funding, hospitals, and doctors' education are
American, the lifestyle and access to care Italian. Health hell: Italian budgets, medical training, and ICUs; American pricing, coverage, Big Macs, drunk driving, weapons-mania, couch potatodom,
and streetcorner opiates.

For one giddy moment around 2012 everything seemed to be
going right, my two countries converging in a virtuous spiral. Italian medicine was being dragged into the modern age by European
Union regulations, while the Affordable Care Act was nudging
Americans toward universal coverage. Now both are a tossup—
the European Union forced austerity budgets down Italy's throat
and now is itself under assault from Brexit and its potential spin-
offs, while the outcome of the 2016 elections threatens to return
American health care policy to the Stone Age.

> Overall health system performance in all Member States:
> Rank 1: France
> Rank 2: Italy
>
> —*World Health Organization*, World Health Report,
>   2000 ratings

A Voyage in the Inferno of Rome Emergency Rooms

—*Il Tempo* headline, 2017

The Italian medical landscape features crumbling hospitals, doctors trained on books rather than patients, pervasive corruption, and per capita spending one third that of the US. But, by any criteria, Italians are healthier.

Because of their top-flight health care system? Hmmm. That stellar World Health Organization ranking was based entirely on two criteria, system fairness (access and cost distribution) and population health, ignoring quality-of-care measures such as medical competence or emergency room efficiency. This credited the system for outcomes far beyond its control.

Italians themselves consider their National Health System to be hopelessly dysfunctional. Visitors often ask over dinner, what's medicine like in Rome? I used to turn the question away with a diplomatic word of praise for the concept of universal free public medicine, but now I can be nearly as scathing about the deficiencies in its daily reality as Italians are themselves, an evolution toward frankness the Italians call losing the hairs on your tongue. Until meritocracy triumphs and the pursestrings are loosened, the National Health Service won't live up to its WHO ratings.

Italians are blessed with long healthy lives nonetheless, thanks to the combination of a world-class lifestyle and universal access to health care, however unreliable it may be. They also benefit from a more uniform distribution of income and wealth, which has been shown to improve health outcomes. In the US, the world's most unequal country, the average income of the top ten percent is nineteen times the average income in the bottom ten percent; in Italy that ratio is only eleven to one. Plus, Italian labor laws ensure that parents can take time off to bond with their children without losing their job, sick people don't have to drag themselves back to work prematurely, and retirement doesn't equal poverty.

Americans enjoy the best health care system in the world.

—George H.W. Bush

71% of Americans say the health care system is in a state of crisis or has major problems

—Gallup poll, 2017

Dream on, George. US hospitals may be excellent, but there must be something profoundly wrong with our health care system if we fall near the bottom of the heap among developed nations on life expectancy, infant mortality, maternal mortality, self-reported health, obesity, drug overdoses, suicide, homicides, disability rates, traffic deaths, almost any indicator you can think of. Lack of access to medical care deserves much of the blame, but even educated, insured, well-off Americans are less healthy than their peers in other rich nations.

In 2011, a young dancer opened my eyes to the existence of a subterranean American medical culture, at the antipodes from our Mayo Clinics and Mass General Hospitals. Jessica hadn't had health insurance since college, but said things looked up when she discovered a LGBT clinic in Manhattan whose sliding scale allowed her to get her Lyme disease treated for twenty-five dollars per visit. She also used alternative medicine, such as acupuncture for her chronic headaches at forty bucks a pop. And then, she said, she sometimes went to an underground MRI clinic. A what? You know, she said, a place where if you think there's something wrong with you anywhere in your body you can go and they'll give you an MRI for $100 without a doctor's order . . .

Health care access in the US has historically been a disgrace. The year before the Affordable Care Act kicked in, one in seven Americans was continuously without any medical insurance, and a giddying forty-four percent of nonelderly adults were uninsured or underinsured at some point. My year-abroad students would often find themselves insured for the first time in their adult lives—I remember performing a first Pap smear on one thirty-five-year-old woman who had been sexually active since age fifteen. Even in Obamacare 2018, the US still has far more uninsured citizens than other high-income countries.

Some of the defects in the US health system are unlikely to

change any time soon. As long as the big players can charge any damn thing they want, pricing will remain insane—emergency rooms that charge $1,000 just for walking in the door, drug companies that make you pay $884 for two pills to rid your child of pinworms (they cost one buck total in Italy). In 2014, an Italian woman who had come down with the flu on vacation made a formal complaint to the Italian Ministries of Health and Foreign Affairs after having been charged $3,700 for a fifteen-minute doctor's visit in her New York hotel room.

Research has shown that Italians, who at most have to toss in a three-dollar co-pay when filling a prescription, are sixty percent more likely than Americans to take their medications as prescribed.

When I was in training in the South Bronx back in the seventies, the wards of Morrisania Hospital were so packed with desperately ill people that the informal motto of the emergency room was, "If they can walk in, they can walk out," occasionally escalated for laughs to, "If they can crawl in, they can crawl out." There was no other source of hospital care within five miles. When in 1976 the City of New York saw fit to trim luxuries from its budget, Morrisania was shuttered with no replacement, and the patients who had previously walked, crawled, and been carried in were left to die on the streets.

What American Healthcare Can Learn from Italy: Three Lessons

It's easy. First, learn to live like Italians. Eat their famous Mediterranean diet, drink alcohol regularly but in moderation, use feet instead of cars, stop packing pistols and dropping drugs.

Second, flatten out the class structure. Shrink the gap between high and low incomes, raise pensions and minimum wages to subsistence level, fix the tax structure to favor the ninety-nine percent. And why not redistribute lifestyle too? Give working stiffs the same freedom to have kids (maternity leave), convalesce (sick leave), and relax (proper vacations) as the rich.

Finally, give everybody access to health care. Not just insurance, but actual doctors, medications, and hospitals. As I write, the future of the Affordable Care Act is uncertain, but surely the country will not fall into the abyss that came before. Once they've had a taste of what it's like not to be one heart attack away from bankruptcy, Americans won't turn back the clock. Even what is lately being called Medicare for All, considered to be on the fringe left a decade ago and slammed as "socialized medicine," is now supported by a majority of Americans, according to some polls.

In practice, there's little hope for Italian lessons one and two—the United States is making only baby steps toward improving its lifestyle, and its income inequality is worse every year. But the third lesson is more feasible. Like Italy, we can provide universal access to treatment and medications with minimal point-of-service payments and with prices kept down by government negotiation. Financial arrangements could be single-payer like Medicare or use private insurance companies as intermediaries like Switzerland, without copying the full Italian model of doctors on government salaries. Despite the death by a thousand cuts currently being inflicted on the Affordable Care Act, I am convinced that Americans will no longer stand for leaving vast numbers of the population uninsured, or denying medical coverage to people whose only sin is to be sick. The health care genie can't be put back in the bottle.

AFTERWORD

From when I first began seeing Italian patients I was fascinated by how different they were from Americans in how they related to their bodies, illnesses, and doctors, and soon I was tripping over the kinks in the local medical system. I started writing a weekly medical column for the now-defunct *Rome Daily American*, and the idea of this book germinated out of what seemed too self-revealing for the column: all those intriguing cultural contrasts. I scrawled notes and stuffed them in a manila envelope until, in November 1988, I took a break from work to type up the first bunch with chilblained fingers, on a Macintosh 128, at a hideaway on the last westward spit of Ireland. I have never stopped scribbling since.

Being a practicing doc provides a privileged vantage point, but the role of participant-observer brings limitations. In addition to rank subjectivity and unbridled speculation, there's the risk of taking the part for the whole, like the proverbial seven blind men with the elephant. When I write "America" you sometimes have to read "New York," and when I say "Italy" it often means "Rome." That can irritate the hell out of a non-Roman Italian, because my adoptive city sits on the cusp between northern and southern Italy: for Sicilians it's practically Germany, while for many Italians from Florence on up it's Africa.

Another potential pitfall is misreading your own moment as eternal reality, an easy trap for a foreign observer. Dazzled by some quirk of local culture, we can mistake a flash-in-the-pan meteorite for a fixed star. And plenty has changed in the half-century since I first visited Italy—in 1970 on country roads you'd drive past mustachioed men on donkeys and women carrying water on scarved heads . . .

Drawing on my office experience also raises ticklish privacy issues. I apologize to any reader who might feel uncomfortable to recognize him- or herself in a story, even when I've altered the details so much that no one else would know whom I'm referring to.

I couldn't have written this book without Michael Mewshaw offering years of support, close reading of a complete draft, and my title; the late Leonard Michaels, who on no good evidence told me I was a writer; Caroline Leaf, who's been in it up to her neck since we shared that cottage in Ireland; Linda Mewshaw, the first to plow through the whole megillah; Katharine Ogden Michaels, who offered deep reading and invaluable advice; Mariateresa Barbieri, my daily sounding board and the reader most charged with keeping me honest; Marcia Angell, Jane Madison, John Murray, Constance Park, and John Spitzer, who made astute comments on draft chapters; and my husband Alvin Curran, who, in addition to contributing his own thoughts, has nurtured me unflaggingly with pep talks and pasta. I'm grateful to many other interlocutors over decades, notably Melina Amato, Vincenzo Bacci, Julian Bees, Garry Bernhardt, Gene Bishop, Harold Bourne, Marianna Brilla, Jack Buckley, Andrea De Arcangelis, Andrea Di Vecchia, Doug Drossman, James and Lisa Fentress, Katherine Flegal, Dvorah Kadish, Daniel Levenstein, Phyllis Levenstein, Steve Locke, Marijo Neumann, Dennis Novack, Lisa Paglin, Cosimo Prantera, Vincenzo Rosselli, Edith Schloss, Henry Shapiro, Carlo Vitelli, Ruth Whetstone, and Fabio Zannoni. Thanks also to Don Thomases for matchmaking, Maureen Fant for writing lessons, and the entire Paul Dry Books team for their unwavering kindness, patience, and professionalism in nurturing this project to fruition. But the greatest debt I owe, by far, is to the thousands of patients who have put their trust in me and made my life worthwhile.